THE KINGDOM OF GOD
IS WITHIN YOU

THE KINGDOM OF GOD
IS WITHIN YOU
BY
LEO TOLSTOY

The Kingdom of God is Within You

White Crow Books is an imprint of
White Crow Productions Ltd
PO Box 1013
Guildford
GU1 9EJ

www.whitecrowbooks.com

This edition copyright © 2010 White Crow Books

Text design and eBook production by Essential Works
www.essentialworks.co.uk

Hardback ISBN 978-1-907661-20-4
Paperback ISBN 978-1-907355-27-1
eBook ISBN 978-1-907355-66-0

Religion & Spirituality

Distributed in the UK by
Lightning Source Ltd.
Chapter House
Pitfield
Kiln Farm
Milton Keynes MK11 3LW

Distributed in the USA by
Lightning Source Inc.
246 Heil Quaker Boulevard
LaVergne
Tennessee 37086

Contents

Preface

IN THIS BOOK I HAVE endeavoured to show that our modern Christianity has been tried and found wanting, that the armed camp of Europe is not Christian, but Pagan, as is latter-day religion, of which the present state of affairs is the outcome. The book contains three principal ideas – the first, that Christianity is not only the worship of God and a doctrine of salvation, but is above all things a new conception of life which is changing the whole fabric of human society; the second, that from the first appearance of Christianity there entered into it two opposite currents – the one establishing the true and new conception of life, which it gave to humanity, and the other perverting the true Christian doctrine and converting it into a Pagan religion, and that this contradiction has attained in our days the highest degree of tension which now expresses itself in universal armaments, and on the Continent in general conscription; and the third, that this contradiction, which is masked by hypocrisy, can only be solved by an effort of sincerity on the part of every individual endeavouring to conform the acts of his life – independent of what are regarded as the exigencies of family, society, and the State – with those moral principles which he considers to be true.

LEO TOLSTOY

The above is an extract (slightly adapted) from an article on Count Tolstoy which appeared in the *London Daily Chronicle* of 26th December 1893. Sent by Miss Tatiana Tolstoy, on behalf of her father, to the original publishers of this edition of his work, it is inserted here as a Preface at the suggestion of Count Tolstoy.

The Kingdom of God is Within You:
Or, Christianity not as a Mystical Doctrine,
But as a New Life-Conception

"And ye shall know the truth, and the truth shall make you free."
John viii: 32

*"And fear not them which kill the body, but are not able to kill
the soul; but rather fear him which is able to destroy both soul
and body in hell." Matthew x: 28*

*"Ye are bought with a price; be not ye the servants of men." I Cor-
inthians vii: 23*

Introduction

IN 1884 I WROTE a book entitled *My Religion*, wherein I
formulated my creed.

While affirming my faith in the doctrine taught by Christ,
I could not refrain from manifesting at the same time the reason
why I look upon the ecclesiastical doctrine commonly called
Christianity as erroneous and to me incredible.

Among the many deviations of the latter from the doctrine
of Christ I called attention to the principal one, namely – the
evasion of the commandment that forbids man to resist evil by
violence, as a striking example of the perversion of the doctrine
of Christ by ecclesiastical interpretation.

I knew but little, no more than other men of what had been
taught or written on the subject of non-resistance informer
times. I was familiar with the opinions of the Fathers of the
Church, Origen, Tertullian, and others; and I also knew of the
existence of certain sects called Mennonites, Herrnhuters, and
Quakers, all of which forbid Christians the use of arms and will

not submit to conscription, but I never knew the arguments by which these sects sought to maintain their views.

My book, as I had anticipated, was prohibited by the Russian censors, but partly in consequence of my reputation as a writer, partly because it excited curiosity, it had a circulation in manuscript, and while on the one hand it called forth from those persons who sympathized with my ideas, information concerning works written on the same subject, on the other, it excited criticisms on the opinions therein maintained.

These two results, together with the historical events of recent years, made many things clear to me, and led me to many new deductions and conclusions which I now desire to set forth.

I shall speak in the first place of the information I received in regard to the history of this matter of non-resistance to evil; and in the second place, of the arguments upon the subject offered by religious critics, that is, by critics who profess the religion of Christ, as well as those of secular critics, that is to say, of men who make no such profession; and finally, the conclusions which I drew from the arguments of both parties, as well as from the historical events of later years.

CHAPTER I

Doctrine of Non-Resistance to Evil From the Origin of Christianity, Has Been, and Still Is, Professed by the Minority of Men

CONCERNING THE BOOK *My Religion* – Information called forth by this book – Letters of Quakers – *Professions* of Garrison – Adin Ballou, his *Works* and *Catechism* – *The Net of Faith* of Helchitsky – Relations of men towards works that explain the teachings of Christ – The book of Dymond *On War* – *Assertion of Non-Resistance* by Musser – Relations of government in 1818 towards those who refused to join the military service – General inimical attitude of governments and liberal men towards those who refused to take a part in the violence of governments and their conscious effort to conceal and ignore these demonstrations of Christian Non-Resistance.

Among the early responses called forth by my book were letters from American Quakers. In these letters, while expressing their sympathy with my ideas in regard to the unlawfulness of violence and war where Christians are concerned, the Quakers made known to me many details in relation to their sect, which for more than two hundred years has professed the doctrine of Christ in the matter of non-resistance, and which never has, nor does it now use weapons for self-defence. Together with the letters, the Quakers sent me many of their pamphlets, periodicals, and books. From these publications I learned that already, many years ago, they had demonstrated the Christian's duty of keeping the commandment of non-resistance to evil by violence and the error of the church which countenances wars and executions.

Having shown by a succession of arguments and texts that war – the slaughter and mutilation of men – is inconsistent with a religion founded on peace and goodwill to men, the Quakers go on to assert that nothing is so conducive to the defamation of Christ's truth in the eyes of the heathen, or so successful in arresting the spread of Christianity throughout the world, as the refusal to obey this commandment, made by men who call themselves Christians, and by the sanction thus given to war and violence. The doctrine of Christ, which has entered into the consciousness of men, not by force or by the sword, as they say, but by non-resistance to evil, by humility, meekness, and the love of peace, can only be propagated among men by the example of peace, love, and concord given by its followers.

A Christian, according to the teaching of the Lord, should be guided in his relations towards men only by the love of peace, and therefore there should be no authority having power to compel a Christian to act in a manner contrary to God's law and contrary to his chief duty towards his fellowmen.

The requirements of the civil law, they say, may oblige men, who, to win some worldly advantages, seek to conciliate that which is irreconcilable, to violate the law of God; but for a Christian, who firmly believes that his salvation depends upon following the teaching of Christ, this law can have no meaning.

My acquaintance with the activity of the Quakers and with their publications, with Fox, Paine, and particularly with a work published by Dymond in 1827, proved to me not only that men have long since recognized the impossibility of harmonizing Christianity and war, but that this incompatibility has been proved so clearly and indubitably, that one can only wonder how it is possible for this incongruous union of Christianity with violence – a doctrine which is still taught by the church – to remain in force.

Beside the information obtained from the Quakers, I also received from America about the same time advice on the subject from another and hitherto unknown source. The son of William Lloyd Garrison, the famous anti-slavery champion, wrote to me, that having read my book, wherein he had found ideas similar to those expressed by his father in 1838, and taking it for granted that I should be interested to know that fact, he sent me a book written by Mr. Garrison some fifty years ago, entitled *Non-Resistance*.

This avowal of principle took place under the following circumstances: in 1838, on the occasion of a meeting of the Society for the Promotion of Peace, William Lloyd Garrison, while discussing means for the suppression of war, arrived at the conclusion that the establishment of universal peace can have no solid foundation save in the literal obedience to the commandment of non-resistance by violence (Matthew v: 39), as understood by the Quakers, with whom Garrison was on friendly terms. Having arrived at this conclusion, he wrote offering to the Society the following proclamation, which at that time, in 1838, was signed by many of its members:

"*Declaration of Sentiments adopted by the Peace Convention, held in Boston, September 18, 19, and 20, 1838:*

"Assembled in Convention, from various sections of the American Union, for the promotion of Peace on earth and Goodwill among men, We, the undersigned, regard it as due to ourselves, to the cause which we love, to the country in which we live, and to the world, to publish a Declaration, expressive of the principles we cherish, the purposes we aim to accomplish, and the measures we shall adopt to carry forward the work of peaceful, universal reformation.

"We cannot acknowledge allegiance to any human government; neither can we oppose any such government by a resort to physical force. We recognize but one King and Lawgiver, one Judge and Ruler of mankind. We are bound by the laws of a Kingdom which is not of this world; the subjects of which are forbidden to fight; in which Mercy and Truth are met together, and Righteousness and Peace have kissed each other; which has no state lines, no national partitions, no geographical boundaries; in which there is no distinction of rank or division of caste, or inequality of sex; the officers of which are Peace, its exactors Righteousness, its walls Salvation, and its gates Praise; and which is destined to break in pieces and consume all other kingdoms. Our country is the world, our countrymen are all mankind. We love the land of our nativity only as we love all other lands. The interests, rights, liberties of American citizens are no dearer to us than are those of the whole human race. Hence, we can allow no appeal to patriotism to revenge any national insult or injury; the Principle of Peace, under whose stainless banner we rally, came not to destroy, but to save, even the worst of enemies.

He has left us an example, that we should follow His steps. God commendeth his love toward us, in that 'while we were yet sinners, Christ died for us.

"We conceive that if a nation has no right to defend itself against foreign enemies, or to punish its invaders, no individual possesses that right in his own case. The unit cannot be of greater importance than the aggregate. If one man may take life, to obtain or defend his rights, the same licence must necessarily be granted to communities, states, and nations. If he may use a dagger or a pistol, they may employ cannon, bomb shells, land and naval forces. The means of self-preservation must be in proportion to the magnitude of interests at stake and the number of lives exposed to destruction. But if a rapacious and blood thirsty soldiery, thronging these shores from abroad, with intent to commit rapine and destroy life, may not be resisted by the people or magistracy, then ought no resistance to be offered to domestic troubles of the public peace or of private security. No obligation can rest upon Americans to regard foreigners as more sacred in their persons than themselves, or to give them a monopoly of wrong doing with impunity.

"The dogma, that all the governments of the world are approvingly ordained of God, and that the powers that be in the United States, in Russia, in Turkey, are in accordance with His will, is not less absurd than impious. It makes the impartial Author of human freedom and equality unequal and tyrannical. It cannot be affirmed that the powers that be, in any nation, are actuated by the spirit or guided by the example of Christ, in the treatment of enemies; therefore, they cannot be agreeable to the will of God; and therefore their overthrow, by a spiritual regeneration of their subjects, is inevitable.

"We register our testimony not only against all wars, whether offensive or defensive, but all preparations for war; against every naval ship, every arsenal, every fortification; against the militia system and a standing army; against all military chieftains and soldiers; against all monuments commemorative of victory over a fallen foe, all trophies won in battle, all celebrations in honour of military or naval exploits; against all appropriations for the defence of a nation by force and army, on the part of any legislative body; against every edict of government requiring of its subjects military service. Hence we deem it unlawful to bear arms, or to hold a military office.

"As every human government is upheld by physical strength, and its laws are enforced virtually at the point of the bayonet, we cannot hold any office which imposes upon its incumbent the obligation to compel men to do right, on pain of imprisonment or death. We therefore voluntarily exclude ourselves from every legislative and judicial body, and repudiate all human politics, worldly honours, and stations of authority. If we cannot occupy a seat in the legislature or on the bench, neither can we elect others to act as our substitutes in any such capacity.

"It follows that we cannot sue any man at law, to compel him by force to restore anything which he may have wrongfully taken from us or others; but if he has seized our coat, we shall surrender up our cloak, rather than subject him to punishment.

"We believe that the penal code of the old covenant, *An eye for an eye, and a tooth for a tooth,*' has been abrogated by Jesus Christ; and that under the new covenant, the forgiveness instead of the punishment of enemies has been enjoined upon all His disciples, in all cases whatsoever. To extort money from enemies, or set them upon a pillory, or cast them into prison, or hang them upon gallows, is obviously not to forgive, but to take retribution. *'Vengeance is mine, I will repay, saith the Lord.'*

"The history of mankind is crowded with evidences proving that physical coercion is not adapted to moral regeneration; that the sinful disposition of men can be subdued only by love; that evil can be exterminated from the earth only by goodness; that it is not safe to rely upon an arm of flesh, upon man whose breath is in his nostrils, to preserve us from harm; that there is great security in being gentle, harmless, long-suffering, and abundant in mercy; that it is only the meek who shall inherit the earth, for the violent who resort to the sword are destined to perish with the sword. Hence, as a measure of sound policy – of safety to property, life and liberty – of public quietude and private enjoyment – as well as on the ground of allegiance to Him who is King of kings and Lord of lords, we cordially adopt the non-resistance principle; being confident that it provides for all possible consequences, will insure all things needful to us, is armed with Omnipotent power, and must ultimately triumph over every assailing force.

"We advocate no Jacobinical doctrine. The spirit of Jacobinism is the spirit of retaliation, violence, and murder. It neither fears God nor regards man. We would be filled with the spirit of Jesus Christ. If we abide by our principles, it is impossible for us to be disorderly, or plot treason, or participate in any evil work; we shall submit to every ordinance of man, for the Lord's sake; obey all the requirements of government, except such as we deem contrary to the commands of the gospel; and in no case resist the operation of law, except by meekly submitting to the penalty of disobedience.

"But while we shall adhere to the doctrine of non-resistance and passive submission, we purpose, in a moral and spiritual sense, to speak and act boldly in the cause of God; to assail iniquity in high places and in low places; to apply our principles to all existing civil, political, legal, and ecclesiastical institutions; and to hasten the time when the kingdoms of this world will have become the kingdoms of our Lord and of his Christ, and He shall reign forever.

"It appears to us a self-evident truth, that, whatever the gospel is designed to destroy at any period of the world, being contrary to it, ought now to be abandoned. If, then, the time is predicted when swords shall be beaten into plough-shares, and spears into pruning hooks, and men shall not learn the art of war any more, it follows that all who manufacture, sell, or wield those deadly weapons, do thus array themselves against the peaceful dominion of the Son of God on earth.

"Having thus briefly stated our principles and purposes, we proceed to specify the measures we propose to adopt in carrying our object into effect.

"We expect to prevail through the foolishness of preaching – striving to commend ourselves unto every man's conscience, in the sight of God. From the press we shall promulgate our sentiments as widely as practicable. We shall endeavour to secure the cooperation of all persons, of whatever name or sect. The triumphant progress of the cause of Temperance and of Abolition in our land, through the instrumentality of benevolent and voluntary associations, encourages us to combine our own means and efforts for the promotion of a still greater cause. Hence, we shall employ lecturers, circulate tracts and publications, form societies, and petition our state and national governments, in relation to the subject of Universal Peace. It will be our leading object to devise ways and means for effecting a radical change in the views, feelings, and practices of society, respecting the sinfulness of war and the treatment of enemies.

"In entering upon the great work before us, we are not unmindful that, in its prosecution, we may be called to test our sincerity even as in a fiery ordeal. It may subject us to insult, outrage, suffering, yea, even death itself. We anticipate no small amount of misconception, misrepresentation, and calumny. Tumults may arise against us. The ungodly and violent, the proud and pharisaic, the ambitious and tyrannical, principalities and powers, and spiritual wickedness in high places, may contrive to crush us. So they treated the Messiah, whose example we are humbly striving to imitate. If we suffer with Him we know that we shall reign with Him. We shall not be afraid of their terror, neither be troubled. Our confidence is in the Lord Almighty, not in man. Having withdrawn from human protection, what can sustain us but that faith which overcomes the world?

We shall not think it strange concerning the fiery trial which is to try us, as though some strange thing had happened unto us; but rejoice, inasmuch as we are partakers of Christ's sufferings. Wherefore, we commit the keeping of our souls to God, in well doing, as unto a faithful Creator. For every one that forsakes house, or brethren, or sisters, or father, or mother, or wife, or children, or lands, for Christ's sake, shall receive a hundred-fold, and shall inherit everlasting life.

"Firmly relying upon the certain and universal triumph of the sentiments contained in this declaration, however formidable may be the opposition arrayed against them – in solemn testimony of our faith in their divine origin – we hereby affix our signatures to it, commending it to the reason and conscience of mankind, giving ourselves no anxiety as to what may befall us, and resolving in the strength of the Lord God calmly and meekly to abide the issue."

Later on, Garrison founded a Non-Resistance Society and started a periodical entitled *The Non-Resistant*, wherein the full significance and consequences of the doctrine were plainly set forth, as has been stated in the proclamation. I gained, subsequently, further information concerning the fate of this society and the periodical from a biography of William Lloyd Garrison, written by his sons.

Neither the periodical nor the society enjoyed a long life. The majority of Garrison's associates in the work of liberating the slaves, apprehensive lest the too radical views expressed in *The Non-Resistant* might alienate men from the practical business of the abolition of slavery, renounced the doctrine of non-resistance as expressed in the declaration, and both periodical and society passed out of existence.

One would suppose that this declaration of Garrison, formulating, as it did, an important profession of faith in terms both energetic and eloquent, would have made a deeper impression on men, and have become a subject for universal consideration. On the contrary, not only is it unknown in Europe, but even among those Americans who honour the memory of Garrison there are but few who are familiar with this.

A similar fate befell another American champion of the same doctrine, Adin Ballou, who died recently, and who for fifty years had preached in favour of non-resistance to evil. How little is known in regard to the question of non-resistance may be gathered from the fact that the younger Garrison (who has written an excellent biography of his father in four large volumes), in answer to my inquiry whether any society for the defence of the principles of non-resistance was yet alive and possessed adherents, wrote me that, so far as he knew, the society had dissolved and its members were no longer interested, while at this very time Adin Ballou, who had shared Garrison's labours, and who had devoted fifty years of his life to the teaching of the doctrine of non-resistance, both by pen and by tongue, was still living in Hopedale, Massachusetts. Afterwards I received a letter from Wilson, a disciple and co-worker of Ballou, and subsequently I entered into correspondence with Ballou himself. I wrote to him, and he sent me his works, from one of which I made the following extract: "Jesus Christ is my Lord and Master," says Ballou in one of his articles, written to show the inconsistency of Christians who believe in the right of defensive and offensive warfare." I have covenanted to forsake all and follow Him, through good and evil report, until death. But I am nevertheless a Democratic Republican citizen of the United States, implicitly sworn to bear true allegiance to my country, and to support its Constitution, if need be, with my life. Jesus Christ requires me to do unto others as I would that others should do unto me. The Constitution of the United States requires me to do unto twenty-seven hundred thousand slaves" (they had slaves then; now they could easily be replaced by workmen) "the very contrary of what I would have them do unto me – *viz.*, assist to keep in a grievous bondage.... But I am quite easy. I vote on. I help govern on. I am willing to hold any office I maybe elected to under the Constitution. And I am still a Christian. I profess on. I find difficulty in keeping covenant both with Christ and the Constitution.

"Jesus Christ forbids me to resist evildoers by taking 'eye for eye, tooth for tooth, blood and life for life. 'My government requires the very reverse, and depends, for its own self-preservation, on the halter, the musket, and the sword, seasonably employed against its domestic and foreign enemies.'"

In the maintenance and use of this expensive life-destroying apparatus we can exemplify the virtues of forgiving our injuries, love our enemies, blessing them that curse us, and doing good to those that hate us. For this reason we have regular Christian chaplains to pray for us and call down the smiles of God on our holy murders.

The Constitution says – "Congress shall have power to declare war, grant letters of marque and reprisal,' and I agree to this, I indorse it. I swear to help carry it through. I vote for men to hold office who are sworn to support all this. What then, am I less a Christian? Is not war a Christian service? Is it not perfectly Christian to murder hundreds of thousands of fellow human beings; to ravish defenceless females, sack and burn cities, and enact all the other cruelties of war? Out upon these new-fangled scruples! This is the very way to forgive injuries, and love our enemies! If we only do it all in true love nothing can be more Christian than wholesale murder!"

In another pamphlet, entitled *How Many Does It Take?* he says – "One man must not kill. If he does, it is murder; two, ten, one hundred men, acting on their responsibility, must not kill. If they do, it is still murder. But a state or nation may kill as many as they please, and it is no murder. It is just, necessary, commendable, and right. Only get people enough to agree to it, and the butchery of myriads of human beings is perfectly innocent. But how many does it take? This is the question. Just so with theft, robbery, burglary, and all other crimes. Man stealing is a great crime in one man, or a very few men only. But a whole nation can commit it, and the act becomes not only innocent, but highly honourable."

The following is, in substance, a catechism of Ballou, compiled for the use of his congregation.

The catechism of non-resistance:

Q. Whence comes the word non-resistance?

A. From the utterance: "But I say unto you, that ye resist not evil." Matthew v: 39.

Q. What does this word denote?

A. It denotes a lofty Christian virtue, commanded by Christ.

Q. Are we to understand the word non-resistance in its broad sense, that is as meaning that one should offer no resistance to evil whatsoever?

A. No; it should be understood literally as Christ taught it – that is, not to return evil for evil. Evil should be resisted by all lawful means, but not by evil.

Q. From what does it appear that Christ gave that meaning to non-resistance?

A. From the words which he used on that occasion. He said: "Ye have heard that it hath been said, an eye for an eye, and a tooth for a tooth. But I say unto you, that ye resist not evil: but whosoever shall smite thee on thy right cheek, turn to him the other also. And if any man will sue thee at the law, and take away thy coat, let him have thy cloak also."

19

Q. Whom did he mean by the words: "Ye have heard that it hath been said"?

A. The patriarchs and the prophets, and that which they spoke and which is contained in the Old Testament, that the Jews generally call the Law and Prophets.

Q. To what laws did Christ allude in the words: "Ye have heard"?

A. To those in which Noah, Moses, and other prophets grant the use of personal violence against those who commit it, for the purpose of punishing and destroying evil deeds.

Q. Mention such commandments.

A. "Who so sheddeth man's blood, by man shall his blood be shed." Genesis ix: 6.

"He that smiteth a man, so that he die, shall be surely put to death. And if any mischief follow, then thou shalt give life for life, eye for eye, tooth for tooth, hand for hand, foot for foot, burning for burning, wound for wound, stripe for stripe." Exodus xxi: 12, 23, 24, 25.

"And he that killeth any man shall surely be put to death. And if a man cause a blemish in his neighbour; as he hath done, so shall it be done to him; breach for breach, eye for eye, tooth for tooth." Leviticus xxiv: 17, 19, 20.

"And the judges shall make diligent inquisition: and, behold, if the witness be a false witness, and hath testified falsely against his brother; then shall ye do unto him, as he had thought to have done unto his brother. And thine eye shall not pity; but life shall go for life, eye for eye, tooth for tooth, hand for hand, foot for foot." Deuteronomy xix: 8, 19, 21.

These are the injunctions of which Jesus speaks.

Noah, Moses, and the prophets taught that he who murders, mutilates, or tortures his neighbour doeth evil. In order to combat and destroy this evil, the evildoer must be chastised by death, mutilation, or some personal torture. Transgressions are to be avenged by transgressions, murder by murder, torture by torture, evil by evil. Thus taught Noah, Moses, and the prophets. But Christ forbids all this. The Gospel says: I say unto you, resist ye not evil, avenge not one transgression by another, but rather bear a repetition of the offence from the evildoer." That which had been allowed is now forbidden. Having understood what resistance we have been taught, we know exactly what Christ meant by non-resistance.

Q. Did the teaching of the Ancients admit of resisting transgression by transgression?

A. Yes, but Christ forbade it. A Christian has no right in any case to take the life of, or to offend against, the evildoer.

Q. May he not kill or wound another in self-defence?

A. No.

Q. May he enter a complaint to the magistrates for the purpose of chastising the offender?

A. No. For that which he does through others, he practically does himself.

Q. May he fight in the army against foreign or domestic enemies?

A. Certainly not. He can take no part in war, or in the preparation there for. He cannot make use of weapons. He cannot resist one transgression by another, whether he is alone or in company, either personally or through other agents.

Q. May he voluntarily select or drill soldiers for the government?

A. He cannot do this, if he wishes to be faithful to the law of Christ.

Q. May he voluntarily contribute money to assist a government which is supported by military power, executions, and violence in general?

A. No; unless the money is to be used for some special purpose justifiable in itself, where the object and the means employed are good.

Q. May he pay taxes to such a government?

A. No, he should not pay taxes on his own accord, but he should not resist the levying of a tax. A tax imposed by the government is levied independently of the will of the citizens. It may not be resisted without recourse to violence, and a Christian should not use violence; therefore he must deliver his property to the forced damage caused by authorities

Q. May a Christian vote at elections and take part in Court of Law or in the government?

A. No. To take a part in elections, Courts of Law, or in the administration of government is the same thing as a participation in the violence of the government.

Q. What is the chief significance of the doctrine of non-resistance?

A. To show that it is possible to extirpate evil from one's own heart, as well as from that of one's neighbour. This doctrine forbids men to do that winch perpetuates and multiplies evil in this world. He who attacks another, and does him an injury, excites a feeling of hatred the worst of all evil. To offend our neighbour because he has offended us, with ostensible motive of self-defence, means but to repeat the evil act against him as well as against ourselves – it means to beget, or at least to let loose, or to encourage the Evil Spirit whom we wish to expel. Satan cannot be driven out by Satan, falsehood cannot be purged by falsehood, nor can evil be conquered by evil. True non-resistance is the only real method of resisting evil. It crushes the serpent's head. It destroys and exterminates all evil feeling.

Q. But admitting that the idea of the doctrine is correct, is it practicable?

A. As practicable as any virtue commanded by the law of God. Good deeds cannot be performed under all circumstances without self-sacrifice, privations, suffering, and in extreme cases without the loss of life itself. But he who prizes life more than the fulfilment of God's will is already dead to the only true life. Such a man in trying to save his life will lose it. Furthermore, wherever non-resistance costs the sacrifice of one's life, or of some essential advantage of life, resistance costs thousands of such sacrifices.

Non-resistance preserves; resistance destroys.

It is much safer to act justly than unjustly; to endure an offence rather than resist it by violence; safer even in regard to the present life. If all men refused to resist evil the world would be a happy one.

Q. But if only a few were to act thus, what would become of them?

A. Even if but one man were to act thus, and the others should agree to crucify him, would it not be more glorious for him to die in the glory of non-resisting love, praying for his enemies, than live wearing the crown of Caesar, be sprinkled with the blood of the murdered? But whether it be one man or thousands of men who are firmly determined not to resist evil by evil, still, whether in the midst of civilized or uncivilized neighbours, men who do not rely on violence are safer than those who do. A robber, a murderer, a villain, will be less likely to harm them if he finds them offering no armed resistance. "All they that take the sword shall perish with the sword," and he who seeks peace, who acts like a friend, who is inoffensive, who forgives and forgets injuries, generally enjoys peace, or if he dies he dies a blessed death.

Hence, if all were to follow the commandment of non-resistance, there would manifestly be neither offence nor evil doing. If even the majority were composed of such men they would establish the rule of love and good will even towards the offenders, by not resisting evil-by-evil nor using violence. Even if such men formed a numerous minority, they would have such an improving moral influence over society that every severe punishment would be revoked, and violence and enmity would be replaced by peace and goodwill. If they formed but a small minority, they would rarely experience anything worse than the contempt of the world, while the world, without preserving it or feeling grateful therefore, would become better and wiser from its latent influence. And if, in the most extreme cases, certain members of the minority might be persecuted unto death, these men, thus dying for the truth, would have left their doctrine already sanctified by the blood of martyrdom.

Peace be with all ye who seek peace; and may the all-conquering love be the imperishable inheritance of every soul who submits of its own accord to the law of Christ.

Resist not evil by violence – Adin Ballou.

For fifty years Ballou wrote and published books chiefly on the subject of non-resistance. In these writings, remarkable for their eloquence and simplicity of style, the question is considered in all its aspects. He proved it to be the duty of every Christian who professes to believe that the Bible is a revelation from God, to obey this commandment.

He enumerates the arguments against the commandment of

non-resistance, drawn from the Old as well as from the New Testament, the expulsion from the Temple, among others, and answers each one in turn. Setting the Bible aside, he points out the practical good sense on which this principle is founded, sums up the arguments against it, and refutes them. For instance, in one chapter of his work he treats of non-resistance to evil in exceptional cases, and affirms that granting the truth of the supposition that there are cases to which the rule of non-resistance cannot be applied, that would prove that the rule in general is inconsistent. Citing such exceptional cases, he proves that these are the very occasions when the application of this rule is both wise and necessary. The question has been viewed from every side, and no argument, whether of opponent or sympathizer, has been neglected or left unanswered. I mention this in order to call attention to the deep interest which works of this class ought to excite in men who profess Christianity; and it would seem therefore that Ballou's zeal should have been recognized, and the ideas he expressed either accepted or disproved. But such was not the case.

The life work of Garrison the father, his founding the Society of the Non-Resistant, and his declaration, convinced me even more than my intercourse with the Quakers, that the divergence of the Christianity of the State from Christ's law of non-resistance by violence has been long since noticed and pointed out, and men have laboured and still do labour to counteract it. Thus Ballou's earnestness has fortified my opinion. But the fate of Garrison, and particularly that of Ballou, almost unknown, notwithstanding fifty years of active and persistent work in one direction, has confirmed me in the belief that there exists a certain unexpressed but fixed determination to oppose all such attempts by a wall of silence.

In August of 1890 Ballou died, and his obituary appeared in *The American Religion Philosophical Journal* of August 23rd.

From this obituary we learn that Ballou was the spiritual leader of a community, that he had preached from 8000 to 9000 sermons, married 1000 couples, and written 500 articles, but in regard to the object of his life's devotion not a word is said; the word "non-resistance" is never mentioned.

All the exhortations of the Quakers for 200 years, all the efforts of Garrison, the father, the foundation of his society, his periodical and his declarations, as well as the life work of Ballou, are the same as if they had never existed.

Another striking example of the obscurity into which a work written for the purpose of explaining the principle of non-resistance, and to denounce those who refuse to recognize this commandment, may fall, is the fate of a book by the Czech Helchitsky, which has only recently been discovered, and which up to the present time has never been printed.

Shortly after the publication of my book in German I received a letter from a Professor of the Prague University, who wrote to tell me of a book which had never been printed, a work written in the fifteenth century by Helchitsky, and entitled *The Net of Faith.* In this work, written four centuries ago, Helchitsky, as the Professor tells me, has expressed exactly the same opinion in regard to true and false Christianity that I did in my work entitled *My Religion.* The Professor wrote that the work of Helchitsky was to appear in print for the first time in the Czech language, in one of the publications of the St. Petersburg Academy of Science. As I was unable to obtain the book, I endeavoured to ascertain all that was known of Helchitsky himself, and this knowledge I gained from a German book sent to me by the same Professor in Prague.

Besides that I learned something from Pipin's *History of Czech Literature.* Pipin says:

"*The Net of Faith* is the doctrine of Christ, wherewith man is to be raised from the gloomy depths of the social sea of iniquity. True faith is to believe the words of God; but we are living in times when men call the true faith heresy; hence it is upon our own reason that we must rely to discover the truth if we possess it not. Darkness has concealed it from men, and they no longer recognize the true law of Christ.

"As an illustration of the law, Helchitsky cites the original social organization of Christian society, which is considered by the Church of Rome of the present time as rank heresy.

"This primitive church was his own ideal of a social order founded upon equality, liberty, and fraternity. Christianity, according to Helchitsky, still preserves this foundation, and has but to return to its pure teaching to render any other social order whose existence requires the authority of pope or king quite superfluous. The law of love will suffice for all.

"Historically, Helchitsky assigns the decadence of Christianity to the time of Constantine the Great, whom the Pope Silvester received into the Church in spite of his pagan life and morals. Constantine in return rewarded the Pope by endowing him with riches and temporal power. Since then these two forces have played into each other's hands, seeking only outward glory. Doctors, men of learning, and the clergy, caring only to maintain their influence over the world, excited the nations one against the other, encouraging the crimes of murder and rapine, and thus destroying Christianity, both in faith and practice. Helchitsky totally denies the right of man to wage war or to exact the penalty of death. According to him, every soldier, even if he be a 'knight,' is only a transgressor, a criminal, and a murderer."

All this, with the addition of some biographical details and extracts from the correspondence of Helchitsky, is related in the German book.

Having thus become acquainted with the essence of Helchitsky's teachings, I awaited with still greater impatience the appearance of *The Net of Faith* in the Academy's periodical. But one, two, three years passed, and the book was not forthcoming. It was only in 1888 that I learned that the printing had been suspended. I obtained the proof sheets of what had been printed and read them. In many respects it was a wonderful book.

Its contents have been accurately summarized by Pipin. Helchitsky's principal idea is, that Christianity in league with sovereignty during the reign of Constantine the Great, and continuing to develop under these conditions, became corrupted and ceased to be Christianity. He called his book *The Net of Faith* because he had chosen for his motto that verse from the New Testament which speaks of the disciples as fishers of men. He carries on the simile thus: "Through His disciples, Christ caught the world in the net of His faith, but the larger fishes, breaking the net, escaped; then others followed through these same holes made by the large fishes, and the net was left almost empty." By the big fish he means the popes, emperors, and sovereigns who, without giving up their authority, accepted Christianity, but not in its reality, but in its semblance.

Helchitsky teaches the same doctrine that is now taught by the Non-Resistant Mennonites and Quakers, and in former times by the Bogomiles, the Paulicians, and other sects. He teaches that Christianity, requiring as it does from its followers humility, gentleness, a forgiving spirit, the turning of the other cheek when one is struck, and the love of one's enemies, is not compatible with that violence which is an essential element of authority. A Christian, according to Helchitsky, should not only refuse to be a commander or a soldier, but he should take no part in government, neither should he become a tradesman, nor even a landowner. He might be an artisan or a farmer. This book is among the few which have been saved from the flame into which books denouncing official Christianity were commonly cast. As all such so-called heretical works were usually burned with their authors, very few of those which denounce official Christianity have been preserved – and for this reason the book of which we speak has a special interest.

But apart from its interest, concerning which there may be differences of opinion, it is one of the most remarkable results of human thought, both on account of its profundity and the wonderful power and beauty of its language, not to mention its antiquity. And yet this book has remained out of print for centuries, and continues to be unknown except to a few specialists.

One would think that works like these of the Quakers, of Garrison, of Ballou, and of Helchitsky – which affirm and prove by the authority of the Bible, that the world misinterprets the teaching of Christ – would arouse an interest, would make a sensation, would give rise to discussions between the clergy and their flocks.

One might suppose that works which deal with the very essence of the Christian doctrine would be reviewed, and either acknowledged to be just, or else refuted and condemned.

Not at all. Every one of these works suffers the same fate. Men of widely differing opinions, believers, and, what is still more surprising, unbelieving liberals, as though by common consent preserve an obstinate silence in regard to them. Thus every attempt to explain the true meaning of Christ's doctrine goes for nothing.

And more astonishing still is the ignorance concerning two works whose existence was made known to me after the publication of my own book. One is a work by Dymond, *On War*, printed for the first time in London in 1824, and the other by Daniel Musser, entitled *Non-Resistance Asserted*, was written in 1864.

The ignorance in regard to these books is amazing; the more so, that apart from their merit, both treat not so much of the theory as of its practical application to life; of the relations of Christianity to military service, which is particularly interesting in view of the system of conscription. It may be asked, perhaps, what action is befitting for a subject who believes that war is incompatible with religion, when his government calls upon him for military service?

One would take this to be a vital question, whose answer, in view of our present system of conscription, becomes one of serious importance. All men, or the majority of mankind, are Christians, and every male is required to do military duty. How man, in his Christian character, is to meet this demand, Dymond gives the following reply: *"It is his duty, mildly and temperately, yet firmly, to refuse to serve."*

"There are some persons who, without any determinate process of reasoning, appear to conclude that responsibility for national measures attaches solely to those who direct them; that it is the business of governments to consider what is good for the community, and that, in these cases, the duty of the subject is merged in the will of the sovereign. Considerations like these are, I believe, often voluntarily permitted to become opiates of the conscience. I have no part, it is said, in the councils of the government, and am not, therefore, responsible for its crimes. We are, indeed, not responsible for the crimes of our rulers, but we are responsible for our own; and the crimes of our rulers are our own, if, whilst we believe them to be crimes, we promote them by our cooperation.

"Those who suppose that obedience in all things is required, or that responsibility in political affairs is transferred from the subject to the sovereign, reduce themselves to a great dilemma. It is to say, that we must resign our conduct and our consciences to the will of others, and act wickedly or well, as their good or evil may preponderate, without merit for virtue, or responsibility for crime."

It is worthy of notice that the same is expressed in a maxim to soldiers, which they are required to memorize. Dymond says that only a commander answers for the consequences of his order. But this is unjust. A man cannot remove the responsibility for his actions from himself. And this is evident from the following: if your superior orders you to kill your child, your neighbour, your father, or your mother, will you obey? If you will not, there is an end of the argument; for if you may reject his authority in one instance, where is the limit to rejection? There is no rational limit but that which is assigned by Christianity, and that is both rational and practicable.

"We think, then, that it is the business of every man who believes that war is inconsistent with our religion, respectfully, but steadfastly, to refuse to engage in it. Let such as these remember that an honourable and an awful duty is laid upon them. It is upon their fidelity, so far as human agency is concerned, that the cause of peace is suspended. Let them, then, be willing to avow their opinions and to defend them. Neither let them be contented with words, if more than words, if suffering also, is required. It is only by the unyielding fidelity of virtue that corruption can be extirpated. If you believe that Jesus Christ has prohibited slaughter, let not the opinions or the commands of a world induce you to join in it. By this steady and determinate pursuit of virtue,' the benediction which attaches to those who hear the sayings of God and do them, will rest upon you, and the time will come when even the world will honour you as contributors to the work of human reformation."

Musser's work, entitled *Non-Resistance Asserted, or Kingdom of Christ and Kingdom of this World Separated*, was published in 1864.

This book deals with the same question, drawing its illustrations from the drafting of the United States citizens during the time of the Civil War. In setting forth the reasons why men should have the right to decline military service, his arguments are no less applicable to the present time. In his introduction the author says: "It is well known that there are great numbers of peoples in the United States who profess to be conscientiously opposed to war. They are mostly called non-resistants, or defenceless Christians, and refuse to defend their country, or take up arms at the call of the government and go forth to battle against its enemies. Hitherto this conscientious scruple has been respected by the government in this country; and those claiming it have been relieved or excused from this service.

"Since the commencement of the present civil war in the United States the public mind has been unusually agitated on this subject. It is not unreasonable that such persons as feel it to be their duty to go forth and endure the hardships of camp life and imperil health, life, and limb in defence of their country and government, should feel some jealousy of those who have, with themselves, long enjoyed the protection and benefits of the government, and yet, in the hour of its need, refuse to share the burden of its defence and protection. Neither is it strange that such a position should be looked upon as most unreasonable and monstrous, and those who hold it be regarded with some suspicion. Many able speakers and writers," says the author,

"Have raided their voices and pens to refute the idea of nonresistance, as both unreasonable and unscriptural. This is not to be wondered at, seeing that those who profess the principle and do not possess it, or correctly understand it, act inconsistently, and thereby bring the profession into disrepute and contempt. However much misapplication or abuse of a principle may prejudice the minds of those who are unacquainted with a subject, it is yet no argument against its truth."

The author at first proves it to be the duty of each Christian to obey the rule of non-resistance. He says that the rule is perfectly explicit, and that it has been given by Christ to all Christianity without any possibility of being misinterpreted. "Judge for yourselves, whether it is right or wrong to obey man more than you do the Lord," said both Peter and John; and in exactly the same way every man who wishes to be a Christian should regard the requirement of his nation to be a soldier, remembering that

Christ has told him, "Do not resist evil."

This, in the opinion of Musser, decides the question of principle. Another point, as to the right of declining military duty while one enjoys the advantages accruing through violence, the author considers in detail, and arrives at the conclusion that should a Christian who follows the teaching of Christ refuse to go to the war, he must also decline to take any position under the government or any part in the elections, neither must he have recourse to any officer of the law for his own personal advantage. Our author goes on to consider the relation between the Old and New Testaments and the significance of government for non-Christians; arguments against the doctrine of non-resistance are enumerated and refuted. The author closes his book with the following words: "Christians need no governments: for they ought not to obey it in those matters therein Christ's teaching is set at nought, and still less should they take an active part in it. Christ has chosen his disciples out of the world. They have no promise of temporal good or happiness, but the contrary. Their promise is in the world to come. The spirit which they possess renders them happy and contented in any sphere of life. So long as the world tolerates them, they are contented; but if it will not let them dwell in peace, they flee to another city or place; and so they are true pilgrims and strangers on earth, having no certain abiding place. They are well contented that the dead may bury their dead, if they are only permitted to follow Christ."

Without deciding upon the merits of this definition of a Christian's duty in regard to war, which we find set down in these two works, we cannot fail to see the urgent need for a decision in regard to the question itself.

There are men – hundreds of thousands of Quakers, Mennonites, our own Duhobortzi, Molokani, men who belong to no sect whatsoever – who believe that violence and therefore military service is incompatible with Christianity; every year, for instance, we see in Russia a number of men refusing to obey the conscription, because of their religious opinions. And how does the government deal with them? Does it release them? Oh no. . . . Does it use force, and in case of disobedience punish them? Not exactly. In 1818, government managed the affair in this wise.

The following is an extract, hardly known to any one in Russia, from a letter of Muraviev-Karsky, which was prohibited by the Russian censor:

"Tiflis, October 2nd, 1818.

"This morning the commander of the fortress told me that five peasants belonging to the landowners of the government of Tambov had been recently sent into the province of Grusia. These men were intended to serve as soldiers, but they refused to obey. They were flogged several times and made to run the gauntlet, but they were ready to give themselves up to the most cruel tortures, yea, even to death itself, to escape military service. Let us go our way and harm us not; we do no harm ourselves. All men are equal. The sovereign is a man like one of us, why should we pay him taxes, and wherefore should we risk our lives to kill in battle those who have never done us any harm? Draw and quarter us, if you will, and we shall never change our minds; we will never wear the uniform, nor mess at the soldier's table. Some pitying soul may give us alms, but from the government we neither have had nor will have anything whatsoever.' Such are the words of these peasants, who assure us that there are many men in Russia like themselves. Four times they were brought before the Committee of Ministers, and it was finally decided that a report be made to the Czar, who ordered them to be sent to Griisia for discipline, and desired the Commander-in-Chief to forward a monthly report of the progress made in bringing these peasants lo a proper frame of mind."

The final result of this discipline is not known, for the matter was kept a profound secret, and the episode may never have been made public.

This was the conduct of the government seventy-five years ago in the greater number of cases, always carefully hiding the truth from the people; and it pursues the same policy at the present day, except in regard to the German Mennonites, who live in the government of Kherson, and who in lieu of military duty serve a corresponding term as foresters – the justice of their refusal to obey the conscription being recognized.

But they are the sole exception; all others who from religious scruples refuse to perform military duty are treated in the manner just described.

At first the government employs all the methods of coercion now in use to discipline and convert the rebels, while at the same time the most profound secrecy envelops all these proceedings. I know of a process which was begun in 1884 against a man who had declined to serve – a long drawn-out trial which was guarded by the Ministry as a great secret.

The first step is usually to send the accused to the priests, and be it said to their shame, they always try to win over the insubordinate. But as the influence exercised in the name of Christ is generally unsuccessful, the delinquent is sent from the clergy to the gendarmes, who finding in him no political offence send him back, whereupon he is despatched to the scientists, the doctors, and thence into the insane hospital. While he is thus sent to and fro, the delinquent, deprived of his liberty like a condemned convict, is made to endure every kind of indignity and suffering. Four such cases have come to my knowledge. The doctors generally release the man from the insane hospital, and then every underhanded and crafty device is employed to delay the accused, because his release might encourage others to follow his example.

He is not allowed to remain among the soldiers lest they discover from him that conscription is not, as they are taught to believe, in accordance with the law of God, but opposed to it. The most satisfactory arrangement for a government would be either to execute the delinquent or beat him with rods until he died, as was done in former times. But it is awkward to condemn a man to public execution because he is true to the doctrine which we all profess to believe. Nor is it possible to take no notice of a man when he refuses to obey. So the government either tortures the man in order to compel him to deny Christ, or tries to rid itself of him by some means which will hide both the man and the crime from the eyes of the world, rather than resort to public execution.

All sorts of cunning manoeuvres and tricks are employed to torment the man. He is either banished to some remote province, or exasperated to disobedience and then imprisoned, or sent to the reform battalion, where he may be subjected to torture, without publicity or restriction; or he is pronounced insane and locked up in the insane asylum. For instance, one was exiled to Tashkent; that is to say, pretence was made of transferring him thither. Another was sent to Omsk, a third was court-martialled for disobedience and imprisoned, and a fourth was put into a house for the insane. The same thing is repeated on every side. Not only the government, but the majority of liberal free-thinkers, as though by preconceived agreement, carefully avoid alluding to what has been said, written, or done in this matter of denouncing the inconsistency of violence, as embodied in its most shocking, crude, and striking form, in the person of a soldier – this readiness to commit murder – not only with the precepts of Christianity, but with the dictates of mere humanity, which the world professes to obey.

Hence, all the information that I have gathered concerning what has been accomplished and what is still going on in this work of explaining the doctrine of Christ and the light in which it is regarded by the ruling powers of Europe and America, has confirmed me in the conviction that a spirit inimical to true Christianity dwells in these authorities, exhibited chiefly by the conspiracy of silence with which they enshroud any manifestation of it.

CHAPTER II

Opinions of Believers and Unbelievers in Regard to Non-Resistance

T HE FATE OF THE BOOK *My Religion* – the evasive answers of religious critics to the questions propounded in that book – 1st answer, Violence does not contradict Christianity – 2nd answer, Necessity of violence for the purpose of repressing evildoers – 3rd answer, Necessity of violence for the defence of one's neighbour – 4th answer, The violation of the commandment of Non-Resistance regarded as a weakness – 5th answer, Evasion of the answer by a pretence that this matter has long since been decided – The cloak of church authority, antiquity, the holiness of religious men, explain for many the contradictions between violence and Christianity, in theory as well as in life – Usual attitude of the clergy and authorities in regard to the profession of true Christianity – General character of Russian secular writers – Foreign secular critics – Incorrectness of the opinions of the former and the latter caused by a failure to understand the true meaning of the doctrine of Christ.

All the criticisms of the statements contained in my own book have given me a similar impression of a wish to ignore the subject.

As I had anticipated, no sooner was the book published than it was prohibited, and should, according to law, have been burned. But instead of being consumed by the flames, every copy was taken by the government officials and circulated in large numbers, both in manuscript and in the lithographed sheets, as well as in translations which were published abroad. It was not long before criticisms began to appear, not only from the clergy, but from the secular world, which the government, so far from forbidding, took pains to encourage. Hence the very refutation of the book, the existence of which they assumed to be unknown, was made the theme of theological controversy.

These criticisms, both foreign and domestic, may be divided

into two classes, religious and secular, the former by persons who consider themselves believers, and the latter by free thinkers. I shall begin by considering the former. In my book I accuse the clergy of inculcating doctrines contrary to the commandments of Christ, plainly and clearly expressed in the Sermon on the Mount, and particularly in regard to the commandment of non-resistance to evil, thereby depriving the doctrine of Christ of all its significance. Do the ministers of the Gospel believe the Sermon on the Mount, including the commandment of non-resistance, to be of divine origin? Having felt themselves obliged to review my book, it would seem as if they must first of all answer the principal charge, and declare at once whether they do or do not consider the Sermon on the Mount and the commandment of non-resistance obligatory upon a Christian. Instead of making the usual reply couched in words such as "Though one cannot deny, neither can one affirm, the more so as," etc., let them give a categorical answer to my question: Did Christ practically require his disciples to do that which he taught in the Sermon on the Mount, and therefore may a Christian appeal to a legal tribunal, either for defence or prosecution, and still remain a Christian? May he consistently take a part in a government which is the instrument of violence? And that most important question, which since the introduction of the general conscription concerns us all: May a Christian remain a Christian and still disobey the direct command of Christ; may he promise to conduct himself in a manner directly opposed to the doctrine of Christ, by entering into military service and putting himself in training to be a murderer?

The questions are put plainly and directly, and would seem to call for plain and direct answers. But no; my book has been received just as all previous denunciations have been, those denunciations of the clergy who have deviated from the law of Christ, with which history abounds since the time of Constantine the Great. Many words have been expended in noting the errors of my interpretation of this or that passage of the Scriptures, of how wrong I am in referring to the Trinity, the Redemption and the Immortality of the soul, but never a word of that vital question: How are we to reconcile those lessons of forgiveness, humility, patience, and love towards all mankind, our neighbours as well as our enemies, taught us by the Teacher, which dwell in the heart of each of us, with the necessities caused by military aggression against our own countrymen as well as against foreigners? All that deserves the name of a response to these questions may be summed up under five headings. I have endeavoured to bring together in this book not only the criticisms upon my book, but everything that has ever been written on this subject.

The first criticisms with which I deal come mostly from men of high position, either in Church or State, who feel quite sure that no one will venture to combat their assertions; should any one make the attempt, they would never hear the arguments. These men, intoxicated for the most part by their authority, have forgotten that there is a Christianity in whose name they hold their places. They condemn as sectarian all that which is truly Christ-like in Christianity, while on the other hand every text in both Old and New Testaments which can be wrested from its meaning so as to justify an anti-Christian or pagan sentiment – upon these they establish the foundation of Christianity. In order to confirm their statement that Christianity is not opposed to violence, these men generally quote with the greatest assurance equivocal passages from the Old and New Testaments, interpreting them in the most anti-Christian spirit – the death of Ananias and Sapphira, the execution of Simon the Sorcerer, etc. All of Christ's words that can possibly be misinterpreted are quoted in vindication of cruelty – the expulsion from the Temple, the words. *"It shall be more tolerable in that day for Sodom than for that city." Luke x: 12* and other passages. According to these men, a Christian is not at all obliged to be guided by the spirit of humility, forgiveness, and love of his enemies. It is useless to try to refute such a doctrine, because men who affirm it refute themselves, or rather they turn away from Christ himself, to invent an ideal and a form of religion all their own, forgetful of Him in whose name both the Church and the offices they hold exist. If men but knew that the Church preaches an unforgiving, murder-loving, and belligerent Christ, they would not believe in that Church, and its doctrines would be defended by none.

The second method, somewhat more awkward, consists in

affirming that though Christ did, in point of fact, teach us to turn the other cheek, and to share our cloak, and that these are indeed lofty moral laws, still . . . the world abounds in evildoers, and if these wretches are not subdued by force, the righteous will perish and the world will be destroyed. I met with this argument for the first time in St. John Chrysostom, and have called attention to its unfairness in my book entitled *My Religion*.

This argument is groundless, because if we allow ourselves to look upon our fellow men as evildoers, outcasts (Raka), we sap the very foundations of the Christian doctrine, which teaches us that we, the children of the Heavenly Father, are brothers and equal one to the other. In the second place, if the same father had permitted us to use violence towards wrongdoers, as there is no infallible rule for distinguishing the good from the evil, every individual or every community might class its neighbours under the head of evildoers, which is practically the case at the present time. In the third place, if it were possible to distinguish the righteous from the unrighteous, even then it would not be expedient in a Christian community to put to death, to cripple, or to imprison the evildoers, as in such a community there would be no one to execute these sentences, since every man in his quality of Christian is forbidden to do violence to a malefactor.

The third mode of reply, more ingenious than the preceding ones, consists in affirming that while to obey the commandment of non-resistance is every Christian's duty, when the injury is a personal one, it ceases to be obligatory when harm is done to one's neighbour, and that in such an emergency a Christian is bound to break the commandment and use force against the evildoer. This assertion is purely arbitrary, and one finds no justification for it throughout the whole body of the doctrine of Christ.

Such an interpretation is not only a narrow one, but actually amounts to a direct negation. If every man has the right to employ violence whenever his neighbour is threatened with danger, then the question becomes reduced to this: how may one define what is called danger to one's neighbour? If, however, my private judgment is to be the arbiter in this matter, then any violence which I might commit on any occasion whatever could be excused by the declaration that my neighbour was in danger.

Magicians have been burned, aristocrats and Girondists put to death, because the men in power considered them dangerous.

If this important condition, which destroys the significance of the commandment, ever entered into the thought of Christ, it would have been formulated somewhere. Not only is no such exception to the commandment to be found throughout the Teacher's life and lessons, but there is on the other hand a warning against an interpretation so false and misleading.

The error and the impracticability of such a definition is vividly illustrated in the Bible story of Caiaphas, who made use of this very same interpretation. He admitted that it was not well to put to death the innocent Jesus, but at the same time he perceived the existence of a danger not for himself, but for all the people, and therefore declared it better for one man to die, rather than that a whole nation should perish.

And we have a still more explicit proof of the fallacy of this interpretation in the words addressed to Peter, when he tried to revenge by violence the attack upon Jesus (Matthew xxvi: 51). Peter was defending not himself, but his beloved and divine Master, and Christ distinctly forbade him, saying, *"For all they that take the sword shall perish with the sword." Matthew xxvi: 52.* One can never justify an act of violence against one's fellow man by claiming to have done it in defence of another who was enduring some wrong, because in committing an act of violence, it is impossible to compare the one wrong with the other, and to say which is the greater, that which one is about to commit, or the wrong done against one's neighbour. We release society from the presence of a criminal by putting him to death, but we cannot possibly know that the former might not have so changed by the morrow as to render the execution a useless cruelty. We imprison another, we believe him a dangerous man, but no later than next day this very man may have ceased to be dangerous, and his imprisonment has become unnecessary. I see a robber, a man known to me, pursuing a girl; I hold a gun in my hand, I wound or perhaps kill the robber and save the girl. The fact that I have either wounded or killed the robber remains, but I know not what might have happened had I not done so. And what a vast amount of harm must and does accrue from the assurance that a man feels of his right to provide against a possible calamity. Ninety-nine percent of the world's iniquity, from the Inquisition to the bomb-throwing of the present day and the execution of tens of thousands of political criminals, so called, result from this very assurance.

The fourth and still more ingenious reply to this question of the Christian's responsibility in regard to the commandment of Christ concerning non-resistance to evil by violence, consists in asserting that this commandment is not denied but acknowledged like all the others; it is only the special significance attributed to it by sectarians that is denied. Our critics declare that the views of Garrison, Ballou, and Dymond, as well as those professed by the Quakers, the Shakers, the Mennonites, the Moravians, the Waldenses, Albigenses, Bogomiles, and Paulicians, are those of bigoted sectarians. This commandment, they say, has the importance, no more and no less, of all the others; and one who through weakness has transgressed against any of the commandments, whether that of non-resistance, or another, does not for that cause cease to be a Christian, provided his creed be true.

This is a very cunning and persuasive subterfuge, especially for those who are willing to be deceived, reducing the direct negation of the commandment to its accidental infraction. One has, however, but to compare the attitude of the clergy towards this or any of the other commandments which they do acknowledge, to be convinced that it is quite different from their attitude towards this one.

The commandment against fornication they acknowledge without reservation, and in no case will they ever admit that this sin is not an evil. There are no circumstances mentioned by the clergy when the commandment against fornication may be broken, and they always insist that the occasions for this sin must be avoided. But in regard to non-resistance it is a very different matter. Every clergyman believes that there are circumstances wherein this commandment may be held in abeyance, and they preach accordingly. So far from teaching their parishioners to avoid the temptations to this sin, chief among which is the oath of allegiance, they take the oath themselves. Clergymen have never been known to advocate the breaking of any other command-ment, but in regard to the doctrine of non-resistance, they dis-tinctly teach that this prohibition must not be taken too literally, that so far from always obeying this commandment, one should on occasion follow the opposite course – that is, one should sit in judgment, should go to war, and should execute criminals. Thus inmost of the cases where non-resistance to evil by violence is in question, the preachers will be found to advocate disobedi-ence. Obedience to this commandment, they say, is difficult, and can only be practicable in a state of society whose members are perfect. But how is it to become less difficult, when its infraction is not only condoned, but also directly encouraged, when legal tribunals, prisons, the implements of warfare, the cannon and muskets, armies and battles, receive the blessing of the Church? Therefore this reply is not true. Evidently, the statement that this commandment is acknowledged by the clergy to be of equal va-lidity with the other commandments cannot be true.

Clergymen do not really acknowledge it, yet, unwilling to admit this fact, they try by evasion to conceal their non-acknowledgment.

Such is the fourth method of answering.

The fifth, more ingenious than its predecessor, is the popular one of all. It consists in quietly evading reply, pretending that the question was solved ages ago, in a cogent and satisfactory man-ner, and that it would be a waste of words to reopen the subject. This method is employed by all the more cultured authors, who, if they made answer at all, would feel themselves bound to be logical. Realizing that the inconsistency between that doctrine of Christ, of which we make a verbal profession, and the scheme of our daily lives is not to be solved by words, and that the more it is talked the more glaring this inconsistency becomes, they evade it with more or less circumspection, pretending that the question of union between Christianity and the law of violence has either been already solved, or else that it cannot be solved at all.

Most of my clerical critics have made use of this method. I might quote scores of criticisms of this class, wherein every-thing is discussed except the vital principle of the book. As a characteristic specimen of these criticisms I will quote from an article by that well-known and scholarly Englishman, the writer and preacher, Canon Farrar, who, like so many other learned theologians, is an expert in the art of silently ignoring and evading a statement. The article appeared in an American magazine, *The Forum*, for October 1888.

After briefly but conscientiously setting forth the subject matter of my book, Farrar says: "After repeated search the central principle of all Christ's teaching seemed to him [Tolstoy] to be, 'Resist not evil' or 'him that is evil.' He came to the conclusion that a coarse deceit had been palmed upon the world when these words were held by civil society to be compatible with war, courts of justice, capital punishment, divorce, oaths, national prejudice, and indeed with most of the institutions of civil and social life. He now believes that the Kingdom of God would come if all men kept these five commandments, which he holds to be the pith of all Christ's teaching – *viz.*: 1. Live in peace with all men. 2. Be pure. 3. Take no oaths. 4. Never resist evil. 5. Renounce national distinctions.

Most of the Bible does not seem to him to reflect the spirit of Christ at all, though it has been brought into artificial and unwarrantable connection with it. Hence he rejects the chief doctrines of the Church: that of the Atonement by blood, that of the Trinity, that of the descent of the Holy Ghost upon the Apostles and the transmission to the priesthood by laying on of hands, that of the need of the seven sacraments for salvation. He sets aside the authority of Paul, of councils, of fathers, popes, or patriarchs, and believes himself to be the immediate disciple of Christ alone. But we are compelled to ask, is this interpretation of Christ a true one? Are all men bound, or is any man bound, to act as this great writer has done?"

One might naturally expect that this vital question, which alone could induce a man to write a dissertation on the book, would be answered either by admitting that my interpretation of the doctrine of Christ is correct and should be accepted, or declaring that it is erroneous, proving his point, and offering a more correct interpretation of the words which I have misconstrued. But no, Farrar merely expresses his belief that "though actuated by the noblest sincerity, Count Tolstoy has been misled by partial and one-sided interpretations of the meaning of the Gospel and the mind and will of Christ." In what this error consists he does not explain, but says: "To enter into the proof of this is impossible in this article, for I have already exceeded the space at my command" And concludes with equanimity: "Meanwhile the reader who feels troubled lest it should be his duty also to forsake all the conditions of his life, and to take up the position and work of a common labourer, may rest for the present on the principle, 'securus judicat orbis terrarum.' With few and rare exceptions the whole of Christendom, from the days of the apostles down to our own, has come to the firm conclusion that it was the object of Christ to lay down great eternal principles, but not to disturb the bases and revolutionize the institutions as well as all inevitable conditions. Were it my object to prove how untenable is the doctrine of communism, based by Count Tolstoy upon the divine paradoxes, which can be interpreted on only historical principles in accordance with the whole method of the teaching of Jesus, it would require an ampler canvass than I have here at my disposal." What a pity that he has no space! And, wonderful to relate, no one for fifteen centuries ever had the space to prove that the Christ whom we profess, said one thing and meant another. And of course they could prove it if they would! But it is not worthwhile to prove what everybody knows to be true. It is enough to say: "*Securus judicat orbis terrarum.*"

The criticisms of all educated believers are very much alike, because realizing, as they must the danger of their position, they feel that their only safeguard lies in the hope that by sheltering themselves behind the authority and holiness of the Church, they may succeed in intimidating their readers, or diverting them from any idea of reading the Bible for themselves or using their own reason to solve this question. And this is a method that succeeds. To whom would it ever occur, indeed, that all these assurances repeated with so much solemnity, century after century, by archdeacons, bishops and archbishops, synods and popes, are a base falsehood, a calumny against the character of Christ, uttered for the purpose of assuring to themselves the money they require to lead a life of ease at the expense of others

— a falsehood and a calumny so palpable, particularly now, that
the only chance of perpetuating this falsehood lies in holding the
people in awe by their arrogance and audacity?

The very same thing has been going on of late years in the Bureau of military conscription. A number of aged officials, decorated and self-important, are at a table, a full-length portrait of
the Emperor with the mirror of justice before them, and while
leisurely chatting with each other they write, call out the names,
and give their orders. Here also, with a cross upon his breast, his
hair blowing over his stole, a genial and venerable-looking priest
dressed in a silk robe sits before a pulpit on which is placed a
golden cross and a Bible with gilt clasps.

Ivan Petrov is called. An untidy, poorly clad youth, with a
frightened expression, twitching muscles, and gleaming eyes
that have a wandering look, steps forward, and in a hesitating,
broken voice almost whispers: "I . . .according to law . . . as a
Christian . . . I . . . I cannot. . . ." "What is he muttering?" asks the
chairman impatiently, squinting and making an effort to hear, as
he raises his head from the book. "Speak louder!" exclaims the
colonel with the glittering shoulder straps. "As a Christian . . . I
. . . I . . ." And at last it becomes plain that the youth refuses to
enter the military service because he is a Christian. "Don't talk
nonsense! Measure him! Doctor, be kind enough to look at the
measure, Will he do?" "He will do." "Holy Father, let him take
the oath."

Not only is there no uneasiness on the part of the officers, but
no one pays the least attention to the muttering of this frightened, pitiable youth. "They always mutter, and we are in a hurry;
we have still so many more to receive."

The recruit tries to speak again. "This is against the law of
Christ!" "Move on! Move on! We know what is lawful and what
is not! Move on! Father, make him understand! Next! Vassili
Nikitin!"

Then the trembling youth is led away. Now which of all these
men — the soldiers, Vassili Nikitin, the new man on the list, or
any other witness of the scene — which of these would ever dream
that the unintelligible, broken utterances of the youth, silenced
forthwith by the magistrates, embodied the real truth, while the

loud, arrogant speeches of the officials, of the priest, uttered with authority, were actually false?

The same impression is made not only by Farrar's essay, but by all those grandiloquent sermons, reviews, and other publications which spring into existence on every side wherever truth is found combating the arrogance of falsehood. At once these orators and writers, subtle or bombastic, begin by dwelling upon points closely allied to the vital question, while preserving an artful silence on the question itself.

And this is the fifth and most efficacious method of accounting for the inconsistent attitude of ecclesiastical Christianity, which, while professing Christ, with its own life denies, and teaches others to deny, this doctrine in the practice of daily life. They who employ the first method of justification by boldly and distinctly affirming that Christ sanctioned violence, meaning wars and murders, put themselves beyond the pale of Christ's teaching; while they who defend themselves according to the second, third, and fourth methods soon become entangled, and are easily convicted of falsehood; but the fifth class, they who condescend not to reason, use their dignity for a screen, and insist that all these questions were settled ages ago, and need no reconsideration; they, apparently invulnerable, will maintain an undisputed authority, and men will repose under the hypnotic suggestion of Church and State, nor seek to throw off the yoke.

Such were the views of the clergy, of the professors of Christianity, in regard to my book, nor could anything different have been expected; they are in bonds to their inconsistent position, believers in the divinity of the Teacher and yet discrediting His plainest words – an inconsistency which they are bound to reconcile in someway. Hence it is not to be supposed that they would give unbiased opinions in regard to the essential question of that change which must take place in the life of one who makes a practical application of the doctrine of Christ to the existing order. From secular critics and free thinkers, who acknowledge no obligation to the doctrine of Christ, and who might be expected to judge them without prejudice, I had prepared myself for criticisms such as these. I thought that the Liberals would look upon Christ not only as the founder of a religion involving personal salvation (as understood by the ecclesiastics and their followers), but, to use their own expression, as upon are former who tears down the old foundations to make way for new ones, and whose reformation is not even yet complete.

To set forth that conception of Christ and his doctrine has been the object of my book. But to my surprise not one out of the many criticisms, Russian or foreign, that have appeared, has accepted my view, or even discussed it from my standpoint, which is, that the teaching of Christ is a philosophical, moral, and social doctrine. (I use the phraseology of the scientists.) The Russian secular critics, conceiving the sum and substance of my book to be a plea in favour of non-resistance to evil, and taking it for granted (probably for the sake of the argument) that the doctrine itself forbade any struggle whatsoever against the wrong, made a virulent and for several years most successful attack upon this doctrine, proving that the teaching of Christ must be false, since it forbids any effort to overcome evil. Their refutations of this so-called false doctrine had all the more chance of success, because the censorship had prohibited not only the book itself but also all articles in its defence, and consequently they knew beforehand that their arguments could not be assailed.

It is worthy of note that here in Russia, where not a word against the Holy Scriptures is allowed by the censor, for several years in succession, the distinct and unmistakable commandment of Christ (Matthew v: 39) was criticized, distorted, condemned, and mocked at in all the leading periodicals.

The Russian secular critics, apparently ignorant of all that had been said and done in regard to non-resistance to evil, seemed to think that I had invented the principle myself, and attacked it as if it were my idea, first distorting and then refuting it with great ardour, bringing forward timeworn arguments that had been analysed and refuted over and over again, showing that the oppressed and downtrodden should be defended by violence, and declaring the doctrine of Christ concerning non-resistance to be immoral.

All the significance that the Russian critics saw in Christ's preaching was, that it seemed expressly intended to hamper them in their struggles against what they believe to be an evil in the present day. Thus it came about that the principle of non-resistance to evil by violence was attacked from two opposite camps: the Conservatives, because this principle interfered with them in their efforts to suppress sedition, and as opposed to all persecution, as well as to the punishment of death; the Revolutionists, because this principle forbade them to resist the oppression of the Conservatives, or to attempt their overthrow. The Conservatives were indignant that the doctrine of non-resistance to evil by violence should thwart an energetic suppression of revolutionary elements, which might imperil the welfare of a nation; the Revolutionists in the like manner were indignant because this same doctrine averted the downfall of the Conservatives, who, in their opinion, imperil the welfare of the people. It is a circumstance worthy of notice that the Revolutionists should attack the principle of non-resistance to evil by violence, for of all the doctrines dreaded by despotism and dangerous to its existence, this is the chief one. Since the creation of the world the opposite principle of resistance by violence has been the corner stone of every despotic institution, from the Inquisition to the fortress of Schlüsselburg.

Moreover, the Russian critics declared that the progress of civilization itself would be checked were this commandment of non-resistance applied to everyday life, by which they mean the civilization of Europe, which is, according to them, the model for all mankind.

Such was the substance of Russian criticism.

Foreign critics start from the same premises, but their deductions differ somewhat from those of the Russian critics; not only are they less captious and more cultivated, but their modes of analysis are not the same.

In discussing my book, and more particularly the Gospel doctrine as it is expressed in the Sermon on the Mount, the foreign critics affirmed that the latter could not really be called Christian doctrine – (they believe that the Christian doctrine is embodied in Catholicism or Protestantism) – and that the precepts of the Sermon on the Mount are only a series of the delightful but unpractical visions of the *"charmant docteur,"* as Renan says, suited to the artless, half-civilized Galileans who lived 1800 years ago, or to the Russian semi-barbarous peasants, to Sutaev and Bondarev, and to the Russian mystic Tolstoy', but which are by no means adapted to the lofty plane of European culture. The foreign secular critics, in a courteous way, in order not to wound my feelings, have endeavoured to show that my belief that mankind may be guided by so simple a doctrine as the Sermon on the Mount, arises partly from my limited knowledge of history and ignorance of the many vain attempts to carry out in daily life the principles of the Sermon on the Mount, which history tells us have always proved an utter failure, and partly from my misconception of the significance of our modern civilization, with its Krupp guns, its smokeless powder, its African colonization, its Home Rule, its parliaments, journalism, strikes, and constitutions, not to mention the Eiffel Tower – on which the entire population of Europe is at present reposing.

Thus wrote Vogue, thus wrote Leroy-Beaulieu, Matthew Arnold, the American writer Talmage, who is also a popular preacher, the free-thinker Ingersoll, and others.

"The teaching of Christ is no longer practicable, because it does not suit our industrial times" Ingersoll ingenuously remarks, and thereby he no doubt gives utterance to the views which this cultured generation holds in regard to the doctrine of Christ. The doctrine has no affinity with the industrialism of the present age, as though industrialism were a sacred institution which can suffer no change. A drunkard might thus reply to one who calls upon him to be sober, that a man in liquor finds such advice absurd.

The arguments of all secular writers, Russian as well as foreign, however varied in form or expression, are substantially alike; they all agree in misapprehending the doctrine of Christ, with its outcome of non-resistance, and in affirming that it is not expedient because it implies a need of a change of life.

The doctrine of Christ is inexpedient, because if we lived up to it our lives could not go on as they have done hitherto; in other words, if we were to begin to live like righteous men, as Christ bids us, we must abandon the wicked ways to which we have grown accustomed. So far from discussing the question of non-resistance of evil by violence, the very mention of the fact that the precepts of Christ include such a command is considered as sufficient proof of the inexpediency of the whole doctrine.

And yet it would seem necessary to offer some solution of this question, as it lies at the root of all that most interests us.

The question is how to settle these differences among men, when the very action that is considered evil by one man is considered good by another. It is no answer to say that I think an action evil although my adversary may consider it a good one. There are but two ways of solving the difficulty. One is to find a positive and indisputable standard of evil, and the other is to obey the command, resist not evil by violence.

Men have tried to achieve the former from the earliest historical ages, and we all know with what unsuccessful results.

The second solution – that is, the non-resistance of what we must consider evil until we have found a universal standard – that solution has been suggested by Christ himself.

It might be thought that the solution suggested by Christ was the wrong one, and a better one might be substituted after the standard had been found which is to define evil once and for all. One might not know of the existence of such a question, as is the case with the barbarous races, but no one can be permitted to pretend, like the learned critics of the Christian doctrine, that no such question does exist, or that the recognition of the right of certain individuals or groups of individuals, and still less of one's own right, to define evil, and to resist it by violence, decides the question, because we all know that such a recognition does not decide it at all, for there are always persons who will refuse to admit that such a prerogative can exist.

And yet this very acknowledgment, that anything that seems evil to us is evil, or else an utter misconception of the question, affords a basis for the conclusions of secular critics concerning the doctrine of Christ; hence not only the utterances of the clerical, but also those of the secular critics in regard to my book, have made it evident to me that most men totally fail to comprehend either the doctrine of Christ, or the questions which it is intended to decide.

CHAPTER III

The Misconception of Christianity
by Non-Believers

T HE MEANING OF THE Christian doctrine, which is
clear for the minority, has become unintelligible for the
majority of men – The cause of it is the false conception of Christianity and the misguided assurance of believers, as
well as of unbelievers, that they apprehend it – The apprehension
of Christianity for believers is concealed by the Church – The
apprehension of Christianity – Its essence and its unlikeness to
the pagan doctrines – Misunderstood at first, it has grown clear
to those who embraced it owing to its correspondence with the
truth – Contemporaneously with it arose the assertion that the
true meaning of the doctrine was understood, and had been confirmed by miraculous transmission – The Council of Disciples
according to the Acts – Authoritative and miraculous assertion
of the true conception of Christ's doctrine has found its logical
conclusion in the acknowledgment of the Credo and the Church
– The Church could not have been established by Christ – Definition of Churches according to the Catechism – There are various Churches, ever antagonistic to one another – What is heresy? – The work of Mr. Arnold concerning heresies – Heresies
are the sign of activity in the Churches – Churches always divide
mankind, and are ever inimical to Christianity – In what the activity of the Russian Church consists – Matthew xxiv: 23 – The
Sermon on the Mount, or the Credo – The Orthodox Church
conceals from the people the true meaning of Christianity – The
same is done by other Churches – All the contemporary external
conditions are such that they destroy the doctrine of the Church,
and therefore Churches use all their efforts to defend it.

The knowledge which I obtained after the publication of my
book in regard to the views which the minority of mankind have
held, and still hold, concerning the doctrine of Christ in its simplicity and real significance, as well as the criticisms of clerical

and secular writers, who deny the possibility of apprehending it in its actual meaning, have convinced me that while the minority has not only always possessed a true conception of this doctrine, and that this conception has grown steadily more and more clear, for the majority, on the other hand, its sense has become more and more vague, reaching at last such a degree of obscurity that men fail to understand the simplest commands expressed in the Bible, even when couched in the plainest possible language.

The inability that prevails at the present time to comprehend the doctrine of Christ in its true, simple, and actual meaning, when its light has penetrated into the remotest recesses of the human understanding, when, as Christ said, they proclaim from the roofs that which He whispered in the ear; when this doctrine penetrates every phase of human life, domestic, economical, civil, politic, and international – this failure to apprehend it would be inexplicable, if one had not discovered the reasons for it.

One of the reasons is, that believers as well as unbelievers are perfectly sure that they long ago understood the doctrine of Christ so completely, unquestionably and finally, that it can have no other meaning but the one which they attribute to it. That is because the tradition of this false conception has been handed down for ages – and therefore its misconception.

The most powerful stream of water cannot add one single drop to a vessel that is already full.

One might succeed in explaining to the dullest of men the most difficult of problems, if he had no previous conception in regard to them; but it is impossible to explain to the cleverest man even the simplest matters, if he is perfectly sure that he knows everything about it.

The Christian doctrine appears to men of the present times to be a doctrine of that kind, known for ages, and never to be questioned in its most trivial details, and which is susceptible to no other interpretation.

At the present time Christianity is conceived by those who profess the doctrines of the Church as a supernatural, miraculous revelation of all that is expressed in the Credo; while unbelievers look upon it as an affair of the past, a manifestation of the demand of humanity for a belief in the supernatural, as an historical fact, which has found its fullest expression in Catholicism, Orthodoxy, and Protestantism, and which has for us no vital meaning. For the believers the real significance of the doctrine is concealed by the Church; for the unbelievers it is hidden by science.

Let us begin by considering the former.

Eighteen hundred years ago, in the pagan world of Rome, there appeared a strange and novel doctrine, unlike any of its predecessors, which was ascribed to the man Christ.

It was a doctrine wholly new in form as well as in substance, both for the Hebrew world from whose midst it had sprung as well as for the Roman world in whose midst it was preached and promulgated.

Among the accurately defined religious precepts of the Jews, where, according to Isaiah, there was precept upon precept, and among the highly perfected Roman legislative assemblies, there appeared a doctrine that not only repudiated all deities, all fear of them, all augury and all faith in it, but also denied the necessity for any human institutions whatsoever. Instead of the precepts and creeds of former times, this doctrine presented only an image of interior perfection, truth and love in the person of Christ, and the attainment of this interior perfection possible for men, and, as a consequence, of the outward perfection foretold by the prophets: the coming of the Kingdom of God, when all enmity shall cease, when every man will hear the word of the Lord and be united with another in brotherly love, and when the lion and the lamb shall lie down together. Instead of threats of punishment for the non-observance of the commandments of the old laws, religious no less than secular, instead of tempting men by promise of rewards to observe these laws, this doctrine attracted mankind only by proclaiming itself to be the truth.

"If any man will do his will, he shall know of the doctrine, whether it be of God, or whether I speak of myself." John vii: 17.

"Which of you convinceth me of sin? And if I say the truth, why do ye not believe me?" John viii: 46.

"But now ye seek to kill me, a man that hath told you the truth." John viii: 40.

"And ye shall know the truth, and the truth shall make you free." John viii: 32.

God must be worshipped in truth. All doctrine will be made plain by the Spirit of Truth. Do as I command you, and you will know whether what I say is the truth.

No evidence was brought to prove the doctrine, except the truth and its harmony therewith. The whole substance consisted in learning the truth and in following its guidance, drawing nearer and nearer to it in the affairs of everyday life.

According to this doctrine, there is no mode of action that can justify a man or make him righteous; as regards interior perfection we have only the image of truth, in the person of Christ, to win our hearts, and outward perfection is expressed by a realization of the Kingdom of God. In order to fulfil the doctrine it needs but to take Christ for our model, and to advance in the direction of interior perfection by the road which has been pointed out to us, as well as in that of exterior perfection, which is the establishment of the Kingdom of God. The degree of human happiness, whether it be more or less, depends, according to this doctrine, not on the degree of perfection at which it arrives, but on the comparative rate of progress towards that perfection.

The advance towards perfection of Zacchaeus the Publican, of the adulteress, of the thief on the cross, is, according to this doctrine, better than the stagnation of the righteous Pharisee. The shepherd rejoices more over the one sheep which was lost and is found than over the ninety and nine which are in the fold. The prodigal returned, the piece of money which was lost and is found, is more precious unto God than that which was never lost.

According to this doctrine each state is but a step on the road towards the unattainable interior and exterior perfection, and therefore it has no significance in itself. The progress of this movement towards perfection is its merit; the least cessation of this movement means the cessation of good works.

"Let not thy left hand know what thy right hand doeth," and *"No man, having put his hand to the plough, and looking back, is fit for the kingdom of God." "Rejoice not, that the spirits are subject unto you; but rather rejoice, because your names are written*

in heaven." "Be ye therefore perfect, even as your Father which is in heaven is perfect." "Seek ye first the kingdom of God, and his righteousness."

The fulfilment of the doctrine lies in a continual progress towards the attainment of a higher truth, and in the growing realization of that truth within one's self, by means of an ever-increasing love; as well as in a more and more keen realization of the kingdom of God in the world around us. It is evident that the doctrine that appeared in the midst of the Hebrew and pagan world could not be accepted by the majority of men, who lived a life so totally unlike the one prescribed by this new doctrine; and even those who did accept it could not comprehend its full meaning, because of its contradiction of all former ideas.

It is only through a series of misapprehensions, errors, one-sided explanations, corrected and supplemented by generations of men, that the meaning of the Christian doctrine has become more and more plain. The Christian world conception and that of the Hebrew and pagan peoples mutually acted and reacted upon each other, and the Christian principle being the more vital, it penetrated deeper and deeper into the Hebrew and pagan principles that had outlived their usefulness, and became more clearly denned, freeing itself from the spurious admixtures imposed upon it. Men understood its meaning better and better, and realized it more and more unmistakably in life.

The older the world grew, the more lucid became its apprehension of Christianity, as must always be the case with any doctrine relating to human life.

Successive generations rectified the mistakes of the preceding ones and approached nearer and nearer to the apprehension of its true meaning. Thus it was from the very beginning of Christianity. And it was then that certain men came to the front who affirmed that the only true interpretation was the one which they themselves proclaimed, adducing the miracles as a proof thereof.

This was the principal cause of its misapprehension in the first place, and of its complete perversion in the second.

The doctrine of Christ was supposed to be transmitted to mankind not like any other truth, but in a peculiar, supernatural manner; hence they propose to prove its authority, not because it satisfies the demands of reason and of human nature in general, but because of the miraculous character of its transmission, which is supposed to be an incontrovertible proof of the validity of its conception.

This idea sprang from a misconception, and the result was that it became impossible to understand it.

It originated at the very beginning, when the doctrine was so imperfectly understood and often so erroneously construed, as, for example, in the Gospels and the Acts. The less men understood it, the more mysterious it appeared, and the greater need was there for visible proof of its authenticity. The rule for doing unto others as you would wish them to do unto you, called for no miraculous proof, neither did it require faith, because the proposition is convincing in itself, both to reason and to human nature. But the proposition that Christ was God needed miraculous testimony.

The more mystical grew the apprehension of Christ's teaching, the more the miraculous element entered into it; and the more miraculous it became, the further it was from its original meaning; and the more complicated, mystical, and remote from its original meaning it came to be, the more necessary it was to declare its infallibility, and the less intelligible it became.

From the very beginning of Christianity one could see from the Gospels, the Acts, and the Epistles how the misapprehension of the doctrine called forth the necessity of proofs – miraculous and beyond human intelligence.

It dated from the time mentioned in the Acts when the disciples went up to Jerusalem to consult with the elders in regard to the question that had arisen as to whether the uncircumcised and those who abstained not from the meat offered to idols, should be baptized.

The very manner of asking the question showed that those who discussed it misconceived the doctrine of Christ, who rejected all external rites, such as the washing of the feet, purification, fasts, and the Sabbath. It is said distinctly: "Not that which goeth into the mouth defileth a man; but those things which proceed out of the mouth come forth from the heart; and they defile the man." And therefore the question in regard to the baptism of those not circumcised could only arise among men who, loving their Teacher and with the intuitive perception of the grandeur of his doctrine, could not as yet comprehend its exact meaning. And so it was.

And in proportion as the members of the assembly failed to comprehend the doctrine, did they stand in need of an outward affirmation of their incomplete conception. And in order to decide the question, whose very proposal proves the misconception of the doctrine, it was that in this assembly for the first time, according to the description given in the Acts, were uttered those awful words, productive of so much harm, by which the truth of certain propositions has been for the first time confirmed: "For it seemed good to the Holy Ghost, and to us," that is to say, it was a declaration that the truth of what they said was witnessed by a miraculous participation of the Holy Ghost, that is – of God.

But the assertion that the Holy Ghost – that is to say, God – had spoken through the Apostles, in its turn required proof. And therefore it became necessary to declare that on the fiftieth day the Holy Ghost in the shape of fiery tongues descended on those who had made this assertion. [In the description the descent of the Holy Ghost precedes the council, but the Acts were written much later than either.] But the descent of the Holy Ghost must also be proved, though it would be difficult to say why a fiery tongue hovering over a man's head should be a proof of the truth of what he says any more than the miracles, the cures, the resurrections, the martyrdoms, and all the rest of those persuasive miracles with which the Acts are filled, and which serve rather to repel than to convince one of the truth of the Christian dogmas. The results of these methods were such that the more pains they took to confirm their state merits, accumulating stories of miracles, the more the doctrine itself deviated from its original meaning, and the less intelligible it became.

Thus it was from the beginning of the Christian era, and thus it continued to increase, until in our own time it has reached its logical consummation in the dogma of transubstantiation, the infallibility of the Pope, the bishops, and Scriptures, which is something utterly incomprehensible and nonsensical, requiring a blind faith, not in God or Christ, nor even in the doctrine, but a faith either in one person, as in Catholicism, or in many persons, as in Orthodoxy, or in a book, as in Protestantism. The more widely spread Christianity became, and the larger the number of uninstructed men it received, the less it was understood, the more the infallibility of its conceptions was insisted upon, and the more slender grew the possibility of understanding its true meaning. Already, about the time of Constantine, the entire conception of the doctrine amounted to the résumé formulated by the temporal power – the outcome of discussions that took place in the council – to the Credo, in which it is said: I believe in this and that, etc., and at the end, "in the one holy, Apostolic and Ecumenical Church," that is, in the infallibility of the persons who constitute it; so that it all amounted to this, that a man believed not in God, nor in Christ, as they revealed themselves to him, but in that which was believed by the Church.

But the Church is holy, and was founded by Christ. God could not allow men to interpret his doctrine as they chose, and therefore He established the Church. All these propositions are so unjust and unfounded, that one is actually ashamed to refute them. In no place, and in no manner whatsoever, save in the assertion of the Church, is it seen that either God or Christ can ever have founded anything like the Church in its ecclesiastical sense. There is a distinct and evident warning in the New Testament against the Church, as an outside authority, in the passage which bids the disciples of Christ call no man father or master. But nowhere is there a word in regard to the establishment of what the ecclesiastics call the Church. The word church is used in the New Testament twice, once in speaking of the assembly which is to decide a dispute; the second time in connection with the obscure words in regard to the rock, Peter, and the gates of hell. From these two references, where the word is used only in the sense of an assembly, men have derived the institution which we recognize at present under the name of the Church.

But Christ could by no means have founded a church, that is, what we understand by that word at the present time, because nothing like our church, as we know it in these days, with the sacraments, the hierarchy, and above all the establishment of infallibility, was to be found either in the words of Christ, or in the ideas of the men of those times.

Because men have called something which has been established since, by the same word that Christ used in regard to another thing, by no means gives them a right to assert that Christ founded only one true church.

Moreover, if Christ had it in his mind to establish a church which was to be the depository of the whole doctrine and faith, He would surely have expressed this so plainly and clearly, and would have given, apart from all stories of miracles which are repeated with every variety of superstition, such signs as would leave no doubt as to its authenticity; yet this was not the case, and now as always, one finds different institutions, each one calling itself the only true church.

The Catholic catechism says: *"L'Eglise est la societe des fideles etablie par N. S. Jesus Christ, repandue sur toute laterre et soumise a l'autorite de pasteurs legitimes, principalement notre S. P. le pape"* – meaning by *"pasteurs legitimes"* a human institution made up of a number of men bound together by a certain organization of which the Pope is the head.

The Orthodox catechism says: *"Our Church is a society established on earth by Jesus Christ, united by the divine doctrine and the sacraments under the government and direction of a hierarchy established by the Lord,"* – those words, "established by the Lord," signifying a Greek hierarchy, composed of certain men who are ordained to fill certain places.

The Lutheran catechism says: *"Our Church is a holy Christian society of believers under Christ, our Master, in which the Holy Ghost, by means of the Bible and the sacraments, offers, communicates, and dispenses the divine salvation,"* meaning by that, that the Catholic Church is in error, and has fallen away from grace, and that the genuine tradition has been preserved in Protestantism.

For Catholics the divine Church is identified with the Pope and the Roman hierarchy. For the Orthodox it is identified with the institution of the Eastern and Russian hierarchy. For Lutherans the divine Church signifies a congregation of men who acknowledge the Bible and the Lutheran catechism

When those who belong to any one of the existing churches speak of the beginnings of Christianity, they generally use the word church in the singular, as though there had never been but one church. This is quite unfair. The Church, which as an institution declares itself to be the depository of infallible truth, did not arise until there were already two.

While the faithful still agreed among themselves, the congregation was united and there was no occasion for calling itself a church. It was only when it separated into two hostile parties, that each party felt obliged to assert its possession of the truth, by claiming infallibility.

During the course of the controversies between the two parties, while each one claimed infallibility for itself and declared its opponent heretical, arose the idea of the one church.

We know that there was a church in the year 51, which granted the admission of the uncircumcised, and we know it only because there was another, the Jewish Church, which denied their right to membership.

If at the present time there is a Catholic Church which asserts its infallibility, it is because there are other churches, namely, the Greek Orthodox and the Lutheran, each one asserting its own infallibility, and thus disowning all other churches. Hence the idea of one church is but the product of the imagination, containing not a shadow of reality.

It is an historical fact that there have existed, and still continue to exist, numerous bodies each one of whom maintains itself to be the true church established by Christ, declaring at the same time that all the others who call themselves churches are heretical and schismatic.

The catechisms of those churches which possess the greatest number of communicants, the Catholic, the Orthodox, and the Lutheran, express this in the plainest language.

The Catholic catechism says: *"Quels sont ceux quisont hors de l'eglise? Les infideles, heretiques, et schismatiques."* By *"schismatiques"* it means the so-called Orthodox, and by heretics the Lutherans; so that, according to the Catholic catechism, the Church is composed only of Catholics.

In the so-called Orthodox catechism it says: *"The name*

Church of Christ means only the Orthodox Church, which has re-mained in perfect union with the universal church." As to the Ro-man Church and the Protestant creeds (they are not even called a church), they cannot belong to the one true church, for they have separated themselves from it."

According to this definition the Catholics and the Protestants are outside of the Church, and only the Orthodox are in it.

The Lutheran catechism says: *"Die wahre Kirche wirddarein erkannt, das in ihr das Wort Gottes lauter undrein ohne Men-schenzusetzung gelehrt und die Sacramententreu nach Christ Einsetzung gewartet werden."*

According to this definition, those who have added anything whatsoever to the teaching of Christ and the apostles, as the Catholic and Greek Churches have done, are outside the Church and the Lutherans alone are in it.

The Catholics assert that the Holy Ghost dwells perpetually with their hierarchy; the Orthodox assert that the same Holy Ghost resides also with them; the Arians claim that the Holy Ghost manifests itself to them (and they have the same right to assert this as have the prevailing religions of the present day); all the denominations of Protestants, Lutherans, Reformed Presby-terians, Methodists, Swedenborgians, and Mormons assert that the Holy Ghost manifests itself only with them.

If the Catholics assert that the Holy Ghost during the separa-tion of the Arian and Greek Churches withdrew from the separat-ing churches and remained in the one true church, then the Prot-estants of any denomination whatsoever may assert with as much right that during the separation of their church from the Catholic, the Holy Ghost left the Catholic Church and entered into their own. And this is exactly what they do say. Every church professes to derive its creed by an unbroken tradition from Christ and the apostles. And certainly every Christian creed derived from Christ must have reached the present generation through tradition of some sort. But this is no proof that any one of these traditions embodies infallible truth, to the exclusion of all others.

Every branch proceeds from the root without interruption; but the fact that each one comes from one root, by no means proves it to be the only branch. And so it is in regard to the churches. The proofs which each church offers of its apostolic succession, and the miracles which are to prove its authenticity, are the same in every case; consequently there is but one exact definition of what is called a church (not the imaginary church which we may desire, but the actual church which has really existed). The Church is a body of men which lays claim to the exclusive possession of the truth. All these various societies which were afterwards transformed by State authority into powerful organizations have really been the chief obstacles to the diffusion of true Christianity. It could not be otherwise; for the principal characteristic which distinguishes the doctrine of Christ from those of earlier times is that the men who accepted it strove to understand and to fulfil it more and more perfectly; whereas the doctrine of the Church affirmed that it was already thoroughly understood and also fulfilled.

However strange this may seem to us, reared as we have been in the false doctrine of the Church, as if it were a Christian institution, and taught to despise heresy, it is nevertheless in that which men called heresy that true progress, that is true Christianity, was manifested, and it only ceased to be such when these heresies were checked, and it was, so to speak, stamped with the immutable imprint of the Church.

What then is heresy? Read all the theological works which treat of heresies, of that subject which above all others calls for an exact definition, for every theologian speaks of the true doctrine in the midst of the false ones by which it is surrounded, and nowhere will you find even the shadow of a definition of heresy.

As an instance of the complete absence of the definition of what is understood by the word heresy, we will quote the opinion of a learned Christian historian, E. de Pressensé, in his *Histoire du Dogme*, with its epigraph *"Ubi Christus, ibi Ecclesia"* (Paris, 1869). This is what he says in his preface (p. 4):

"I know that they dispute our right to qualify thus" (that is, to pronounce them heretical) *"the tendencies which were so actively resisted by the early Fathers. The very name of heresy seems an attack upon liberty of conscience and thought. We cannot share these scruples, for they would simply deprive Christianity of any individual character."*

And having said that after Constantine the Church did in fact abuse its authority to describe the dissenters as heretics and to persecute them, he says, in speaking of the early ages of Christianity: "The Church is a free association; there is an advantage to be gained in separating from it The controversy against error is based on feelings and ideas; no uniform body of dogma has as yet been adopted; differences of secondary importance appear in the East and West with perfect freedom; theology is not limited by unalterable formulas. If amid these varying opinions a common groundwork of faith is discerned, have we not the right to see in this, not a definite system devised and formulated by the representatives of a school, but faith itself in its most unerring instinct and spontaneous manifestation? If this very unanimity which is revealed in the essential matters of faith is found to be antagonistic to certain tendencies, have we not the right to infer that these tendencies disagreed with the fundamental principles of Christianity? Will not this supposition become a certainty if we recognize in the doctrine rejected by the Church the characteristic features of one of the religions of the past? If we admit that Gnosticism or Ebionitism are legitimate forms of Christian thought, we must boldly declare that Christian thought does not exist, nor does it possess any specific characteristic by which it may be recognized. We should destroy it even while pretending to enlarge its limits. In the time of Plato no one would have dared to advocate a doctrine which would leave no room for the theory of ideas, and he would have been subjected to the well-deserved ridicule of Greece, if he attempted to make of Epicurus or of Zeno a disciple of the Academy. Let us then admit that if there exists a religion or a doctrine called Christianity, it may have its heresies."

The writer's argument amounts to this, that every opinion which does not accord with the code of dogmas that we have professed at any given time, is a heresy. At a certain time and in a certain place men make a certain profession, but this profession can never be a fixed criterion of the truth. All is summed up in the *"Ubi Christus, ibi Ecclesia," and Christ is wherever we are.*

Every so-called heresy which claims that what it professes is the actual truth, may likewise find in the history of the Church a consistent explanation of the faith it professes, and apply all the arguments to its own use. Pressense simply calls his own creed Christian truth, precisely as every heretical sect has done.

The primary definition of the word heresy is the name given by a society of men to any opinion contradicting any part of the doctrine professed by the society. A more specific meaning is an expression of an opinion which denies the truth of the creed, established and maintained by the temporal power.

There is a remarkable, although little-known work entitled *Unpartheyische Kirchen und Ketzer-Historie*, 1729, by Gottfried Arnold, which treats of this subject, and points out the illegality, the perversity, the lack of sense, and the cruelty of employing the word heresy in the sense of refutation. This book is an attempt to relate the history of Christianity in the form of a history of heresies.

In his introduction the author asks a series of questions: (1) Of those who make heretics (Von denen Ketzermachern Selbst); (2) Of those who have become heretics; (3) Of the subjects of heresy; (4) Of the ways of making heretics; and (5) Of the aims and consequences of the making of heretics. To each of these points he adds scores of other questions, giving the answers from the works of well-known theologians, but principally leaving it to the reader to draw his own deductions from the contents of the book. As instances of questions which are to a certain extent their own answers I will quote the following: Concerning the 4th question, of the methods for making heretics, he asks in one of the questions (the 7th): "Does not all history tend to show us that the greatest makers of heretics, the adepts in the art, were those very wiseacres from whom the Father concealed his secrets – that is the hypocrites, the Pharisees, and the Scribes, or utterly godless and evil-minded men? (Questions 20–21.) And in the corrupted times of Christianity did not the hypocrites and envious ones reject the very men, talented and especially endorsed by the Lord, who would have been highly esteemed in periods of pure Christianity? (21) And on the other hand, would not those men who during the decadence of Christianity rose above all others, and set themselves up as teachers of the purest Christianity, would not they, during the times of the Apostles of Christ and his disciples, have been considered as the shameful heretics and anti-Christians? "Among other things, while expressing the idea that the verbal declaration of the essence of faith which was required by the Church, the abjuration of which was regarded as a heresy, could never cover all the ideas and beliefs of the faithful, and that hence the requirement that faith shall be expressed by a certain formula of words is the immediate cause of heresy, he says in the 21st question:

"And supposing that holy acts and thoughts appear to a man so high and so profound that he finds no adequate words wherewith to convey them, should he be considered a heretic if he is unable to formulate his conception? (33) And was not this the reason why there were no heresies in the early times of Christianity, because Christians judged each other not by their words, but by their hearts and by their deeds, enjoying a perfect freedom of expression, without the fear of being called heretic?" "Was it not one of the convenient and easiest methods of the Church" (he asks in the 31st question) "when the ecclesiastics wished to rid themselves of any one, or ruin his reputation, to excite suspicion in regard to the doctrine he held, and by investing him in the garment of heresy, condemn and cast him out?"

"Although it is true that among so-called heretics sins and errors have been committed, it is no less true, as the numerous examples here quoted bear testimony" (that is to say, in the history of the Church and of heresies)"that there has never been a sincere and conscientious man of any importance whose safety has not been endangered through the envy of the ecclesiastics."

This was the interpretation of heresy almost 200 years ago, and the same meaning is attached to it today, and so long as the idea of the Church shall exist it will never change. Where the Church exists there must also exist the idea of heresy. The Church is a body of men claiming possession of indisputable truth. A heresy is the opinion of men who do not acknowledge the truth of the Church to be indisputable.

Heresy is the manifestation of a movement in the Church; it is an attempt to destroy the immutable assertion of the Church, the attempt of a living apprehension of the doctrine. Each advance that has been made towards the comprehension and the practice of the doctrine has been accomplished by heretics: Tertullian, Origen, Augustine, and Luther, Huss, Savonarola, Helchitsky, and others were all heretics. It could not be otherwise.

A disciple of Christ, who possesses an ever-growing sense of the doctrine and of its progressive fulfilment as it advances towards perfection, cannot either for himself or others affirm, simply because he is a disciple of Christ, that he understands and practises the doctrine of Christ to its fullest extent; still less could he affirm this in regard to any body of men. To whatsoever state of comprehension and perfection he may have arrived he must always feel the inadequacy both of his conception and of its application, and must ever strive for something more satisfactory. And therefore to claim for one's self, or for any body of men whatsoever, the possession of a complete apprehension and practice of the doctrine of Christ is in direct contradiction to the spirit of Christ's doctrine itself.

However strange this statement may appear, every church, as a church, has always been, and always must be, an institution not only foreign, but absolutely hostile to the doctrine of Christ. It is not without reason that Voltaire called it *"l'infâme"*; it is not without reason that all so-called Christian sects believe the Church to be the Scarlet Woman prophesied by the Revelation; it is not without reason that the history of the Church is the history of cruelties and horrors.

Churches in themselves are, as some persons believe, institutions based upon a Christian principle, from which they have deviated to a certain extent; but considered in the light of churches, of bodies of men claiming infallibility, they are anti-Christian institutions. Between churches in the ecclesiastical sense and Christianity, not only is there nothing in common except the name, but they are two utterly contradictory and hostile elements. One is pride, violence, self-assertion, inertia, and death. The other is meekness, repentance, submission, activity, and life.

No man can serve these two masters at the same time; he must choose either the one or the other.

The servants of the churches of every creed, especially in these modern times, strive to represent themselves as the partisans of progress in Christianity; they make concessions, they try to correct the abuses that have crept into the Church, and protest that it is wrong to deny the principle of the Christian Church on account of these abuses, because it is only through the medium of the Church that unity can be obtained, and that the Church is the only mediator between God and man. All this is untrue. So far from fostering the spirit of unity, the churches have ever been the fruitful source of human enmity, of hatred, wars, conflicts, inquisitions, Eves of St. Bartholomew, and so on; neither do the churches act as the mediators between God and man – an office, moreover, quite unnecessary, and directly forbidden by Christ himself, who has revealed his doctrine unto each individual; it is but the dead formula and not the living God which the churches offer to man, and which serves rather to increase than diminish the distance between man and his Creator. The churches, which were founded upon a misconception, and which preserve this misconception by their immutability, must of necessity harass and persecute any new conception, because they know, however they may try to conceal it, that every advance along the road indicated by Christ is undermining their own existence.

Whenever one reads or listens to the essays and sermons in which ecclesiastical writers of modern times belonging to the various creeds discuss the Christian truths and virtues, when one hears and reads these artificial arguments, these exhortations, these professions of faith elaborated through centuries, that now and then sound sincere, one is almost ready to doubt if the churches can be inimical to Christianity." It cannot be possible that men like John Chrysostom, Fenelon, Butler, and other Christian preachers, could be inimical to it" One would like to say: "The churches may have gone astray from Christianity, may have committed errors, but they cannot have been hostile to it." But one must first see the fruit before he can know the tree, as Christ has taught, and one sees that their fruits were evil, that the result of their works has been the distortion of Christianity; and one cannot help concluding that, however virtuous the men may have been, the cause of the church in which these men served was not Christian. The goodness and virtue of certain individuals who served the churches were peculiar to themselves

66

and not to the cause which they served. All these excellent men, like Francis of Assisi and Francis de Sales, Tichon Zadonsky, Thomas à Kempis and others, were good men, even though they served a cause hostile to Christianity, and they would have been still more charitable and more exemplary had they not yielded obedience to false doctrines.

But why do we speak of, or sit in judgment on, the past, which may be falsely represented, and is in any event but little known to us? The churches, with their principles and their works, are not of the past; we have them with us today, and can judge them by their works and by their influence over men.

What then constitutes their power? How do they influence men? What is their work in the Greek, the Catholic, and in all the Protestant denominations? And what are the consequences of such work?

The work of our Russian, so-called Orthodox Church is visible to all. It is a factor of primary importance, which can neither be concealed nor disputed.

In what manner is the activity of the Russian Church displayed – that vast institution which labours with so much zeal, that institution which numbers among its servants half a million men, and costs the people tens of millions?

The activity of the Church consists in forcing, by every means in its power, upon the one hundred millions of Russian people those antiquated, timeworn beliefs which have lost all significance, and which were formerly professed by foreigners, with whom we had nothing in common, beliefs in which nearly every man has lost his faith, even in some cases those very men whose duty it is to inculcate them.

The endeavour to force upon the people those formulas of the Byzantine clergy, marvellous to them, and senseless to us, concerning the Trinity, the Virgin, the sacraments, grace, and so forth, embraces one province of the activity of the Russian Church; another function is the encouragement given to idolatry in the literal sense of the word: the veneration of holy relics and holy images, the sacrifices offered to them in the faith that they will hear and grant prayers. I will pass over in silence what is written in the ecclesiastical magazines by the clergy who possess a semblance of learning and liberality, and will speak only of what is really done by the clergy throughout the immense extent of Russia, among its one hundred millions of inhabitants. What is it that is taught to the people with such unremitting pains and endeavour, and with so much earnestness? What is required of them for the sake of the so-called Christian religion?

I will start at the beginning, with the birth of the child. When a child is born we are taught that a prayer must be read over the mother and child in order to purify them, for without that prayer the mother remains unclean. For that purpose, and facing the icons of the saints, whom the common people simply call gods, the priest takes the infant in his arms, reads the exhortation, and by that mean she is supposed to cleanse the mother. Then the parents are instructed, nay, even ordered, under penalty of punishment in the event of non-compliance, to christen the child – that is, to let the priest immerse it three times in the water, while words unintelligible to all present are read, and still less intelligible ceremonies are performed, such as the application of oil to different parts of the body, the cutting of the hair, the blowing and spitting of the sponsors at the imaginary devil. All this is necessary to cleanse the child and make a Christian of him. Then the parents are told that the child must receive the holy sacrament – that is, he is to swallow, in the form of bread and wine, a particle of the body of Christ, by which means the child will receive the blessing of Christ, and so on. Then they are told that as the child grows it must be taught to pray, which means that he is to stand in front of boards upon which the faces of Christ, the Virgin, and the saints are painted, bow his head and body, while with his right hand, his fingers being folded in a peculiar manner, he touches his forehead, his shoulders and his stomach, and utters certain Slavonic words, the commonest of which, those which all children learn, are the following: *"Mother of God . . . . Virgin, rejoice,"* etc. Then the child is taught that he must repeat this – that is, that he must make the sign of the cross whenever he sees a church or an icon. Furthermore, he is taught that on a holiday (holidays are either the day on which Christ was born, although no one knows when that took place, or the day of his circumcision, or that on which the Virgin died, or when the cross or the icon was brought, or when some fanatic beheld a vision, etc.) he should array himself in his best clothes, go to church, buy candles and set them up before the icons of the saints, give to the priest memoranda bearing the names of the dead who are to be prayed for, receive bread with triangular pieces cut out of it, pray repeatedly for the health and welfare of the Czar and bishops, as well as for himself and his own affairs, and then kiss the cross and the hand of the priest.

Thus is he taught to pray; and besides this, he is also taught that he must perform his devotions once a year. To perform one's devotions means to go to church and tell one's sins to the priest, it being assumed that this recital of one's sins to a stranger will have a purifying effect on a man; then he is to swallow a spoonful of bread and wine, which will purify him still more. Moreover, men are told that if a man and woman desire to have their sexual relation sanctified they must come to church, put crowns of metal upon their heads, swallow some wine, walk three times round a table, accompanied by the sound of singing, and this will make their sexual relation holy and entirely different from any others.

In daily life the observation of the following rules is enjoined: to eat no meat nor drink no milk on certain days, to say *Te Deums* and Requiems on certain other days, to invite the priest to one's house on holidays and present him with money; to take from the church several times a year boards upon which are painted the images of the saints, and to carry them on towels through fields and houses. Before death a man must without fail receive a spoonful of bread and wine; and if there be time to be anointed with oil, that is still better, for it insures his welfare in the future life. After his death his relatives are told that, in order to save his soul, it is well to place in his hand a printed prayer; it is also a good thing to read a certain book over the dead, and/or his name to be mentioned in church at stated times.

This is what constitutes every man's religious obligation. But if any one wishes to take a special care of his soul, this creed teaches that the greatest amount of happiness may be secured in the next world by bequeathing money for churches and monasteries, thereby obliging the saints to pray for one. According to this faith it is also well to visit monasteries and kiss the miraculous icons and the relics.

These are believed to impart a peculiar holiness, strength, and grace; and to be near these objects, as one must be in kissing them, placing tapers before them, crawling under them and repeating *Te Deums* before them, greatly promotes salvation.

And this is the faith called Orthodox, this is the true faith, the one which under the garb of a Christian religion has been energetically taught to the people for many centuries, and is inculcated at the present time more vigorously than ever.

Let it not be said that the Orthodox teachers look upon all this as an ancient form of faith which it was not considered worthwhile to abolish, and that the essence of the doctrine abides elsewhere. This is not the truth. Throughout Russia, and lately with increased energy, the entire Russian clergy teaches this faith, and this alone. Nothing else is taught. Men may write about other doctrines and discuss them in the capitals, but among the hundred million inhabitants this, and only this, is taught. The ecclesiastics may discuss other doctrines, but only this is what is taught.

All this – the worship of relics and shrines – is included in theology and the catechism; the people are carefully instructed in all this, theoretically and practically, by every kind of solemnity, splendour, authority, and violence; the people are compelled to believe in it all; they are hypnotized, and the faith is jealously guarded against any attempt to deliver them from these foolish superstitions.

As I said in my book, I have during the course of many years had frequent opportunities to remark the ridicule and rude jests that have been applied to Christ's words and doctrine, and the ecclesiastics not only failed to condemn it, they even encouraged this scoffing; but let a man venture to say one disrespectful word of the ugly idol called the Iverskaya, sacrilegiously carried around Moscow by intoxicated men, and a groan of indignation will rise from these same Orthodox ecclesiastics. In fact, it is only an external worship in the form of idolatry that is propagated. And let it not be said that the one does not exclude the other, that "All therefore whatsoever they bid you observe, that

70

observe and do; but do not ye after their works: for they *"say, and do not" Matthew xxiii: 3*. This is said concerning the Pharisees, who fulfilled all the outward commands of the law, and therefore the words," whatsoever they bid you observe, that observe and do," refer to acts of benevolence and charity; whereas the words, *"do not ye after their works, for they say and do not,"* refer to their observances of the rites and their indifference to works of charity, and directly contradicts the clerical interpretation of this passage, which explains it as a commandment which has to do only with the rites. An external worship is hardly compatible with the service of charity and truth; one is apt to exclude the other. It was so with the Pharisees, and the same may be said of our professing Christians.

If a man is to be saved by redemption, the sacraments, and prayer, good works are no longer of any value to him. It must be either the Sermon on the Mount or the Credo. No man can believe in both, and the ecclesiastics have chosen the latter. The Credo is taught and recited as a prayer in the churches, while the Sermon on the Mount is excluded even from selections from the Bible which are read in churches, so that the congregation never hear it, except on the days when the entire Bible is read. It is inevitable; the men who can believe that a cruel and unreasonable God had condemned humanity to eternal death and sacrificed his own Son, and who had destined a certain portion of mankind to everlasting torture, cannot believe in a God of love. A man who believes in God, in the Christ who is coming in his glory to judge and punish the dead and the living, cannot believe in a Christ who commands us to turn the other cheek to the offender, who forbids us to sit in judgment, and who bids us to forgive our enemies and to love them. A man who believes in the inspiration of the Old Testament and in the holiness of David, who on his deathbed ordered the murder of an old man who had offended him, and whom he could not kill himself because he was bound by an oath (I Kings ii. 8, 9), and many other horrors of a similar character, in which the Old Testament abounds, cannot believe in the moral law of Christ; a man who believes in the doctrine and sermons of the church, wherein the practice of war and the penalty of death are reconciled with Christianity, cannot believe in the brotherhood of humanity.

But, above all, a man who believes in salvation through faith, in redemption, and in the sacraments, cannot strive with all his might to live up to the moral precepts of Christ. A man who has been taught by the Church the sacrilegious doctrine that he is to be saved through a certain medium, and not by his own efforts, will surely have recourse to that medium; he will not trust to his own efforts, on which, he has been assured, it is sinful to rely. Every church, with its doctrines of redemption and salvation, and above all, the Orthodox faith, with its idolatry, excludes the doctrine of Christ. But it is said, *"This has always been the faith of the people, and that they will continue to hold it is proved by the whole history of the Russian nation. It would be wrong to deprive them of their traditions."* Herein lies the fallacy. The people, it is true, did once upon a time profess something like what is at present professed by the Church; but besides this worship of images and relics, the people had always a profound moral conception of Christianity never possessed by the Church, and only met with in her noblest representatives; but the people, in the better class, and in spite of the obstacles raised by the State and the Church, has long since abandoned the cruder phase of belief, a fact that is proved by the rationalistic sects that are beginning to spring up on every side, sects that Russia is filled with at the present day, and against which the ecclesiastics wage so hopeless a warfare. The people are beginning to recognize the moral, vital side of Christianity more and more plainly. And now the Church appears, failing to give them a moral support, but forcibly teaching old-time paganism – the Church, with its immutable formulas, endeavouring to thrust men back into the gloom from which they are struggling so earnestly to escape.

The ecclesiastics say: "We are teaching nothing new; it is the same faith which the people already hold, only we teach it in a more perfect manner." It is like binding a chicken and trying to put it back into the shell from which it came. I have often been struck by the spectacle, which would be simply absurd were not its results so terrible, of men travelling, so to speak, in a circle, deceived and deceiving, but wholly unable to escape from the charmed circle.

The first question, the first doubt, that enters the head of every Russian when he begins to reason, is a suspicion of the miraculous icons, and principally of the relics: is it true that they are incorruptible, and that they perform miracles? Hundreds and thousands of men ask these questions, and are at a loss for an answer, especially since bishops and metropolitans and other eminent persons kiss both the relics and the miraculous images. Ask the bishops and other personages of importance why they do this, and they will tell you that they do it in order to impress the masses, and the masses do it because the bishops and other magnates do it. The activity of the Russian Church, despite the veneer of modernity and the scientific and spiritual standards which its members have begun to establish by their essays, their religious reviews, and their sermons, consists not only in encouraging the people in a coarse and grotesque idolatry, but in strengthening and promulgating superstition and religious ignorance, and in endeavouring to destroy the vital conception of Christianity that exists in the people side by side with this idolatry.

I remember being once in a bookshop of the monastery of Optinae Desert while an old peasant was selecting spiritual reading for his educated grandson. The monk was offering him a description of relics, of holy days, of miraculous icons, the Book of Psalms, and the like. I asked the old man if he had a Bible. "No," he replied. "Give him a Russian Bible," I said to the monk. "We don't sell that to them," said the monk. This, in short, is the activity of our Church.

But the European or American reader may say, "That only happens in barbaric Russia," and the remark will be correct, but only so far as it applies to the government, which supports the Church to maintain in our land its stupefying and demoralizing influence.

It is true that there is nowhere in Europe a government so despotic, or that is in more perfect accord with the established Church. Therefore in Russia the government authorities play an important part in demoralizing the people; but it is not true that the Russian Church differs from other churches in respect to its influence over the people.

Churches are everywhere alike, and if the Catholic, Anglican, and Lutheran have not at their beck so submissive a government as the Russian, we may be sure that they would not fail to take advantage of it were it within their reach.

The Church as a Church, whether it be Catholic, Anglican, Lutheran, or Presbyterian, or any denomination whatsoever, inasmuch as it is a Church, cannot help striving after the same object as the Russian Church – namely, to conceal the true meaning of the doctrine of Christ and to substitute a meaning of its own, which imposes no obligations, which excludes the possibility of understanding the true, living doctrine of Christ, and which above all justifies the existence of a priesthood living at the expense of the people.

Do we not find Catholicism with its prohibition against reading the Bible, and with its demand for implicit obedience to the clergy and the infallible Pope? Wherein does Catholicism differ in its preaching from the Russian Church? The same external worship, the same relics, miracles, and statues, miracle-performing Madonnas and processions; the same vague and mystical utterances concerning Christianity in books and sermons, and all in support of the grossest idolatry.

And is it not the same in the Anglican or in the Lutheran, or in any other Protestant denomination with an established form of church?

The same demands that the congregation shall acknowledge a belief in dogmas which were defined in the fourth century, and which have lost all meaning for the men of our time; the same call for idol worship, if not of relics or icons, at least of the Sabbath and the letter of the Bible; the same endeavour to conceal the real requirement of Christianity and the substitution of exterior rites, and *"cant,"* as the English so happily define the tendency which finds such sway among them.

This activity is more noticeable in Protestantism, because that creed has not even the excuse of antiquity. And is not the same thing going on in the present "Revivalism," are generated Calvinism, which has given birth to the Salvation Army? Inasmuch as the attitude of all ecclesiastical dogmas towards the doctrine of Christ is very much the same, so are their methods of a similar character.

The attitude they have taken obliges them to make every effort to conceal the doctrine of that Christ in whose name they speak.

The disparity between ecclesiastical creeds and the doctrine of Christ is so great that a special effort is required to keep mankind in ignorance. Indeed, one needs but to consider the position of any adult, I do not say educated, but one who has assimilated superficially the current notions concerning geology, physics, chemistry, cosmography, and history, when for the first time he actually reflects on the faith impressed upon him in his childhood, and maintained by the Church, concerning the creation of the world in six days – the appearance of light before the sun was created, the story of Noah's ark and the animals preserved in it, concerning Jesus and his divine origin as the Son of God who created all things before time existed; that this God came down to earth because of Adam's sin; that he rose from the dead, ascended into heaven, and sits on the right hand of the Father; that he will come in the clouds to judge the living and the dead, etc.

All these ideas evolved by the men of the fourth century, which had for them a certain meaning, have none whatever for us. The present generation may repeat these words, but it can never believe in them, because the statements that God dwells in heaven, that the heavens opened and a voice was heard to utter certain words, that Christ arose from the dead and ascended into heaven, that he will come again from some place in the clouds, etc, have no meaning for us.

It was possible for a man who believed that heaven was a substantial arch of limited dimensions to believe or to disbelieve that God created it, that it opened, and that Christ ascended thither – but for us there is no sense in such ideas. Men of our time can only affirm that it is one's duty to believe all this – which they do. But they cannot really believe in what has no meaning in it for them.

But if all these utterances are supposed to have an allegorical significance and are only intended as similes, then we know in the first place that all the churchmen will not agree to this – on the contrary, the majority insist on taking the Scriptures literally; and in the second place, that these interpretations differ greatly, and are supported by no reliable authority.

And even if a man wished to believe the doctrine of the Church as it is taught, the increase of culture, the reading of the Bible, and the intercourse among the members of different churches, form a greater and more in surmountable obstacle to belief.

Nowadays a man has but to buy the Bible for threepence, and to read the simple, indisputable words of Christ to the Samaritan woman, that the Father seeketh worshippers neither in Jerusalem nor in this or that mountain, but worshippers in spirit and truth; or the words, that a Christian should pray not like the heathen in the temples, nor at the corners of streets, but in the secrecy of his closet; or, that a disciple of Christ may call no one father or mother – one has but to read these words to be indubitably convinced that priests who call themselves teachers in opposition to the teaching of Christ, and dispute among themselves, cannot be authorities, and that that which they teach is not Christian.

But this is not enough. If the modern man were to go on believing in miracles and never read the Bible, the fellowship with men of other creeds and professions, which is so much a matter of course in these days, will compel him to question the truth of his religion. It was natural enough for a man who had never met a believer in a creed different from his own, to think that his was the only faith; but an intelligent man has but to encounter – and that is an everyday occurrence – good and bad men of all creeds, who criticize each other's beliefs, in order to question the truth of his own religion. Now, only a man either totally ignorant or indifferent to the problems of life as dealt with by religion can remain in the faith of the Church.

What shrewdness is needed, and what efforts must the churches make in order to go on in the face of all these faith-destroying influences, building temples, saying masses, preaching, instructing, converting, and above all receiving for this the large compensations which all those priests, pastors, stewards, superintendents, abbots, archdeacons, bishops, and archbishops receive!

A special and supernatural effort is called for, and to this the Church responds, exerting herself more and more. In Russia, besides many other measures, they employ a simple, rude violence, by virtue of the power invested in the Church. People who shrink from an outward observance of faith and who do not conceal the fact are simply punished or deprived of their civil rights; and to those who strictly comply with the rites, privileges and rewards are granted.

So much for Orthodoxy; but every church, without exception, makes the most of the means at its disposal, and hypnotism is one of the chief agents.

Every art, from architecture to poetry, is enlisted, in order to move and intoxicate the human soul. This hypnotic and mesmerizing influence is markedly displayed in the activity of the Salvation Army, which employs novel, and to us abnormal methods, such for instance as drums, horns, singing, banners, uniforms, processions, dancing, outbursts of tears, and dramatic gestures.

Still these methods are startling simply because of their novelty. Is not the familiar form of worship in cathedrals, with their peculiar illumination, the golden pomp, the candles, choirs, organs, bells, vestments, the weeping preachers, etc., of a similar nature? And yet, however powerful may be the influence of this hypnotism, it is by no means the chief or most harmful form which the activity of the Church assumes. Its most malign activity is that which is devoted to deceiving the children – those little ones of whom Jesus has said, *"Woe be unto him who tempts the least of these."* From the earliest awakening of a child's intelligence he is deceived and formally taught that which his teachers no longer believe themselves, and this goes on until the delusion becomes from habit a part of his nature. A child is systematically deceived concerning the most important affair in life, and when this deception has become so incorporated with his being that it is difficult to uproot it, then the world of science and reality is opened to him – a world that is wholly at variance with the faith which he has imbibed from his teachers – and he is left to reconcile these contradictions as best he may.

Given the problem of how to muddle a man so that he will be unable to discriminate between two antagonistic conceptions that have been taught to him since his childhood, one could never have devised anything more effectual than the education of every young man in our so-called Christian society.

Shocking as it is to contemplate the work of the churches among men, still, if we consider their position, we shall see that they cannot act otherwise. They are face to face with a dilemma: the Sermon on the Mount or the Nicene Creed; the one excludes the other. If a man sincerely believes the Sermon on the Mount, the Nicene creed must inevitably lose all its meaning for him, and the same would hold true as regards the Church and its representatives; but if a man accepts the Nicene creed, that is to say the Church, or those who call themselves its representatives, then he will find no use for the Sermon on the Mount. Hence it is incumbent on the churches to make every effort to obscure the meaning of the Sermon on the Mount and to endeavour to draw the people towards them. It is only due to their intense activity in that direction that the influence of the churches has not decreased. Let the Church but pause in this effort to influence the masses by hypnotizing men and deceiving children forever so short a time, and men will comprehend the doctrine of Christ, and this comprehension will do away with churches and their influence. Therefore the churches cease not for one moment their compulsory activity through the hypnotism of adults and the deception of children. And it is this activity of the churches that gives people a false conception of Christ's doctrine, and prevents the majority of men, these so called believers, from understanding it.

CHAPTER IV

Misconception of Christianity
by Scientists

T HE RELATION OF SCIENTISTS to religions in general – What are religions, and their significance to human life – Three conceptions of life – The Christian doctrine is the expression of the divine life-conception – The misconception of Christianity by scientists who study its outward manifestations due to the fact that they consider it from the standpoint of the social life-conception – Opinion resulting there from, that the teaching of Christ is exaggerated and unpractical – The expression of the life-conception of the Gospel – Erroneous judgments of scientists concerning Christianity are based upon the assurance that they possess an infallible criterion of knowledge – Hence arise two misapprehensions in regard to the Christian doctrine – The first misapprehension concerning the impracticability of the doctrine arises from the fact that the Christian doctrine presents a conduct of life different from that of the social life-conception – Christianity offers not a rule, but an ideal – Christ adds the consciousness of a divine power to that of an animal power – Christianity seems to exclude the possibility of life only when the indication of the ideal is taken for the rule – An ideal cannot be belittled – According to the doctrine of Christ, life is movement – The ideal and the commandments – The second misapprehension arises from the attempt to replace the love of God and his service by the love and service of humanity – Scientists believe that Christianity and their doctrine concerning the service of humanity are identical – The doctrine of love towards humanity has for its foundation the social life-conception – The love for humanity which springs logically from love for the individual has no meaning, because humanity is a fiction – Christian love springing from the love of God has for its object not only humanity but the whole world – Christianity teaches a life in accordance with its divine nature

– It indicates that the essence of a man's soul is love, and that its good is obtained from its love of God, whom he feels to be within him through love.

Let us now turn our attention to another fallacious conception of Christianity, which is antagonistic to its actual principles – the scientific conception.

The Christianity of the churchmen is something which they have evolved for themselves, and which they believe to be the only true interpretation of Christian doctrine.

The scientists take the professions of faith of the various churches for Christianity, and assuming that these dogmas embody an exhaustive definition of Christian doctrine, they affirm that Christianity has had its day.

One needs but to take into consideration the important part which all religion's and especially Christianity, have played in the life of man, and the significance which science attaches to them, to see at once how impossible it would be to obtain any just apprehension of Christian doctrine through these conceptions. As each individual must possess certain impressions in regard to the meaning of his life, and, though often unconsciously, conform his conduct thereunto, so mankind in the aggregate, or groups of men living under the same conditions, must likewise possess a conception of the meaning of their common life and its consequent activities. As an individual passing from one period of life to another inevitably changes his ideas, the point of view of a grown-up man differs from that of a child, so also mankind in the aggregate – the nation – inevitably, and in conformity with its age, changes its views of life and the activity that springs there from.

The difference in this respect between an individual and mankind in general lies in the fact that while the individual, in forming his conception of the significance and responsibilities of that new period of life upon which he is about to enter, may avail himself of the advice of his predecessors who have already passed that stage, mankind can have no such advantage, because it is advancing along an unbeaten track and there is no one of whom it can ask for the clue to the mystery of life, or how it shall demean itself under these unfamiliar conditions to which no nation has ever yet been subjected.

The married man with a family of children will not continue to view life as he did when he was a child, neither is it possible for mankind, with the many changes that have taken place – the density of the population, the constant intercourse of nations, the perfected means of combating the forces of nature, and the increase of knowledge generally – to view the life of the present day in the light of the past; hence it becomes necessary to evolve a life-conception from which activities corresponding with a new system which is to be established will naturally develop.

And this need is supplied by that peculiar capacity of the race for producing men able to impart a new significance to human life – a significance developing a different set of activities.

The birth of the life-conception, which always takes place when mankind enters upon new conditions and its subsequent activities, is what we call religion.

Therefore, in the first place, religion is not, as science regards it, a phenomenon which formerly travelled hand in hand with the development of mankind, and which has since been left behind; on the contrary, it is a phenomenon inherent to human existence itself, and never more distinctly manifested than at the present day. In the second place, religion defines future rather than past activities, therefore it is evident that an investigation of the phenomena of the past can by no means touch the essence of religion.

The longing to typify the forces of nature is no more the essence of religion than is the fear of those same forces, or the need of the miraculous and its outward manifestations, as the scientists suppose. The essence of religion lies in the power of man to foreknow and to point out the way in which mankind must walk. It is a definition of a new life which will give birth to new activities.

This faculty of foreknowledge concerning the destiny of humanity is more or less common, no doubt, to all people; still from time to time a man appears in whom the faculty has reached a higher development, and these men have the power clearly and distinctly to formulate that which is vaguely conceived by all men, thus instituting a new life-conception from which is to flow an unwonted activity, whose results will endure for centuries to come. Thus far there have been three of these life-conceptions; two of them belong to a bygone era, while the third is of our down time and is called Christianity. It is not that we have merged the various conceptions of the significance of life into three arbitrary divisions, but that there really have been but three distinct conceptions, by which the actions of mankind have been influenced, and save through these we have no means of comprehending life.

These three life-conceptions are – firstly, the individual or animal; secondly, the social or pagan; and thirdly, the universal or divine.

According to the first of these, a man's life is his personality, and that only, and his life's object is to gratify his desires. According to the second, his life is not limited to his own personality; it includes the sum and continuity of many personalities – of the family, of the race, and of the state, and his life's object is to gratify the will of the communities of individuals. And according to the third, his life is confined neither to his personality nor to that of the aggregate of individuals, but finds its significance in the eternal source of all life – in God himself.

These three life-conceptions serve as the basis for the religions of every age.

The savage sees life only through the medium of his own desires. He cares for nothing but himself, and for him the highest good is the full satisfaction of his own passions. The incentive of his life is personal enjoyment. His religion consists of attempts to propitiate the gods in his favour, and of the worship of imaginary deities, who exist only for their own personal ends.

A member of the pagan world recognizes life as something concerning others besides himself; he sees it as concerning an aggregate of individuals – the family, the race, the nation, the state, and is ready to sacrifice himself for the aggregate. The incentive of his life is glory. His religion consists in honouring the chiefs of his race, his progenitors, his ancestors, his sovereigns, and in the worship of those gods who are the exclusive patrons of his family, his tribe, his race, and his state.

The man who possesses the divine life-conception neither looks upon life as centred in his own personality nor in that of mankind at large, whether family, tribe, race, nation, or state, but rather does he conceive of it as taking its rise in the eternal life of God, and to fulfil His will he is ready to sacrifice his personal, family, and social well-being. Love is the impelling motive of his life, and his religion is the worship in deed and in truth of the beginning of all things – of God himself.

History is but the transcript of the gradual transition from the animal life-conception of the individual to the social, and from the social to the divine. The history of the ancients, for thousands of centuries, culminating in that of Rome, is the history of the evolution from the animal life-conception of the individual to that of society and the state. From the advent of Christianity and the fall of Imperial Rome we have the history of that change which is still going on from the social to the divine life-conception.

The latter, together with the Christian doctrine which, is based upon it, and by which our lives are shaped, and our activities, both practical and scientific, are quickened, is regarded by the pseudo scientists, who judge it only by its outward signs, as something outlived, which has lost all meaning for us.

According to scientists this doctrine is embodied in the dogmas of the Trinity, the Redemption, the miracles, the Church and its sacraments, etc., and is only one of the many religions which have arisen during the progress of human history, and now, having played its part and outlived its time, is vanishing before the dawn of science and true enlightenment.

The grossest of human errors spring in most cases from the fact that men who stand on a low intellectual plane, when they encounter phenomena of a higher order, instead of trying to rise to the higher plane from which these phenomena may be fitly regarded, and making an effort to understand them, judge them by their own low standard, and the less they know of what they speak the more bold and determined are their judgments.

Most scientists who treat of the moral doctrine of Christ from the lower standpoint of a social life-conception, regard it as nothing more than an amalgam without cohesion of the asceticism of

India with the doctrines of the Stoics and Neo-Platonists, and of vague anti-social dreams, devoid of all serious meaning in these latter days; they simply see its outward manifestation in the form of dogmas in Catholicism, in Protestantism, and in its struggle with the powers of the world. Interpreting the design of Christianity from its outward aspects, they are like unto deaf men, who judge of the meaning and excellence of music by the movements of the musicians.

Hence it is that all such men, from Comte and Strauss to Spencer and Renan, not understanding the purport of Christ's words, knowing nothing whatever of their intention, ignorant of the question to which they serve as an answer, and taking no pains to learn it – such men, if they are inimical to Christianity, utterly deny the sense of the doctrine; but if they are leniently inclined, then, from the height of their superior wisdom, they amend it, taking for granted that Christ would have said what they think He meant, had He known how to express himself. They treat His doctrine just as men of overweening self-conceit treat their inferiors, correcting them in their speech: "You mean so and so." And the spirit of emendation is always such as to reduce the doctrine of the higher, the divine life-conception, to that of the lower and the social conception.

It is usually admitted that the moral teaching of Christianity is good but exaggerated; that in order to make it perfect, its hyperboles, which are incompatible with our present mode of life, should be discarded. "A doctrine which requires so much that is impracticable is more hurtful than one which demands of men only what is in proportion to their strength." Thus declare the learned interpreters of Christianity, thus unwittingly reiterating the assertion of those who misunderstood the Christian doctrine long years ago and crucified the Master.

The Hebrew law, *"An eye for an eye, and a tooth for a tooth,"* the retributive justice known to mankind thousands of years ago, seems far better suited to the court of contemporary scientists than the law of love which Christ preached 1800 years ago, and which was to replace this identical law of justice.

It would seem that every action of those men who accepted the teaching of Christ in its literal sense, and lived up to it, all the words and deeds of sincere Christians, and all the agencies which under the guise of socialism and communism are now transforming the world, are merely exaggeration, not worth discussing. Nations which have lived under Christian influences, and which are now represented by their advanced thinkers, the scientists, have arrived at the conclusion that the Christian doctrine is a matter of dogma; that its practical teaching has been a mistake and an exaggeration, inimical to the just requirements of morality that are in accord with human nature, and that the very doctrine which Christ repudiated, and for which he substituted a dogma of his own, is far better suited to us. The scientist considers the commandment of non-resistance to evil by violence an exaggeration, and even an act of folly. It would be far better, in his opinion, to reject it, never dreaming that it is not the doctrine of Christ which he is contradicting, but something which he assumes to be the doctrine in question. He does not realize when he says that the commandment of non-resistance in the doctrine of Christ is an exaggeration, that he is like one who, teaching the theory of the circle, declares that the equality of the radii is an exaggeration. It is just as if one who has no idea of the form of a circle were to affirm that the law which requires that each point of its circumference shall be equidistant from its centre, is an exaggeration. As a suggestion to reject or modify the proposition concerning the equality of the radii of a circle signifies an ignorance in regard to the circle itself, so also does the idea of rejecting or modifying, in the practical teaching of Christ, the commandment of non-resistance to evil by violence signify a misunderstanding of the doctrine.

And those who entertain these views do not really comprehend the doctrine. They do not understand that it is the unfolding of a new conception of life, corresponding to the new phase of existence upon which the world entered 1800 years ago, and a definition of the new activity to which it gave birth. Either they do not believe that Christ said what He meant to say, or that what is found in the Sermon on the Mount and elsewhere He said either from His enthusiasm or lack of wisdom and simplicity of character.

Matthew vi: 25–34. 25 Therefore I say unto you, Take no thought for your life, what ye shall eat, or what ye shall drink; nor yet for your body, what ye shall put on. Is not the life more than meat, and the body than raiment?

26 Behold the fowls of the air: for they sow not, neither do they reap, nor gather into barns; yet your heavenly Father feedeth them. Are ye not much better than they?

27 Which of you by taking thought can add one cubit unto his stature?

28 And why take ye thought for raiment? Consider the lilies of the field, how they grow; they toil not, neither do they spin:

29 And yet I say unto you, that even Solomon in all his glory was not arrayed like one of these.

30 Wherefore, if God so clothe the grass of the field, which to-day is, and tomorrow is cast into the oven, shall he not much more clothe you, O ye of little faith?

31 Therefore take no thought, saying, what shall we eat? Or, What shall we drink? Or, Where withal shall we be clothed?

32 (For after all these things do the Gentiles seek:) for your heavenly Father knoweth that ye have need of all these things.

33 But seek ye first the kingdom of God, and his righteousness; and all these things shall be added unto you.

34 Take therefore no thought for the morrow: for the morrow shall take thought for the things of itself. Sufficient unto the day is the evil thereof.

Luke xii: 33–34. 33 Sell that ye have, and give alms; provide yourselves bags which wax not old, a treasure in the heavens that faileth not, where no thief approacheth, neither moth corrupteth.

34 For where your treasure is, there will your heart be also.

Matthew xix: 21 "Go and sell that thou hast, and give to the poor, and thou shall have treasure in heaven: and come and follow me."

Mark viii: 34 "Whosoever will come after me, let him deny himself and take up his cross, and follow me"

John iv: 34 "My meat is to do the will of him that sent me, and to finish his work"

Luke xxii: 42 "Not my will, but thine, be done."

Not what I wish, but what Thou wishest, and not as I wish, but as Thou wishest. Life consists in doing not your own will, but the will of God.

All these doctrines are regarded by men who adhere to the lower life-conception as expressions of enthusiastic exaltation with no special reference to daily life. And yet these doctrines are no less the natural outcome of the Christian life-conception than is the idea of giving one's labour for the common good, or of sacrificing one's life to defend one's country, the outcome of the social life-conception.

As the believer in the social life-conception says to the savage: "Rouse yourself! Consider what you are doing! The life that man lives for himself alone cannot be the true one, for life is fleeting and full of woe. It is the life of the community at large, the race, the family, the state, that endures; therefore a man must sacrifice his personality for the life of the family and the state;" Christianity in like manner says unto him who believes in a social life-conception of the community: "Repent, arouse yourself, consider your ways, else shall you perish. Know you that this bodily, animal life is born today and dies tomorrow, nothing can assure its permanence, no outward expedients, no system whatsoever can give it stability. Consider your ways and learn that the life you live is not the real life, that neither family, social, nor state life will save you from perdition. An honest rational life is possible for man provided that he be, not a participant of the life of the family or life of the state, but a partaker of the source of all life – that of the Father himself; then his life is united to the life of the Father." Such is beyond a doubt the meaning of the Christian conception of life, clearly set forth in every maxim of the New Testament.

One may not share such a conception of life, one may deny it, or prove it to be inaccurate and fallacious; but no man can possibly judge a doctrine without having first made himself familiar with the life-conception which forms its basis; and still more impossible is it to judge a lofty subject from a low standpoint, to pronounce upon the belfry from a knowledge of the foundation. Yet this is precisely what is done by contemporary scientists. And this is because they are labouring under an error similar to that of the clergy, in believing that they possess such infallible methods of studying their subject, that if they but bring their so-called scientific methods to bear upon the subject under consideration, there can be no doubt as to the accuracy of their conclusion.

The possession of a guide to knowledge, which they believe to be infallible, is really the chief obstacle to the comprehension of the Christian doctrine among unbelievers and so-called scientists, by whose opinions the great majority of unbelievers, the so-called educated classes, are guided. All the errors of the scientists concerning Christianity, and especially two strange misapprehensions that avail more than anything else to blind men to its real signification, arise there from.

One of these misapprehensions is that the doctrine of a Christian life not being practical, it remains optional with the individual whether he take it for his guide or no; and if he chooses to do so, it may then be modified to suit the exigencies of our social life. The second misapprehension is, that the Christian doctrine of love of God, and therefore of the service due to Him, is a mystical requirement, neither clearly expressed nor offering any well-defined object of love; consequently the more definite and intelligible doctrine of love of man and of the service of humanity may be substituted for it.

The first misapprehension which relates to the impracticability of the Christian doctrine arises from the fact that men who believe in the social life-conception, not comprehending the rule obeyed by men who hold the Christian doctrine, and mistaking the Christian standard of perfection for the guiding principle of life, believe and declare that it is impossible to follow the teaching of Christ, because implicit obedience to this doctrine would end by destroying life. "If man were to fulfil the precepts of Christ, he would destroy his life; and if all the world were to fulfil them, the human race would soon become extinct. If you were to take no thought for the morrow, neither of what ye shall eat or drink, nor what ye shall put on; if one may not resist evil by violence or defend one's life, nor even give up one's life for his friend; if one is to preserve absolute chastity, mankind could not long exist;" so they believe and affirm.

And they are right, if one takes the incentives to perfection offered by the teaching of Christ as laws which each man must obey, just as, for instance, in the social order every man must pay his taxes, and some must serve in the courts of law, and so on.

The misapprehension consists in overlooking the fact that the doctrine of Christ, and the doctrine formulated by a lower life-conception, guide men in very different ways. The doctrines of the social life-conception guide men in fulfilling the requirements of the law. The doctrine of Christ guides men by manifesting the infinite perfection of the Heavenly Father, to which it is natural for every man to aspire, whatever may be his shortcomings.

The misconception of those who judge the Christian doctrine by the standard of the state or civil doctrine is this – that they imagine that the perfection of which Christ speaks may be attained in this life, and ask themselves, just as they would ask concerning some law of the state, what will happen when all this shall be fulfilled? This hypothesis is fallacious, because the perfection indicated by Christianity is infinite and can never be attained; and Christ promulgates his doctrine, knowing that although absolute perfection will never be attained, yet the aspiration towards it will ever contribute to the welfare of mankind, that this welfare may by this means be everlastingly increased.

Christ is not teaching angels, but men who live and move in an animal life, and whose impulses are of an animal nature. And to this animal impulse Christ, so to speak, adds another force by communicating to man a sense of the divine perfection, guiding the current of life between these two forces.

To take it for granted that human life is to follow the direction indicated by Christ would be like expecting the boatman, who, crossing a swift river, steers almost directly against the current, to float in that direction.

Christ recognizes the fact that a parallelogram has two sides, and that a man's life is controlled by two indestructible forces: his animal nature and his consciousness of a filial relationship to God. Disregarding the factor of the animal life, which never looses its hold, and is beyond man's control, Christ speaks of the divine consciousness, urging man to its fuller recognition, its complete emancipation from all that fetters it, and to its utmost development.

Man's true life, according to the precepts of Christ, is only

THE KINGDOM OF GOD IS WITHIN YOU

to be found in this emancipation and in the growth of the divine consciousness. According to the old dispensation, a true life meant the fulfilment of the precepts of the law; but according to Christ, it means the closest approach to the divine perfection which has been manifested to every man, and which every man recognizes – a closer and closer union of his will to the will of God; a union which every man is striving to attain, and which would utterly destroy the life we now lead.

God's perfection is the asymptote of human life, towards which it is forever aspiring and drawing nearer, although it can only reach its goal in the infinite.

It is only when men mistake the suggestion of an ideal for a rule of conduct that the Christian doctrine seems at odds with life. Indeed, the reverse is true, for it is by the doctrine of Christ, and that alone, that a true life is rendered possible. "It is a mistake to require too much," men usually say, when discussing the demands of the Christian religion." One ought not to be required to take no thought for the morrow, as the Bible teaches, but of course one should not be over-anxious; one cannot give all that he possesses to the poor, still he should bestow a certain portion of his goods in charity; one ought not to remain unmarried, but let him avoid a dissolute life; one need not renounce his wife and children, although one must not idolize them."

These arguments are equivalent to telling a man who is crossing a swift river and steering his boat against the current, that no one can cross a river by steering against the current, but that he must direct his boat in a straight line towards the point he wishes to reach.

The doctrine of Christ differs from former doctrines in that it influences men not by outward observances, but by the interior consciousness that divine perfection may be attained.

It is this illimitable and divine perfection that absorbs the soul of man, not restricted laws of justice and philanthropy. It needs but the aspiration towards this divine perfection to impel the course of human life from the animal to the divine, so far as may be humanly possible.

In order to land at any given point one must steer beyond it. To lower the standard of an ideal means not only to lessen the chances of attaining perfection, but to destroy the ideal itself. The ideal that influences mankind is not an ingenious invention; it is something that dwells in the soul of each individual. It is this ideal of utter and infinite perfection that excites men and urges them to action. A possible degree of perfection would have no appeal to the souls of men.

It is because the doctrine of Christ requires illimitable perfection, that is to say, the blending of the divine essence, which is in each man's soul, with the will of God, the union of the son with the Father, that it has authority. It is only the emancipation of the Son of God, who dwells with each one of us, from the animal element within us, and the drawing near to the Father, that can in the Christian sense of the word be called life.

The presence of the animal element in man is not enough of itself to constitute human life. Neither is a spiritual life, which is guided only by the will of God, a human life. A true human life is composed of an animal and of a spiritual life united to the will of God, and the nearer this component life approaches to the life of God, the more it has life.

According to the Christian doctrine, life is a condition of progress towards the perfection of God; hence no one condition can be either higher or lower than another, because each is in itself a certain stage in human progress towards the unattainable perfection, and therefore of equal importance with all the others. Any spiritual quickening, according to this doctrine, is simply an accelerated movement towards perfection. Therefore the impulse of Zacchaeus the publican, of the adulteress and the thief on the cross, show forth a higher order of life than does the passive righteousness of the Pharisee. This doctrine therefore can never been forced by obligatory laws. The man who, from a lower plane, lives up to the doctrine he professes, ever advancing towards perfection, leads a higher life than one who may perhaps stand on a superior plane of morality, but who is making no progress towards perfection.

Thus the stray lamb is dearer to the Father than those which are in the fold; the prodigal returned, the coin that was lost and is found again, more highly prized than those that never were lost.

Since the fulfilment of this doctrine is an impulse from self towards God, it is evident that there can be no fixed laws for its movement. It may spring from any degree of perfection or of imperfection; the fulfilment of rules and fulfilment of the doctrine are by no means synonymous; there could be no rules or obligatory laws for its fulfilment.

The difference between social laws and the doctrine of Christ is the natural result of the radical dissimilarity between the doctrine of Christ and those earlier doctrines which had their source in a social life-conception. The latter are for the most part positive, enjoining certain acts, by the performance of which men are to be justified and made righteous, whereas the Christian precepts (the precept of love is not a commandment in the strict sense of the word, but the expression of the very essence of the doctrine), the five commandments of the Sermon on the Mount, are all negative, only meant to show men who have reached a certain degree of development what they must avoid. These commandments are, so to speak, mile stone son the infinite road to perfection, towards which humanity is struggling, they mark the degrees of perfection which it is possible for it to attain at a certain period of its development.

In the Sermon on the Mount Christ expressed the eternal ideal to which mankind instinctively aspires, showing at the same time the point of perfection to which human nature in its present stage may attain.

The ideal is to bear no malice, excite no ill will, and to love all men. The commandment which forbids us to offend our neighbour is one which a man who is striving to attain this ideal must not do less than obey. And this is the first commandment.

The ideal is perfect chastity in thought, no less than indeed; and the commandment which enjoins purity in married life, forbidding adultery, is one which every man who is striving to attain this ideal must not do less than obey. And this is the second commandment.

The ideal is to take no thought for the morrow, to live in the present, and the commandment, the fulfilment of which is the point beneath which we must not fall, is against taking oath or making promises for the future. Such is the third commandment.

The ideal – to use no violence whatsoever – shows us that we must return good for evil, endure injuries with patience, and give up the cloak to him who has taken the coat. Such is the fourth commandment.

The ideal is to love your enemies, to do good to them that despitefully use you. In order to keep the spirit of this commandment one must at least refrain from injuring one's enemies, one must speak kindly of them, and treat all one's fellow creatures with equal consideration. Such is the fifth commandment.

All these commandments are reminders of that which we, in our striving for perfection, must and can avoid; reminders, too, that we must labour now to acquire by degrees habits of self-restraint, until such habits become second nature. But these commandments, far from exhausting the doctrine, do not by any means cover it. They are but stepping-stones on the way to perfection, and must necessarily be followed by higher and still higher ones, as men pursue the course towards perfection.

That is why a Christian doctrine would make higher demands than those embodied in the commandments, and not in the least decrease its demands, as they who judge the Christian doctrine from a social life-conception seem to think.

This is one of the mistakes of the scientists in regard to the significance of Christ's doctrine. And the substitution of the love of humanity for the love and service of God is another, and it springs from the same source.

In the Christian doctrine of loving and of serving God, and (as the natural consequence of such love and service) of loving and serving one's neighbour, there seems to the scientific mind a certain mysticism, something at once confused and arbitrary, and, believing that the doctrine of love for humanity rests on a firmer basis and is altogether more intelligible, they utterly reject the requirement of love and service of God.

The theory of a scientist is that a virtuous life, a life with a purpose, must be useful to the world at large; and in a life of this kind they discover the solution of the Christian doctrine, to which they reduce Christianity itself. Assuming their own doctrine to be identical with that of Christianity, they seek and believe that they find in the latter an affirmation of their own views.

This is a fallacy. The Christian doctrine, and the doctrine of the Positivists, and of all advocates of the universal brotherhood of man, founded on the utility of such a brotherhood, have nothing in common, and especially do they differ in that the doctrine of Christianity has a solid and a clearly defined foundation in the human soul, whereas love of humanity is but a theoretical conclusion reached through analogy.

The doctrine of the love of humanity has for its basis the social life-conception.

The essence of the social life-conception consists in replacing the sense of individual life by that of the life of the group. In its first steps, this is a simple and natural progression, as from the family to the tribe; from the family to the race is more difficult, and requires special education – which has arrived at its utmost limits when the state has been reached.

It is natural for every man to love himself, and he needs no incentive thereto; to love his tribe, which lends both support and protection; to love his wife, the delight and comfort of his daily life; the children, who are his consolation and his future hope; his parents, who gave him life and cherished him – all this, although not so intense as love of self, is natural and common to mankind.

To love one's race, one's people, for their own sake, although not so instinctive, is also common. To love one's ancestors, one's kinsfolk, through pride, is also natural and frequent; and a man may feel love for his fellow countrymen, who speak the same language and profess the same faith as himself, although the emotion is less strong than love of self or love of family. But love for a nation, Turkey, for instance, or Germany, England, Austria, Russia, is almost impossible, and notwithstanding the training given in that direction, it is only a fictitious semblance; it has no real existence. At this aggregate ceases man's power of transfusing his innermost consciousness; for such a fiction he can feel no direct sentiment. And yet the Positivists and all the preachers of the scientific fraternity, not taking into consideration the fact that this feeling is weakened in proportion to the expansion of its object, continue to theorize on the same lines. They say: "If it were to the advantage of an individual to transfuse his consciousness into the family, and thence into the nation and the state, it follows that it will be to his further advantage to transfuse his consciousness into the universal entity, mankind, that all men may live for humanity, as they have lived for the family and for the state."

And theoretically they are right.

After having transferred the consciousness and love for the individual to the family, and from the family to the race, the nation, and the state, it would be perfectly logical for men, in order to escape the strife and disasters that result from the division of mankind into nations and states, to transfer their love to humanity at large. This would appear to be the logical outcome, and it has been offered as a theory by those who forget that love is an innate sentiment, which can never be inspired by preaching; that it must have a real object, and that the entity which men call humanity is not a real object, but a fiction.

A family, a race, even a state, are no inventions of men; these things have formed themselves like a hive of bees, or a colony of ants, and possess an actual existence. The man who loves his family, after a human fashion, knows whom he is loving – Ann, Maria, John, or Peter. The man who loves his ancestors, and is proud of them, knows that he loves the Guelphs, for instance, or the Ghibellines; the man who loves his country knows that he loves France from the Rhine to the Pyrenees, that he loves its capital, Paris, and all its history. But the man who loves humanity, what is it that he loves? There is a state, there is a people, there is the abstract conception of man. But humanity as a concrete conception is impossible.

Humanity? Where is its limit? Where does it end and where does it begin? Does it exclude the savage, the idiot, the inebriate, the insane? If one were to draw a line of demarcation so as to exclude the lower representatives of the human race, where ought it to be drawn? Ought it to exclude the Negro, as they do in the United States, or the Hindus, as some Englishmen do, or the Jews, as does another nation? But if we include all humanity without exception, why should we restrict ourselves to men? Why should we exclude the higher animals, some of whom are superior to the lowest representatives of the human race?

We do not know humanity in the concrete, nor can we fix its limits. Humanity is a fiction, and therefore it cannot be loved.

Indeed, it would be advantageous if men could love humanity as they love the family. It would be very useful, as the communists say, to substitute a community of interests for individual competition, or the universal for the personal; in a word, to make the whole world a mutual benefit society – only that there are no motives to bring about such a result. The Positivists, communists, and all the exponents of the scientific fraternity exhort us to extend the love which men feel for themselves, their families, their fellow countrymen, over humanity at large, forgetting that the love of which they speak is a personal love, which may be kindled for the family, and even extend to include one's native country, but which expires altogether when it is appealed to in behalf of an artificial state, such as Austria, England, or Turkey; and when claimed for that mystical object, humanity in general, one cannot even grasp the idea.

"A man loves himself, his physical personality, he loves his family, he even loves his country. Why should he not also love mankind? It would seem such a happy consummation! And it so happens that Christianity inculcates the same precept." These are the opinions of the positivist, the communist, and the socialist fraternities.

It would indeed be fortunate, but it is impossible, because love founded on a personal and social life-conception can go no further than the love of country.

The flaw in the argument arises from the fact that the social life-conception, the basis of family love and of patriotism, is itself an individual love, and such a love, in its transference from a person to a family, a race, a nation, and a state, gradually loses its efficiency, and in the state has reached its final limit, and can go no further.

The necessity for widening the sphere of love is not to be denied, and yet it is the very attempt to satisfy this requirement that destroys its possibility, and proves the inadequacy of personal human love.

And here it is that the advocates of the positivist, communist, and socialist brotherhood offer as a prop to the humanitarianism that has proved its inefficiency, a Christian love, not in its essence, but only in its results; in other words, not the love of

God, but the love of man.

But there can be no such love; it has no raison d'être. Christian love comes only from a Christian life-conception, whose sole manifestation is the love and service of God.

By a natural sequence in the extension of love from the individual to the family, and thence to the race, the nation, and the state, the social life-conception has brought men not to the consciousness of love for humanity – which is illimitable – the unification of every living creature – but to a condition which evokes no feeling in man, to a contradiction for which it provides no reconciliation.

It is only the Christian doctrine which, by lending to human life a new significance, is able to solve the difficulty. Christianity presents the love of self and the love of the family, as well as patriotism and the love of humanity, but it is not to be restricted to humanity alone; it is to be given to every living creature; it recognizes the possibility of an indefinite expansion of the kingdom of love, but its object is not to be found outside itself, in the aggregate of individuals, neither in the family, nor in the race, nor in the state, nor in mankind, nor all the wide world, but in itself, in its personality – a divine personality, whose essence is the very love which needed a wider sphere.

The distinction between the Christian doctrine and those which preceded it may be thus defined. The social doctrine says: Curb thy nature (meaning the animal nature alone); subject it to the visible law of the family, of society, and of the state. Christianity says: Live up to thy nature (meaning the divine nature); make it subject to nothing; neither to thine own animal nature, nor to that of another, and then thou shalt attain what thou seekest by subjecting thine outward personality to visible laws. The Christian doctrine restores to man his original consciousness of self, not the animal self, but the Godlike self, the spark of divinity, as the son of God, like unto the Father, but clothed in a human form. This consciousness of one's self as a son of God, whose essence is love, satisfies at once all those demands made by the man who professes the social life-conception for a broader sphere of love. Again, in the social life-conception the enlargement of the domain of love was a necessity for the salvation of the individual; it was attached to certain objects, to one's self, to one's family, to society, and to humanity. With the Christian world conception love is not a necessity, neither is it attached to any special object; it is the inherent quality of a man's soul; he loves because he cannot help loving.

The Christian doctrine teaches to man that the essence of his soul is love; that his well-being may be traced not to the fact that he loves this object or that one, but to the fact that he loves the principle of all things – God, whom he recognizes in himself through love, and will by the love of God love all men and all things.

This is the essential difference between the Christian doctrine and that of the positivists and all other non-Christian theorists of a universal brotherhood.

Such are the two chief misapprehensions in regard to the Christian doctrine, and from those most of the false arguments on the subject have originated.

One is, that the doctrine of Christ, like the doctrines which preceded it, promulgates rules which men must obey, and that these rules are impracticable. The other, that the whole meaning of Christianity is contained in the doctrine of a cooperative union of mankind, in one family, to attain which, leaving aside the question of love of God, one should obey only the rule of love of one's fellowmen.

Finally, the mistake of scientists, in supposing that the doctrine of the supernatural contains the essence of Christianity, that its life-teaching is not practicable, together with the general misapprehensions that result from such a misconception, further explains why men of our time have so misunderstood Christianity.

CHAPTER V

Contradiction of Our Life and Christian Consciousness

MEN CONSIDER THAT they may accept Christianity without changing their life – The pagan life-conception no longer corresponds to the present age of humanity, which the Christian life-conception alone can satisfy – The Christian life-conception is still misunderstood by men, but our life itself necessitates its acceptance – The requirements of a new life-conception always seem unintelligible, mystical, and supernatural – Such, for the majority of men, seem the requirements of the Christian life-conception – The acceptance of a Christian life-conception will inevitably be accomplished both through spiritual and material agencies – The fact that men, conscious of a higher life-conception, continue to entertain the lower forms of life, causes contradiction and suffering, which embitter life and require its alteration – Contradictions of our life – The economical contradiction, and the suffering it causes to the working men and to the rich – The contradiction of State, and the sufferings that arise from obedience to State laws – The international contradiction, and its acknowledgment by contemporary writers, Komarovsky, Ferri, Booth, Passy, Lawson, Wilson, Bartlett, Defourny, Moneta – The military contradiction the extreme.

Many causes have contributed towards the misunderstanding of the teaching of Christ. One of these is that men assumed to understand the doctrine, when, like the faithful of the church, they accepted the statement that it had been transmitted in a supernatural manner; or, like the scientists, after having investigated certain of its outward manifestations. Another reason may be found in the conviction that it is impracticable, and that it may be replaced by the doctrine of love of humanity. But the principal reason of all such misconceptions is that men look upon the doctrine of Christ as one that may be accepted or rejected, without any special change in one's life.

Men, attached by habit to the existing order, shrink from attempting to change it, hence they agree to consider this doctrine as a mass of revelations and laws that may be accepted without making any change in one's life; whereas the doctrine of Christ is not a doctrine of rules for man to obey, but unfolds a new life-conception, meant as a guide for men who are now entering upon a new period, one entirely different from the past.

The life of humanity continues its course and has its stages, like the life of an individual; each age has its own life-conception, which a man must adopt whether he will it or not. Those who do not adopt it consciously, adopt it unconsciously. The same change that takes place in the views of the individual, as life goes on, occurs also in the existence of nations and of humanity in general.

If a father were to conduct his affairs like a child, his life would certainly become so unbearable that he would cast about for a different plan of life, and would eagerly grasp at one better suited to his years.

And the human race is at the present time passing through a similar experience, in its transition from a pagan to a Christian life-conception. A man of the society of the present day finds that the pagan life-conception is no longer suited to the times, hence he is induced to submit to the requirements of the Christian religion, whose truths, however misunderstood and falsely interpreted they may be, are yet familiar to his ears, and seem to offer the only practical solution of the contradictions that beset his path. If the demands of the Christian doctrine seem unintelligible, peculiar, and dangerous to a man who has hitherto held the social life-conception, the demands of the latter seemed none the less so to a savage of a previous age, who neither fully apprehended them, nor was able to foresee their consequences.

The savage reasoned thus: "It would be folly for me to sacrifice my peace or my life to defend an incomprehensible, intangible, and uncertain ideal, family, race, country, and, above all, it would be dangerous to deliver myself into the hands of an unknown power." But there came a time in the life of the savage when, on the one hand, he had begun, although vaguely, to understand the meaning of social life, as well as that of its chief incentive – social approval or condemnation: glory – while, on the other hand, the sufferings of his personal life had become so severe that it was no longer possible for him to go on believing in the truth of his former life-conception; whereupon he accepted the social and State doctrine and submitted to its laws.

And he who holds the social life-conception is now undergoing a similar experience.

"It is madness" – thus reasons the man holding such views – "to sacrifice one's interests or those of one's family and of one's country, in order to fulfil the requirements of a law that would compel one to renounce the most natural and praiseworthy feelings towards one's self, one's family, and one's country, and, above all, the guarantee of protection afforded by the State."

But there comes a time when, on the one hand, a vague awakening consciousness stirs the soul, the consciousness of the higher law, love of God and one's neighbour, and the sufferings a man endures from the contradictions of life, compel him to renounce the social life-conception and to adopt the new Christian life-conception which is offered him. And this time has now arrived.

To us, who underwent the transition from the individual to the social life-conception thousands of years ago, this transition appears to have been both natural and inevitable, just as the present transition, through which we have been passing these last 1800 years, seems arbitrary, unnatural, and overwhelming. But it seems so for the simple reason that the former change is a thing of the past, and has fixed in us certain habits, whereas we are still practically accomplishing the present transition, and have to accomplish it consciously.

It was centuries, indeed thousands of years, before the social life-conception was adopted by all mankind; it passed through various phases, and we ourselves possess it through heredity, education, and unconscious habit, hence it seems natural to us. But 5000 years ago it seemed as strange and unnatural to men as the Christian doctrine in its true meaning seems to them now.

The universal brotherhood of man, the equality of races, the abolition of property, the anomalous doctrine of non-resistance, all these requirements of the Christian religion seem to us impossibilities. But in olden times, thousands of years ago, not only the requirements of the state, but even those of the family, as, for instance, the obligation of parents to feed their children, of children to support their aged parents, and that of conjugal fidelity, seemed equally impossible. And still more unreasonable seemed the demands of the State, requiring citizens to submit to established authority, to pay taxes, to perform military duty in defence of their country, etc. We find no difficulty in comprehending these requirements now; they seem perfectly simple and natural, with nothing mystical or alarming in their aspect; but five, or even three thousand years ago, such demands seemed intolerable.

Thus the social life-conception served as a foundation for religion, for at the time when it was first manifested to men it seemed to them to be utterly incomprehensible, mystical, and supernatural. Now that we have passed that phase of human life, we can understand the reasons for the aggregation of men into families, communities, and states. But in the early ages the demand for these aggregations was made in the name of the supernatural, and its fulfilment assured by the same authority.

The patriarchal religion deified the family, the race, the people. State religions deified the sovereigns and the state. Even at the present day the uneducated masses, the Russian peasants, for instance, who call the Czar a God upon earth, obey the laws from religious instinct, not because their reason counsels them to do so, nor because they have the least idea of a State.

And to those men of our own times who hold the social life-conception the Christian doctrine seems to be a supernatural religion, whereas in reality there is nothing mystical or supernatural about it; it is only a doctrine concerning human life, corresponding with the degree of development which man has attained, and one which he cannot refuse to accept.

The time will come, and it is already near at hand, when the Christian foundations of life – equality, brotherly love, community of goods, non-resistance of evil by violence – will seem as natural and simple as the foundations of family, social, and state life appear to us at the present time.

There can be no retrogression for humanity. Men have

outgrown the lower life-conception of the family and the state, and must press forward to embrace the next higher conception, as they have already begun to do.

This movement is accomplished in two ways: consciously, by moral causes; unconsciously, by material ones. It rarely happens that a man changes his mode of life at the dictates of reason; however conscious he may be of the new design and purpose revealed to him by his reason, he goes on in the old fashion until his life has become intolerably inconsistent and therefore distressing. Likewise, the larger portion of mankind, after learning through its religious teachers a new conception of life and its object, to which it has yet to adjust itself, will for a long time pursue its wonted course, and only make the change in the end because its former life has become impossible.

In spite of the necessity for a change of life, acknowledged and proclaimed by our religious guides and admittedly the wisest men; in spite of the religious respect entertained for these guides, the majority of men continue to be influenced in life, now additionally complicated, by their former views. It is as if the father of a family, knowing well enough how to conduct himself properly, should through force of habit or thoughtlessness continue to live as if he were still a child.

At this very moment we are experiencing one of these transitions. Humanity has outgrown its social, its civic age, and has entered upon a new epoch. It knows the doctrine that must underlie the foundations of life in this new epoch; but, yielding to inertia, it still clings to its former habits. From this inconsistency between the theory of life and its practice follow a series of contradictions and sufferings that embitter man's life and compel him to make a change.

One needs but to compare the practice of life with its theory to be horrified at the extraordinary contradictions between the conditions of life and our inner consciousness.

Man's whole life is a continual contradiction of what he knows to be his duty. This contradiction prevails in every department of life, in the economical, the political, and the international As though his intelligence were forgotten and his faith temporarily eclipsed – for he must have faith, else would his life have no permanence – he acts in direct opposition to the dictates of his conscience and his commonsense.

In our economical and international relations we are guided by the fundamental principles of bygone ages – principles quite contradictory to our mental attitude and the conditions of our present life.

It was right for a man who believed in the divine origin of slavery, and in its necessity, to live in the relation of a master to his slaves. But is such a life possible in these days? A man of antiquity might believe himself justified in taking advantage of his fellowman, oppressing him for generations, merely because he believed in diversity of origin, noble or base, descent from Ham or Japheth. Not only have the greatest philosophers of ancient times, the teachers of mankind, Plato and Aristotle, justified the existence of slavery and adduced proofs of its legality, but no longer than three centuries ago those who described an ideal state of society could not picture it without slaves.

In ancient times, and even in the Middle Ages, it was honestly thought that men were not born equal, that the men worthy of respect were only Persians, only Greeks, only Romans, or only Frenchmen; but no one believes it now. And the enthusiastic advocates of the principles of aristocracy and patriotism at this present day cannot believe in their own statements.

We all know, and cannot help knowing, even if we had never heard it defined and never attempted to define it ourselves, that we all possess an inherent conviction deep in our hearts of the truth of that fundamental doctrine of Christianity, that we are all children of one Father, yea, every one of us, wheresoever we may live, whatsoever language we may speak; that we are all brothers, subject only to the law of love implanted in our hearts by our common Father.

Whatever may be the habits of thought or the degree of education of a man of our time, whether he be an educated liberal, whatsoever his shade of opinion, a philosopher, whatsoever may be his system, a scientist, an economist of any of the various schools, an uneducated adherent of any religious faith – every man in these days knows that in the matter of life and worldly goods all men have equal rights; that no man is either better or worse than his fellowmen, but that all men are born free and equal. Every man has an instinctive assurance of this fact, and yet he sees his fellow beings divided into two classes, the one in poverty and distress, which labours and is oppressed, the other idle, tyrannical, luxurious; and not only does he see all this, but, whether voluntarily or otherwise, he falls in line with one or the other of these divisions – a course repugnant to his reason. Hence he must suffer both from his sense of the incongruity and his own share in it.

Whether he be master or slave, a man in these days is forever haunted by this distressing inconsistency between his ideal and the actual fact, nor can he fail to perceive the suffering that springs there from.

The masses – that is to say, the majority of mankind, who suffer and toil, their lives dull and uninteresting, never enlivened by a ray of brightness, enduring numberless privations – are those who recognize most clearly the sharp contrasts between what is and what ought to be, between the professions of mankind and their actions.

They know that they work like slaves, that they are perishing in want and in darkness, that they may minister to the pleasures of the minority. And it is this very consciousness that enhances its bitterness; indeed, it constitutes the essence of their suffering.

A slave in old times knew that he was a slave by birth, whereas the working man of our day, while he feels himself to be a slave, knows that he ought not to be one, and suffers the tortures of Tantalus from his unsatisfied yearning for that which not only could be granted him, but which is really his due. The sufferings of the working classes that spring from the contradictions of their fate, are magnified tenfold by the envy and hatred which are the natural fruits of the sense of these contradictions.

A working man in our period, even though his work may be less fatiguing than the labour of the ancient slave, and even were he to succeed in obtaining the eight-hour system and twelve-and-sixpence a day, still has the worst of it, because he manufactures objects which he will never use or enjoy; he is not working for himself; he works in order to gratify the luxurious and idle, to increase the wealth of the capitalist, the mill-owner, or manufacturer. He knows that all this goes on in a world where men acknowledge certain propositions such as the economic principle that labour is wealth, that it is an act of injustice to employ another man's labour for one's own benefit, that an illegal act is punishable by law, in a world, moreover, where the doctrine of Christ is professed – that doctrine which teaches us that all men are brothers, and that it is the duty of a man to serve his neighbour and to take no unfair advantage of him.

He realizes all this, and must suffer keenly from the shock in contradiction between the world as it should be and the world as it is. "According to what I am told and what I hear men profess," says a working man to himself, "I ought to be a free man equal to any other man, and loved; I am a slave, hated and despised." Then he in his turn is filled with hatred and seeks to escape from his position, to overthrow the enemy that oppresses him, and to get the upper hand himself.

They say: "It is wrong for a workman to wish himself in the place of a capitalist, or for a poor man to envy the rich." But this is false. If this were a world where God had ordained masters and slaves, rich and poor, it would be wrong for the working man or the poor man to wish himself in the place of the rich; but this is not so; he wishes it in a world which professes the doctrine of the Gospel, whose first principle is embodied in the relation of the son to the Father, and consequently of fraternity and equality. And however reluctant men may be to acknowledge it, they cannot deny that one of the first conditions of Christian life is love, expressed not in words but in deeds.

The man of education suffers even more from these inconsistencies. If he has any faith whatever he believes, perhaps in fraternity – at least in the sentiment humanity; and if not in the sentiment humanity, then in justice, and if not in justice, then surely in science; and he cannot help knowing all the while that the conditions of his life are opposed to every principle of Christianity, humanity, justice, and science.

He knows that the habits of life in which he has been bred, and whose abandonment would cause him much discomfort, can only be supported by the weary and often suicidal labour of the downtrodden working class – that is, by the open infraction of those principles of Christianity, humanity, justice, and even of science (political science), in which he professes to believe. He affirms his faith in the principles of fraternity, humanity, justice, and political science, and yet the oppression of the working class is an indispensable factor in his daily life, and he constantly employs it to attain his own ends, in spite of his principles; and he not only lives in this manner, but he devotes all his energies to maintain a system which is directly opposed to all his beliefs.

We are brothers, but every morning my brother or my sister performs for me the most menial offices. We are brothers, but I must have my morning cigar, my sugar, my mirror, or what not – objects whose manufacture has often cost my brothers and sisters their health, yet I do not for that reason forbear to use these things; on the contrary, I even demand them. We are brothers, and yet I support myself by working in some bank, commercial house, or shop, and am always trying to raise the price of the necessities of life for my brothers and sisters. We are brothers; I receive a salary for judging, convicting, and punishing the thief or the prostitute, whose existence is the natural outcome of my own system of life, and I fully realize that I should neither condemn nor punish. We are all brothers, yet I make my living by collecting taxes from the poor, that the rich may live in luxury and idleness. We are brothers, and yet I receive a salary for preaching a pseudo Christian doctrine, in which I do not myself believe, thus hindering men from discovering the true one. I receive a salary as priest or bishop for deceiving people in a matter which is of vital importance to them. We are brothers, but I make my brother pay for all my services, whether I write books for him, educate him, or prescribe for him as a physician. We are all brothers, but I receive a salary for fitting myself to be a murderer, for learning the art of war, or for manufacturing arms and ammunition and building fortresses.

The whole existence of our upper classes is utterly contradictory, and the more sensitive a man's nature the more painful is the incongruity.

A man with a sensitive conscience can enjoy no peace of mind in such a life. Even supposing that he succeeds in stifling the reproaches of his conscience, he is still unable to conquer his fears.

Those men and women of the dominant classes who have hardened themselves and have succeeded in stifling their consciences must still suffer through their fear of the hatred they inspire. They are quite well aware of its existence among the labouring classes; they know that it can never die; they know, too, that the working men realize the deceits practised upon them, and the abuses that they endure; that they have started organizations to throw off the yoke, and to take vengeance on their oppressors. The happiness of the upper classes is poisoned by fear of the impending calamity, foreshadowed by the unions, the strikes, and First of May demonstrations. Recognizing the calamity that threatens them, their fear turns to defiance and hatred. They know that if they relax for one moment in this conflict with the oppressed, they are lost, because their slaves, already embittered, grow more and more so with every day's oppression. The oppressors, though they may see it, cannot cease to oppress. They realize that they themselves are doomed from the moment they abate one jot of their severity. So they go on in their career of oppression, notwithstanding their affectation of interest in the welfare of the working men, the eight-hour system, the laws restricting the labour of women and children, the pensions and the rewards. All this is mere pretence, or at best the natural anxiety of the master to keep his slave in good condition; but the slave remains a slave all the while, and the master, who cannot live without the slave, is less willing than ever to set him free. The governing classes find themselves in regard to the working men very much in the position of one who has overthrown his opponent, and who holds him down, not so much because he does not choose to let him escape, but because he knows that should he for one moment lose his hold on him, he would lose his own life, for the vanquished man is infuriated and holds a knife in his hand.

Hence our wealthy classes, whether their consciences be tender or hardened, cannot enjoy the advantages they have wrung from the poor, as did the ancients, who were convinced of the justice of their position. All the pleasures of life are poisoned either by remorse or fear.

Such is the economic inconsistency. Still more striking is that of the civil power.

A man is trained first of all in habits of obedience to state laws. At the present time every act of our lives is under the supervision of the State, and in accordance with its dictates a man marries and is divorced, rears his children, and in some countries accepts the religion it prescribes. What is this law then that determines the life of mankind? Do men believe in it? Do they consider it true? Not at all. In most cases they recognize its injustice, they despise it, and yet they obey it. It was fit that the ancients should obey their law> It was chiefly religious, and they sincerely believed it to be the only true law, to which all men owed obedience. Is that the case with us? We cannot refuse to acknowledge that the law of our state is not the eternal law, but only one of the many laws of many states, all equally imperfect, and frequently wholly false and unjust – a law that has been openly discussed in all its aspects by the public press. It was fit that the Hebrew should obey his laws, since he never doubted that the finger of God Himself had traced them; or for the Roman, who believed that he received them from the nymph Egeria; or even for those peoples who believed that the rulers who made the laws were anointed of God; or, that Legislative Assemblies have both the will and the ability to devise laws as good as possible. But we know that laws are the offspring of party conflicts, false dealing, and the greed of gain, that they are not, and can never be, the depository of true justice; and therefore it is impossible for people of the present day to believe that obedience to civil or state laws can ever satisfy the rational demands of human nature. Men have long since realized that there is no sense in obeying a law whose honesty is more than doubtful, and therefore they must suffer when, though privately denying its prerogative, they still conform to it. When a man's whole life is held in bondage by laws whose injustice, cruelty, and artificiality he plainly discerns, and yet is compelled to obey these laws under penalty of punishment, he must suffer; it cannot be otherwise.

We recognize the disadvantages of custom houses and import duties, but we are yet obliged to pay them; we see the folly of supporting the Court and its numerous officials, we admit the harmful influence of church preaching, and still we are compelled to support both; we also admit the cruel and iniquitous punishments inflicted by the courts, and yet we play our part in them; we acknowledge that the distribution of land is wrong and immoral, but we have to submit to it; and despite the fact that we deny the necessity for armies or warfare, we are made to bear the heavy burden of supporting armies and waging war.

These contradictions, however, are but trifling in comparison with the one which confronts us in the problem of our international relations, and which cries aloud for solution, since both human reason and human life are at stake, and this is the antagonism between the Christian faith and war.

We, Christian nations, whose spiritual life is one and the same, who welcome the birth of every wholesome and profitable thought with joy and pride, from whatsoever quarter of the globe it may spring, regardless of race or creed; we, who love not only the philanthropists, the poets, the philosophers, and the scientists of other lands; we, who take as much pride in the heroism of a Father Damien as if it was our own; we, who love the French, the Germans, the Americans, and the English, not only esteeming their qualities, but ready to meet them with cordial friendship; we, who not only would be shocked to consider war with them in the light of an exploit – when we picture to ourselves the possibility that at some future day a difference may arise between us that can only be reconciled by murder, and that any one of us may be called upon to play his part in an inevitable tragedy – we shudder at the thought.

It was well enough for a Hebrew, a Greek, or a Roman to maintain the independence of his country by murder, and even to subdue other nations by the same means, because he firmly believed himself a member of the one favoured people beloved by God, and that all the others were Philistines and barbarians. Also, in the times of the Middle Ages men might well have held these opinions, and even they who lived towards the end of the last century and at the beginning of this. But we, whatever provocation may be offered us, we cannot possibly believe as they did; and this difficulty is so painful for us in these times that it has become impossible to live without trying to solve it.

"We live in a time replete with contradictions," writes Count Komarovsky, the Professor of International Law, in his learned treatise. "Everywhere the tone of the public press seems to indicate a general desire for peace, and shows the need of it for all nations. And the representatives of the government, in their private as well as in their public capacity, in parliamentary speeches and diplomatic negotiations, express themselves in the same temper. Nevertheless, the governments increase the military force year after year, impose new taxes, negotiate loans, and will leave as a legacy to future generations the responsibilities of the present mistaken policy. How are the word and the deed at variance!

"By way of justification the governments claim that all their armaments and the consequent outlay are simply defensive in their character, but to the uninitiated the question naturally suggests itself – whence is to come the attack if all the great powers are devoting themselves to a defensive policy? It certainly looks as if each one of them lived in hourly expectation of attack from his neighbour, and the consequence is strife between the different governments to surpass each other in strength. The very existence of this spirit of rivalry favours the chances of war: the nations, no longer able to support the increased armament, will sooner or later prefer open war to the tension in which they live and the ruin which menaces them, so that the slightest pretext will avail to kindle in Europe the conflagration of a general war. It is a mistake to suppose that such a crisis will heal the political and economic ills under which we groan. The experience of late wars shows us that each one served only to exacerbate the animosity of the nations against each other, to increase the unbearable burden of military despotism, and has involved the political and economic situation of Europe in a more melancholy and pitiable plight than ever."

"Contemporary Europe keeps under arms 9 millions of men," says Enrico Ferri, "and a reserve force of 15 million, at a cost of 4 milliards of francs a year. By increasing its armament it paralyses more and more the springs of social and individual welfare, and may be compared to a man who, in order to obtain weapons, condemns himself to anaemia, thereby depriving himself of the strength to use the weapons he is accumulating, whose weight will eventually overpower him."

Charles Booth has expressed the same idea in his address delivered in London, July 26, 1887, before the Association for the Reform and Codification of National Laws. Having mentioned the same numbers – over nine million in active service and 15 million in reserve, and the enormous sums required to support these armies and armaments – he says, in substance: "These numbers represent but a small part of the actual expenditure, because outside of the expenses enumerated in the budgets of the nations we must take into consideration the great losses to society from the removal of so many able-bodied men, lost to industry in all its branches, and moreover, the interest on the enormous sums spent in military preparations, which yield no returns. As might be expected, the constantly increasing national debts are the inevitable result of these outlays in preparation for war. By far the greater proportion of the debt of Europe has been contracted for munitions of war. The sum total is 4 milliards of pounds, or 40 milliards of roubles, and these debts are increasing every year."

Komarovsky, whom we lately quoted, says elsewhere: "We are living in hard times. Everywhere we hear complaints of the stagnation of commerce and industry and of the wretched economical situation. They tell us of the hard conditions of life among the labouring classes and the general impoverishment of the people. But regardless of this, governments, determined to maintain their independence, go to the utmost limits of folly. Additional taxes are levied on every side, and the financial oppression of the people knows no bounds. If we glance at the budgets of European states for the last hundred years, we shall be struck with their constantly increasing figures. How can we explain this abnormal condition, that sooner or later threatens to overwhelm us with inevitable bankruptcy?"

Most assuredly it is caused by the expense of maintaining armies, which absorbs one-third, or even one-half, of the budget of all European nations. The saddest part of it however is, that there is no end to this increase of budgets and consequent impoverishment of the masses. What is socialism but a protest against the abnormal situation in which the majority of mankind of our continent finds itself?"

"We are being ruined," says Frédéric Passy, in a paper read before the last Peace Congress in London (1890), "to enable us to take part in the senseless wars of the future, or to pay the interest of debts left us by the criminal and insane wars and contests of the past We shall perish with hunger, to have success in murder."

Going on to speak of the opinion of France in regard to this matter, he says: "We believe that now, a hundred years after the proclamation formulating the belief in the rights of men and citizens, the time has come to declare the rights of nations and to repudiate once and for all time those undertakings of fraud and violence, which, under the name of conquests, are actually crimes against humanity, and which, however much the pride of nations or the ambition of monarchs may seek to justify them, serve only to enervate the conquerors."

"I am always very much surprised at the way religion is carried on in this country," says Sir Wilfrid Lawson before the same Congress. "You send a boy to the Sunday School, and you tell him: 'My dear boy, you must love your enemies; if any boy strikes you, don't strike him again; try to reform him by loving him.' Well, the boy goes to the Sunday school till he is fourteen or fifteen years of age, and then his friends say, 'Put him in the Army.' What has he to do in the Army? Why, not love his enemies, but whenever he sees an enemy, to run him through the body with a bayonet is the nature of all religious teaching in this country. I do not think that that is a very good way of carrying out the precepts of religion. I think if it is a good thing for the boy to love his enemy, it is a good thing for the man to love his enemy."

"In Europe great Christian nations keep among them 28,000,000 of armed men to settle quarrels by killing one another, instead of by arguing. This is what the Christian nations of the world are doing at this moment. It is a very expensive way also; for in a publication which I saw – I believe it was correct – it was made out that since the year 1812 these nations had spent the almost incredible amount of 1,500,000,000 of money in preparing and settling their quarrels by killing one another. Now

it seems to me that with that state of things one of two positions must be accepted, either that Christianity is a failure, or
that those who profess to expound Christianity have failed in
expounding it properly."

"So long as our men-of-war are not disarmed and our army
not disbanded, we have no right to be called a Christian nation,"
said Mr. F. L. Wilson.

In a conversation in regard to the duty of Christian ministers
in the matter of preaching against war, Mr. G. D. Bartlett re-
marked, among other things:

"If I understand the Scriptures, I say that men are only playing
with Christianity when they ignore this question.... I have lived
a long life, I have heard many sermons, and I can say without any
exaggeration that I never heard universal peace recommended
from the pulpit half-a-dozen times in my life.... Some twenty
years ago I happened to stand in a drawing room where there
were forty or fifty people, and I dared to make the proposition
that war was incompatible with Christianity. They looked upon
me as an arrant fanatic. The idea that we could get on without
war was regarded as unmitigated weakness and folly."

A Catholic priest, the Abbé Defourny, has spoken in a similar spirit. "One of the first commandments of the eternal law,
engraved in every man's conscience," says the Abbé Defourny,
"forbids a man to take his neighbour's life or shed his blood"
(without sufficient cause, being forced to it by stress of circumstance). "This is a commandment more deeply engraved in the
human heart than all the others.... But as soon as it becomes
a question of war, that is, a question of the wholesale shedding
of human blood, men in these days do not wait for a sufficient
cause. Those who are active in war forget to ask themselves if
there is any justification for the numerous manslaughters that
take place, whether they are just or unjust, legal or illegal, innocent or criminal, or whether they break the principal law that
forbids us to commit murder" (without just cause). "Their conscience is silent.... War has ceased to be a matter connected
with morality. The soldier, amid all the fatigues and dangers he
undergoes, knows no joy but conquest, no sorrow but defeat.
Don't tell me that they serve the country. A great genius has

long ago answered this statement in words that have since become a proverb: 'Take away justice, and what is then a nation but a great band of robbers? And is not a band of robbers in itself a small state? They, too, have their laws. They, too, fight for booty and even honour.'

"The aim of this organization" (it was a question of establishing international tribunals) "is to influence the European nations until they cease to be nations of thieves, and their armies bands of robbers. Yes, our armies are nothing less than a rabble of slaves belonging to one or two monarchs and their ministers, who, as we all know, rule them tyrannically and without any responsibility other than nominal, as we know."

It is the characteristic of a slave that he is a tool in the hands of his master. Such are the soldiers, officers, and generals, who at the beck of their sovereign go forth to slay or to be slain. There is a military slavery, and it is the worst of all slaveries, particularly now, when by means of conscription it forges chains for the necks of all the free and strong men of the nation, in order to use them as instruments of murder, to make them executioners and butchers of human flesh, since that is the sole reason why they are drafted and drilled.

"Two or three potentates in their cabinets make treaties, without protocols, without publicity, and therefore without responsibility, sending men to the slaughter."

'Protests against increased armaments began before our time,' said Signor E. G. Moneta. 'Listen to Montesquieu. France' (for France we might now substitute Europe) 'is perishing from an overgrown army. A new disease is spreading throughout Europe. It has affected kings, and obliges them to maintain an incredible number of troops. It is like a rash, and therefore contagious; for no sooner does one nation increase its troops than all the others follow suit. Nothing can result from this condition of affairs but general calamity.

"Each government maintains as many troops as it would require if its people were threatened with destruction, and this state of tension is called peace. Europe is in truth ruined. If private individuals were reduced to such straits as these, the richest man among them would be practically destitute. The wealth of the world and its commerce are in our hands, and yet we are poor."

This was written almost 150 years ago. It seems like a picture of the present. One thing alone has changed – the form of government. In the time of Montesquieu it was said that the reason for the maintenance of large armies might be found in the unlimited power of kings, who carried on war in the hope of increasing their private property and their glory.

"Then it was said: 'Ah! If the people could but choose representatives who would have a right to refuse the governments when they called for soldiers and money – there would be an end of a military policy.' Now, almost everywhere in Europe there are representative governments, and still the military expenditure in preparation for war has increased in frightful proportion.

"It looks as though the folly of the rulers had passed into the ruling classes. Now they no longer fight because one king has been rude to another king's mistress, as in the time of Louis XIV but by exaggerating the importance of national dignity and patriotism – emotions which are natural and honourable in themselves – and exciting the public opinion of one country against the other, until they have arrived at such a pitch of sensitiveness that it is enough to say, for instance (even were the report to prove false), one country has refused to receive the ambassador of another, to precipitate the most frightful and disastrous war. Europe maintains under arms at the present time more soldiers than were in the field during the great wars of Napoleon. Every citizen on our continent, with a few exceptions, is forced to spend several years in the barracks. Fortresses, arsenals, men-of-war are built, new firearms are invented, which in a short time are replaced by others, because science, which should always be devoted to the promotion of human welfare, contributes, it must be regretfully acknowledged, to human destruction, inventing ever new means of killing greater numbers of men in the shortest possible time.

"In these stupendous preparations for slaughter, and in the maintenance of these vast numbers of troops, hundreds of millions are yearly expended – sums that would suffice to educate the masses, and to carry on the most important works of public improvement, thereby contributing towards a perfect solution of the social problem.

"Therefore, notwithstanding all our scientific victories, Europe finds herself in this respect not one whit better off than she was in the most barbarous times of the Middle Ages. Every one laments a state of things which is neither war nor peace, and longs to be delivered from it. The heads of governments emphatically affirm that they desire peace, and eagerly emulate each other in their pacific utterances, but almost immediately thereafter they propose to the legislative assemblies measures for increasing the armament, asserting that they take these precautions for the preservation of peace.

"But this is not the sort of peace we care for, and the nations are not deceived by it. True peace has for its foundation mutual confidence, whereas these appalling armaments show, if not a declared hostility, at least a secret distrust among the different nations. What should we say of a man who, wishing to show his friendly feelings to his neighbour, should invite him to consider a certain scheme, holding a loaded pistol while he unfolds it before him?

"It is this monstrous contradiction between the assurances of peace and the military policy of the governments, that good citizens wish to put an end to, at any cost."

One is amazed to learn that there are 60,000 suicides reported in Europe, not including Turkey and Russia, every year, and these are all well substantiated cases; but it would be far more remarkable if the number were less. Any man in these times, who investigates the antagonism between his convictions and his actions, finds himself in a desperate plight. Setting aside the many other contradictions between actual life and conviction which abound in the life of a man of the present day, to view the military situation in Europe in the light of its profession of Christianity is enough to make a man doubt the existence of human reason, and drive him to escape from barbarous and insane world by putting an end to his own life. This inconsistency, which is the very quintessence of all the others, is so shocking, that one can only go on living and taking any part in it, by dint of trying not to think about it, to forget it all.

What can it mean? We are Christians, who not only profess to love one another, but are actually leading one common life; our pulses beat in harmony; we meet each other in love and sympathy, deriving support and counsel from our mutual intercourse.

Were it not for this sympathy life would have no meaning. But at any moment some demented ruler may utter a few rash words, to which another gives reply, and lo! I am ordered to march at the risk of my life, to slay those who have never injured me, whom I really love. And it is no remote contingency, but an inevitable climax for which we are all preparing ourselves.

Fully to realize this, is enough to drive one to madness and to suicide, and this is but too common an occurrence, especially among soldiers.

A moment's reflection shows us why this seems an inevitable conclusion.

It explains the frightful intensity with which men plunge into all kinds of dissipation, wine, tobacco, cards, newspaper reading, travel, all manner of shows and pleasures. They pursue all these amusements in deadly earnest, as if they were serious avocations, as indeed they are. If men possessed none of these distractions, half of them would kill themselves out of hand, for to live a life that is made up of contradictions is simply unbearable, and such is the life that most of us lead at the present day. We are living in direct contradiction to our inmost convictions. This contradiction is evident both in economic and in political relations; it is manifested most unmistakably in the inconsistency of the acknowledgment of the Christian law of brotherly love and military conscription, which obliges men to hold themselves in readiness to take each other's lives – in short, every man to be at once a Christian and a gladiator.

CHAPTER VI

The Attitude of Men of the Present Day Towards War

MEN DO NOT ENDEAVOUR to destroy the contradiction between life and consciousness by a change of life, but educated men use all their power to stifle the demands of consciousness and to justify their lives, and thus degrade society to a condition worse than pagan, to a state of primeval savagery – Uncertainty of the attitude of our leading men towards war, universal armament, and general military conscription – Those who regard war as an accidental political phenomenon easily to be remedied by external measures – The Peace Congress – Article in the *Revue des Revues* – Proposition of Maxime du Camp – Significance of Courts of Arbitration and Disarmament – Relations of governments to these, and the business they pursue – Those who regard war as a cruel inevitable phenomenon – Maupassant – Rod – Those who regard it as indispensable, even useful – Camille Doucet, Claretie, Zola, Vogtie.

The contradictions of life and of consciousness may be solved in two ways: by change of life, or by change of consciousness; and it would seem as if there could be no hesitation in a choice between the two.

When a man acknowledges a deed to be evil he may refrain from the deed itself, but he can never cease to regard it as evil. Indeed, the whole world might cease from evil doing, and yet have no power to transform, or even to check for a season, the progress of knowledge in regard to that which is evil, and which ought not to exist. One would think that the alternative of a change of life to accord with consciousness might be settled without question, and that it would therefore seem unavoidable for the Christian world of the present day to abandon those pagan forms which it condemns, and regulate its life by the Christian precepts which it acknowledges.

Such would be the result, were it not for the principle of inertia (a principle no less unalterable in human life than in the world of matter), which finds its expression in the psychological law defined in the Gospel by the words: "Men loved darkness rather than light, because their deeds were evil" John iii: 19. Most persons, in conformity to this principle, do not use their reason in order to ascertain the truth, but rather to persuade themselves that they possess it, and that their daily life, which is pleasant for them, is in harmony with the precepts of truth.

Slavery conflicted with all the moral principles taught by Plato and Aristotle, and yet neither of them perceived this, because the disavowal of slavery must have destroyed that life by which they lived. And the same thing is repeated in our times.

The division of mankind into two classes, the existence of political and military injustice, is opposed to all those moral principles which our society professes, and yet the most progressive and cultivated men of the age seem not to perceive this.

Almost every educated man at the present day is striving unconsciously to preserve the old-time conception of society, which justifies his attitude, and to conceal from others and from himself its inconsistencies, chief among which is the necessity of adopting the Christian ideal, which is subversive of the very structure of our social existence. It is this antiquated social system, in which they no longer believe, because it is really a thing of the past, that men are trying to uphold.

Contemporary literature, philosophical, political, and artistic – all contemporary literature affords a striking proof of the truth of my statement. What wealth of imagination, what form and colour, what erudition and art, but what a lack of serious purpose, what reluctance to face any exact thought! Ambiguity of expression, indirect allusion, witticisms, vague reflection, but no straightforward or candid dealing with the subject they treat of, namely, life.

Indeed, our writers treat of obscenities and improprieties; in the guise of refined paradox they convey suggestions which thrust men back to primeval savagery, to the lowest dregs not only of pagan life, but of animal life, which we outlived 5000 years ago. Delivering themselves from the Christian life-conception, which for some simply interferes with the accustomed current of their lives, while for others it interferes with certain advantages, men must of necessity return to the pagan life-conception and to the doctrines to which it gave rise. Not only are patriotism and the rights of the aristocracy preached at the present time as they used to be 2000 years ago, but also the coarsest Epicureanism and sensuality, with this difference only, that the teachers of old believed in the doctrines they taught, whereas those of the present day neither do nor can possess any faith in what they utter, because there is no longer any sense in it. When the ground is shifting under our feet, we cannot stand still, we must either recede or advance. It sounds exaggerated to say that the enlightened men of our time, the advanced thinkers, are speciously degrading society, plunging it into a condition worse than pagan – into a state of primeval barbarism.

In no other matter has this tendency of the leading men of our time been so plainly shown, as in their attitude towards that phenomenon in which at present all the inconsistency of social life is concentrated – towards war, universal armament, and military conscription.

The equivocal, if not unscrupulous attitude of the educated men of our time towards this question is a striking one. It may be stated from three points of view. Some regard this phenomenon as an accidental state of affairs, which has sprung from the peculiar political situation of Europe, and believe it to be susceptible of adjustment by diplomatic and international mediation, without injury to the structure of nations. Others look upon it as something appalling and cruel, fatal yet unavoidable – like disease or death. Still others, in cold blood, calmly pronounce war to be an indispensable, salutary, and therefore desirable event.

Men may differ in their views in regard to this matter, but all discuss it as something with which the will of the individuals who are to take part in it has nothing whatever to do; therefore they do not even admit the natural question which presents itself to most men, viz. "Is it my duty to take part in it?" In the opinion of these judges there is no reason in such a question, and every man, whatever may be his personal prejudices in regard to war, must submit in this matter to the demands of the ruling powers.

The attitude of those in the first category, who expect deliverance from war by means of diplomatic and international mediation, is well defined in the results of the London Peace Congress, and in an article together with letters concerning war from prominent writers which maybe found in the *Revue des Revues* (No. 8, 1891).

These are the results of the Congress.

Having collected from all parts of the globe the opinions of scientists, both written and oral, the Congress, opening with a *Te Deum* in the Cathedral, and closing with a dinner and speeches, listened for five days to numerous addresses, and arrived at the following conclusions:

Resolution I. The Congress affirms its belief that the brotherhood of man involves as a necessary consequence a brotherhood of nations, in which the true interests of all are acknowledged to be identical. The Congress is convinced that the true basis for an enduring peace will be found in the application by nations of this great principle in all their relations one to another.

II. The Congress recognizes the important influence which Christianity exercises upon the moral and political progress of mankind, and earnestly urges upon ministers of the Gospel and other teachers of religion and morality the duty of setting forth these principles of Peace and Goodwill, which occupy such a central place in the teaching of Jesus Christ, of philosophers and of moralists, and recommends that the third Sunday in December in each year be set apart for that purpose.

III. The Congress expresses its opinion that all teachers of history should call the attention of the young to the grave evils inflicted on mankind in all ages by war, and to the fact that such war has been waged, as a rule, for most inadequate causes.

IV. The Congress protests against the use of military drill in connection with the physical exercises of schools, and suggests the formation of brigades for saving life rather than any of quasi-military character; and it urges the desirability of impressing on the Board of Examiners, who formulate the questions for examination, the propriety of guiding the minds of children into the Principles of Peace.

V. The Congress holds that the doctrine of the universal rights of man requires that aboriginal and weaker races shall be guarded from injustice and fraud when brought into contact with civilized peoples, alike as to their territories, their liberties, and their property, and that they shall be shielded from the vices which are so prevalent among the so-called advanced races of men. It further expresses its conviction that there should be concert olfaction among the nations for the accomplishment of these ends. The Congress desires to express its hearty appreciation of the conclusions arrived at by the late Anti-Slavery Conference, held in Brussels, for the amelioration of the condition of the peoples of Africa.

VI. The Congress believes that the warlike prejudices and traditions which are still fostered in the various nationalities, and the misrepresentations by leaders of public opinion in legislative assemblies, or through the press, are not infrequently indirect causes of war. The Congress is therefore of opinion that these ends should be counteracted by the publication of accurate statements and information that would tend to the removal of misunderstanding amongst nations, and recommends to the Inter-Parliamentary Committee the importance of considering the question of starting an international newspaper, which should have such a purpose as one of its primary objects.

VII. The Congress proposes to the Inter-Parliamentary Conference that the utmost support should be given to every project for the unification of weights and measures, of coinage, tariffs, postal and telegraphic arrangements, means of transport, etc., which would assist in constituting a commercial, industrial, and scientific union of the peoples.

VIII. In view of the vast moral and social influence of woman, the Congress urges upon every woman throughout the world to sustain, as wife, mother, sister, or citizen, the things that make for peace; as otherwise she incurs grave responsibilities for the continuance of the systems of war and militarism, which not only desolate but corrupt the homelife of the nation. To concentrate and to practically apply this influence, the Congress recommends that women should unite themselves with societies for the promotion of international peace.

IX. This Congress expresses the hope that the Financial

Reform Association and other similar societies in Europe and America should unite in convoking at an early date a conference to consider the best means of establishing equitable commercial relations between States by the reduction of import duties as a step towards Free Trade. The Congress feels that it can affirm that the whole of Europe desires Peace, and is impatiently waiting for the moment when it shall see the end of those crushing armaments which, under the plea of defence, become in their turn a danger, by keeping alive mutual distrust, and are, at the same time, the cause of the general economic disturbance which stands in the way of settling in a satisfactory manner the problems of labour and poverty, which should take precedence of all others.

X. This Congress, recognizing that a general disarmament would be the best guarantee of Peace, and would lead to the solution, in the general interest, of those questions which now must divide States, expresses the wish that a Congress of Representatives of all the States of Europe may be assembled as soon as possible to consider the means of effecting a gradual general disarmament, which already seems feasible.

XL. This Congress, considering that the timidity of a single Power or other cause might delay indefinitely the convocation of the above mentioned Congress, is of the opinion that the Government which should first dismiss any considerable number of soldiers would confer a signal, benefiting Europe and mankind, because it would oblige other Governments, urged on by public opinion, to follow its example, and by the moral force of this accomplished fact would have increased rather than diminished the conditions of its national defence.

XII. This Congress, considering the question of disarmament, as well as the Peace question generally, depends upon public opinion, recommends the Peace Societies here represented and all friends of Peace to carry on an active propaganda among the people, especially at the time of Parliamentary elections, in order that the electors should give their votes to those candidates who have included in their programme Peace, Disarmament, and Arbitration.

XIII. This Congress congratulates the friends of Peace on the resolution adopted by the International American Conference (with the exception of the representatives of Chile and Mexico) at Washington in April last, by which it was recommended that arbitration should be obligatory in all controversies concerning diplomatic and consular privileges, boundaries, territories, indemnities, right of navigation, and the validity, construction, and enforcement of treaties, and in all other causes, whatever their origin, nature, or occasion, except only those which, in the judgment of any of the nations involved in the controversy, may imperil its independence.

XIV. This Congress respectfully recommends this resolution to the statesmen of Europe, and expresses the ardent desire that treaties in similar terms be speedily entered into between the other nations of the world.

XV. This Congress expresses its satisfaction at the adoption by the Spanish Senate, on June 18th last, of a project of law authorizing the Government to negotiate general or special treaties of arbitration for the settlement of all disputes, except those relating to the independence and internal government of the States affected; also at the adoption of resolutions to a like effect by the Norwegian Storting, on March 6th last, and by the Italian Chamber on July 11th.

XVI. That a committee of five be appointed to prepare and address communications, in the name of the Congress, to the principal religious, political, economical, labour, and peace organizations in civilized countries, requesting them to send petitions to the governmental authorities of the irrespective countries, praying that measures be taken for the formation of suitable tribunals for the adjudication of international questions, so as to avoid the resort to war.

XVII. Seeing (i) that the object pursued by all Peace Societies is the establishment of juridical order between nations:

(2) That neutralization by international treaties constitutes a step towards this juridical state, and lessens the number of districts in which war can be carried on:

This Congress recommends a larger extension of the rule of neutralization, and expresses the wish:

(1) That all treaties which at present assure to certain States

the benefit of neutrality remain in force, or, if necessary, be amended in a manner to render the neutrality more effective, either by extending neutralization to the whole of the State, of which a part only may be neutralized, or by ordering the demolition of fortresses, which constitute rather a peril than a guarantee for neutrality.

(2) That new treaties, provided that they are in harmony with the wishes of the populations concerned, be concluded for establishing the neutralization of other States.

XVIII. The Committee Section proposes:

(1) That the next Congress be held immediately before or immediately after the next session of the Inter-Parliamentary Conference, and at the same places.

(2) That the question of an international Peace Emblem be postponed sine die.

(3) The adoption of the following resolutions:

(a) Resolved, that we express our satisfaction atthe formal and official overtures of the Presbyterian Church in the United States of America, addressed to the highest representatives of each church organization in Christendom, inviting the same to unite with itself in a general conference, the object of which shall be to promote the substitution of international arbitration for war.

(b) That this Congress, assembled in London from the14th to the 19th July, desires to express its profound reverence for the memory of Aurelio Saffi, the great Italian jurist, a member of the Committee of the International League of Peace and Liberty.

(4) That the memorial to the various heads of the civilized States adopted by this Congress, and signed by the President, should, so far as practicable, be presented to each Power by an influential deputation.

(5) That the Organization Committee be empowered to make the needful verbal emendations in the papers and resolutions presented.

(6) That the following resolutions be adopted:

(a) A resolution of thanks to the Presidents of the various sittings of the Congress.

(b) A resolution of thanks to the chairman, the secretary, and the members of the Bureau of this Congress.

(c) A resolution of thanks to the conveners and members of the sectional committees.

(d) A resolution of thanks to Rev. Canon Scott Holland, Rev. Dr. Reuan Thomas, and Rev. J. Morgan Gibbon, for their pulpit addresses before the Congress, and that they be requested to furnish copies of the same for publication; and also Stamford Hall Congregational Church, for the use of those buildings for public services.

(e) A letter of thanks to Her Majesty for permission to visit Windsor Castle.

(f) And also a resolution of thanks to the Lord Mayor and Lady Mayoress, to Mr. Passmore Edwards, and other friends who have extended their hospitality to the members of the Congress.

XIX. This Congress places on record a heartfelt expression of gratitude to Almighty God for the remarkable harmony and concord which have characterized the meetings of the Assembly, in which so many men and women of varied nations, creeds, tongues, and races have gathered in closest cooperation; and in the conclusion of the labours of this Congress it expresses its firm and unshaken belief in the ultimate triumph of the cause of Peace, and of the principles which have been advocated at these meetings.

The fundamental idea of the Congress is – firstly, that its necessary to disseminate by all means among all men the belief that war is not advantageous for mankind, and that peace is a great benefit; and secondly, to influence governments, impressing upon them the advantages and necessity of disarmament.

To accomplish the first end the Congress advises teachers of history, women, and ministers of the Gospel, to teach people, every third Sunday of December, the evils of war and the benefits of peace; to accomplish the second the Congress addresses itself to governments, suggesting to them disarmament and arbitration.

To preach the evils of war and the benefits of peace! But the evils of war are so well known to men, that from the earliest ages the most welcome greeting was always: "Peace be unto you!"

Not only Christians but all pagans were fully aware of the benefits of peace and of the evils of war thousands of years ago, so that the advice to the ministers of the Gospel top reach against the evils of war and to advocate the benefits of peace every third Sunday in December is quite superfluous.

A real Christian cannot do otherwise than preach thus, constantly, as long as he lives. But if there are those who are called Christians, or Christian preachers, who do not do this, there must be a cause for it, and so long as this cause exists no advice will avail. Still less effective will be the advice to governments to disband armies and have recourse to International Courts of Arbitration. Governments know very well all the difficulties and burdens of conscription and of maintaining armies, and if in the face of such difficulties and burdens they still continue to do so, it is evident that they have no means of doing otherwise, and the advice of a Congress could in no way bring about a change. But scientists will not admit this, and still hope to find some combination of influences by means of which those governments which make war may be induced to restrain themselves.

"Is it possible to avoid war?" writes a scientist in the *Revue des Revues* (No. 8 of 1891). "All agree in recognizing the fact that if war should ever break out in Europe, its consequences would be similar to those of the great invasions. It would imperil the very existence of nations; it would be bloody, atrocious, and desperate. This consideration, and the consideration of the terrible nature of the engines of destruction at the command of modern science, retards its declaration and temporarily maintains the present system – a system which might be continued indefinitely, if it were not for the enormous expenses that burden the European nations and threaten to culminate in disasters fully equal to those occasioned by war."

Impressed with these thoughts, men of all nationalities have sought for means to arrest, or at least to diminish, the shocking consequences of the carnage that threatens us.

"Such are the questions which are to be debated by the next Congress of Universal Peace to be held in Rome, which have already been discussed in a recently published pamphlet on Disarmament."

Unfortunately, it is quite certain that with the present organization of the greater number of the European states, isolated one from the other and controlled by different interests, the absolute cessation of war is an illusion which it would be folly to cherish. Still, the adoption of somewhat wiser rules and regulations in regard to these international duels would at least tend to limit their horrors. It is equally Utopian to build one's hope on projects of disarmament, whose execution, owing to considerations of a national character, which exist in the minds of all our readers, is practically impossible." [This probably means that France cannot disarm until she has retaliated.] "Public opinion is not prepared to accept them, and, furthermore, the international relations make it impossible to adopt them. Disarmament demanded by one nation of another, under conditions imperilling its security, would be equivalent to a declaration of war.

"Still, we must admit that an exchange of opinions between the nations interested may to a certain extent aid in establishing an international understanding, and also contribute to lessen the military expenses that now crush European nations, to the great detriment of the solution of social questions, the necessity of the solution of which is realized by each nation individually, under the penalty of being confronted by a civil war, due to the efforts made to prevent a foreign one."

"One may at least hope for a decrease of the enormous expenses necessary for the present military organization, which is maintained for the purpose of invading a foreign territory in twenty-four hours, or of a decisive battle a week after the declaration of war."

It ought not to be possible for one nation to attack another and take possession of its territory within twenty-four hours. This practical sentiment was expressed by Maxime du Camp, and is the conclusion of his study of the subject.

Maxime du Camp offers the following propositions: "Ist. A Diplomatic Congress, to assemble every year. "2nd. No war to be declared until two months after the incident which gave rise to it." [Here the difficulty lies in determining the nature of the incident that kindled the war – that is, every declaration of war is caused by several circumstances, and it would be necessary to determine from which one the two months are to be reckoned.]

"3rd. No war shall be declared until the vote of the people shall have been taken.

"4th. Hostilities must not begin until a month after the declaration of war."

"No war shall be declared . . .." etc. But who is to prevent hostilities beginning? Who will compel men to do this or that? Who will compel governments to wait a certain stated time? Other nations. But all the other nations are in the very same position, requiring to be restrained and kept within bounds, in other words, coerced. And who will coerce them? And how is it to be done? By public opinion? But if public opinion has sufficient influence to force a nation to postpone its action until a stated time, this public opinion can prevent it from waging war at any time.

But, it is said, there might be a balance of power, which would oblige nations to restrain themselves. This very experiment has been and is still being tried; this was the object of the Holy Alliance, the League of Peace, etc.

But all would agree to this, it is said. If all would agree to this then wars would cease, and there would be no need of Courts of Appeal or of Arbitration.

"A Court of Arbitration would take the place of war. Disputes would be decided by a Board of Arbitrators, like that which pronounced on the Alabama claims. The Pope has been requested to decide the question concerning the Caroline Islands: Switzerland, Belgium, Denmark, and Holland have declared that they prefer the decision of a Court of Arbitration to war."

I believe Monaco has expressed a similar wish. It is a pity that Germany, Russia, Austria, and France have thus far shown no sign of imitating their example.

It is astonishing how easily men can deceive themselves when they feel inclined.

The governments will agree to allow their disputes to be decided by a Board of Arbitration and to dismiss their armies. The trouble between Russia and Poland, England and Ireland, Austria and the Czechs, Turkey and the Slavs, France and Germany, will be settled by mutual consent. This is very much like suggesting to merchants and bankers that they shall sell at cost price, and devote their services gratuitously to the distribution of property.

Of course the essence of commerce and banking consists in buying cheap and selling dear, and therefore the suggestion to sell at cost price and the consequent overthrow of money amounts to a proposal of self-destruction.

The same is true in regard to governments.

The suggestion to governments to desist from violence, and to adjust all differences by arbitration would be to recommend a suicidal policy, and no government would ever agree to that. Learned men found societies (there are more than one hundred of them), they assemble in Congresses (like those held in London and Paris, and the one which is to be held in Rome), they read essays, hold banquets, make speeches, edit journals devoted to the subject, and by all these means they endeavour to prove that the strain upon nations who are obliged to support millions of soldiers has become so severe that something must be done about it; that this armament is opposed to the character, the aims, and the wishes of the populations; but they seem to think that if they consume a good deal of paper, and devote a good deal of eloquence to the subject, that they may succeed in conciliating opposing parties and conflicting interests, and at last effect the suppression of war.

When I was a child I was told that if I wished to catch a bird I must put salt on its tail. I took a handful and went in pursuit of the birds, but I saw at once that if I could sprinkle salt on their tails I could catch them, and that what I had been told was only a joke. Those who read essays and works on Courts of Arbitration and the disarmament of nations must feel very much the same.

If it were possible to sprinkle salt on a bird's tail it would be tantamount to saying that the bird could not fly, and therefore it would be no effort to catch it. If a bird has wings and does not wish to be caught, it will not allow any salt to be put on its tail, for it is the nature of a bird to fly. Likewise it is the nature of a government not to be ruled, but to rule its subjects. And a government rightly is named such only when it is able to rule its subjects, and not be ruled by them. This, therefore, is its constant aim, and it will never voluntarily resign its power. And as it derives its power from the army it will never give up the army, nor will it ever renounce that for which the army is designed – war.

The misapprehension springs from the fact that the learned jurists, deceiving themselves as well as others, depict in their books an ideal of government — not as it really is, an assembly of men who oppress their fellow citizens, but in accordance with the scientific postulate, as a body of men who act as the representatives of the rest of the nation. They have gone on repeating this to others so long that they have ended by believing it themselves, and they really seem to think that justice is one of the duties of governments. History, however, shows us that governments, as seen from the reign of Caesar to those of the two Napoleons and Prince Bismarck, are in their very essence a violation of justice; a man or a body of men having at command an army of trained soldiers, deluded creatures who are ready for any violence, and through whose agency they govern the State, will have no keen sense of the obligation of justice.

Therefore governments will never consent to diminish the number of those well-trained and submissive servants, who constitute their power and influence.

Such is the attitude of certain scientists towards that self-contradiction under which the world groans, and such are their expedients for its relief. Tell these scientists that the question deals only with the personal relations of each individual towards the moral and religious question, and then ask them what they think of the lawfulness or unlawfulness of taking part in the general conscription, and their sole reply will be a shrug of the shoulders; they will not even deign to give a thought to your question. Their way of solving the difficulty is to make speeches, write books, choose their presidents, vice presidents, and secretaries; assembled in a body, to hold forth in one city or another. They think that the result of their efforts will be to induce governments to cease to recruit soldiers, on whom all their power depends; they expect that their appeals will be heard, and that armies will be disbanded, leaving governments defenceless, not only in the presence of neighbours, but of their subjects; that they, like highwaymen who, having bound their defenceless victims in order to rob them, no sooner hear the outcries of pain than they loosen the rope that causes it, and let their prisoners go free.

And there really are men who believe in this, who spend their time in promoting Leagues of Peace, in delivering addresses, and in writing books; and of course the governments sympathize with it all, pretending that they approve of it, just as they pretend to support temperance, while they actually derive the larger part of their income from intemperance; just as they pretend to maintain liberty of the constitution, when it is the absence of liberty to which they owe their power; just as they pretend to care for the improvement of the labouring classes, while on oppression of the workman rest the very foundations of the State; just as they pretend to uphold Christianity, when Christianity is subversive of every government.

In order to accomplish these ends they have long since instituted laws in regard to intemperance that can never avail to destroy it; educational projects that not only do not prevent the spread of ignorance, but do everything to increase it; decrees in the name of liberty that are no restraint upon despotism; measures for the benefit of the working man which will never liberate him from slavery; they have established a Christianity which serves to prop the government rather than destroy it. And now another interest is added to their cares – the promotion of peace. Governments, or rather those rulers who are going about at present with their ministers of state, making up their minds on such radical questions as, for instance, whether the slaughter of millions shall begin this year or next – they are quite well assured that discussions on peace are not going to prevent them from sending millions of men to slaughter whenever they see fit to do so. They like to hear these discussions; they encourage them, and even take part themselves.

It does no harm to the government; on the contrary, it is useful, by way of diverting observation from that radical question: when a man is drafted, ought he or ought he not to fulfil his military duty?

Thanks to all these unions and congresses, peace will presently be established; meanwhile put on your uniforms and be prepared to worry and harass each other for our benefit, say the governments. And the scientists, the essayists, and the promoters of congresses take the same view.

This is one way of looking at it, and so advantageous for the State that all prudent governments encourage it.

The way another class has of regarding it is more tragic. They declare that although it is the fate of humanity to be forever striving after love and peace, it is nevertheless abnormal and inconsistent. Those who affirm this are mostly the sensitive men of genius, who see and realize all the horror, folly, and cruelty of war, but by some strange turn of mind never look about them for any means of escape, but who seem to take a morbid delight in realizing to the utmost the desperate condition of mankind. The view of the famous French writer, Maupassant, on the subject of war, affords a noteworthy example of this kind. Gazing from his yacht upon a drill-and-target practice of French soldiers, the following thoughts arise in his mind:

"I have but to think of the word 'war' and a paralysing sense of horror creeps over me, as though I were listening to stories of witchcraft, or tales of the Inquisition, or of things abominable, monstrous, unnatural, of ages past.

"When people talk of cannibals we smile contemptuously with a sense of superiority to such savages. But who are the savages, the true savages? Those who fight that they may drive off the conquered, or those who fight for the pure pleasure of killing? Those sharp shooters running over yonder are destined to be killed like a flock of sheep who are driven by the butcher to the slaughter house. Those men will fall on some battlefield with a sabre-cut in the head, or with a ball through the heart. Yet they are young men, who might have done useful work. Their fathers are old and poor; their mothers, who have idolized them for twenty years as only mothers can idolize, will learn after six months, or perhaps a year, that the son, the baby, the grown-up child on whom so much love and pains were lavished, who was reared at such an expense, has been torn by a bullet, trampled under foot, or crushed by a cavalry charge, and finally flung like a dead dog into some ditch. Why must her boy, her beautiful, her only boy, the hope and pride of her life, why must he be killed? She knows not; she can but ask why.

"War! . . . The fighting! . . . The murdering; the slaughter of men! . . . And today, with all our wisdom, civilization, with the advancement of science, the degree of philosophy to which the human spirit has attained, we have schools where the art of murder, of aiming with deadly accuracy and killing large numbers of men at a distance, is actually taught, killing poor, harmless devils who have families to support, killing them without even the pretext of the law.

It is stupefying that the people do not rise up in arms against the governments. What difference is there between monarchies and republics? It is stupefying that society does not revolt as a unit at the very sound of the word war.

"Alas! We shall never be free from oppression of the hateful, hideous customs, the criminal prejudices, and the ferocious impulses of our barbarous ancestors, for we are beasts; and beasts we shall remain, moved by our instincts and susceptible of no improvement.

"Anyone but Victor Hugo would have been banished when he uttered his sublime cry of freedom and truth:

"Today force is called violence, and the nations condemn it; they inveigh against war. Civilization, listening to the appeal of humanity, undertakes the case and prepares the accusation against the victors and the generals. The nations begin to understand that the magnitude of a crime cannot lessen its wickedness; that if it be criminal to kill one man, the killing of numbers cannot be regarded in the light of extenuation; that if it be shameful to steal, it cannot be glorious to lead an invading army."

'Let us proclaim these absolute truths, let us dishonour the name of war!'

"But the wrath and indignation of the poet are all in vain," continues Maupassant. "War is more honoured than ever."

A clever expert in this business, a genius in the art of murder, Von Moltke, once made to a peace delegate the following astonishing reply:

'War is sacred; it is a divine institution; it fosters every lofty and noble sentiment in the human heart: honour, self-sacrifice, virtue, courage, and saves men, so to speak, from settling into the most shocking materialism.'

"Assembling in herds by the hundred thousand, marching night and day without rest, with no time for thought or for study, never to read, learning nothing, of no use whatsoever to any living being, rotting with filth, sleeping in the mud, living like a wild beast in a perennial state of stupidity, plundering cities, burning villages, ruining whole nations; then to encounter another mountain of human flesh, rush upon it, cause rivers of blood to flow, and strew the fields with the dead and the dying, all stained with the muddy and reddened soil, to have one's limbs severed, one's brain scattered as wanton waste, and to perish in the corner of a field while one's aged parents, one's wife and children are dying of hunger at home – this is what it means to be saved from falling into the grossest materialism!"

Soldiers are the scourge of the world. We struggle against nature, ignorance, all kinds of obstacles, in the effort to make our wretched lives more endurable. There are men, scientists and philanthropists, who devote their whole lives to benefit their fellow men, seeking to improve their condition. They pursue their efforts tirelessly, adding discovery to discovery, expanding the human intelligence, enriching science, opening new fields of knowledge, day by day increasing the well being, comfort, and vigour of their country.

"Then war comes upon the scene, and in six months all the results of twenty years of patient labour and of human genius are gone for ever, crushed by victorious generals.

"And this is what they mean when they speak of man's rescue from materialism!

"We have seen war. We have seen men maddened; returned to the condition of the brutes, we have seen them kill in wanton sport, out of terror, or for mere bravado and show. Where right exists no longer, and law is dead, where all sense of justice has been lost, we have seen innocent men shot down on the highway, because they were timid and thus excited suspicion. We have seen dogs chained to their masters' doors killed by way of target practice, we have seen cows lying in a field fired at by the mitrailleuses, just for the fun of shooting at something." And this is what they call saving men from the most shocking materialism!

"To invade a country, to kill the man who defends his home because he wears a blouse and does not wear a *kepi*, to burn the dwellings of starving wretches, to ruin or plunder a man's household goods, to drink the wine found in the cellars, to violate the women found in the streets, consume millions of francs in powder, and to leave misery and cholera in their track." This is what they mean by saving men from the most shocking materialism!"

What have military men ever done to prove that they possess the smallest degree of intelligence? Nothing whatever. What have they invented? The cannon and the musket; nothing more.

"Has not the inventor of the wheelbarrow, by the simple and practical contrivance of a wheel and a couple of boards, accomplished more than the inventor of modern fortification?

"What has Greece bequeathed to the world? Its literature and its marbles. Was she great because she conquered, or because she produced? Was it the Persian invasion that saved Greece from succumbing to the most shocking materialism?

"Did the invasions of the Barbarians save and regenerate Rome?

"Did Napoleon I continue the great intellectual movement started by the philosophers at the end of the last century?

"Very well then; can it be a matter of surprise, since governments usurp the rights of life and death over the people, that the people from time to time assume the right of life and death over their governments?"

They defend themselves, and they have the right. No man has an inalienable right to govern others. It is allowable only when it promotes the welfare of the governed. It is as much the duty of those who govern to avoid war, as it is that of a captain of a ship to avoid shipwreck.

"When a captain has lost his ship he is indicted, and if he is found to have been careless or even incompetent, he is convicted. As soon as war has been declared why should not the people sit in judgment upon the act of the government?

"If they could once be made to understand the power that would be theirs, if they were the judges of the rulers who lead them on to slay their fellowmen, if they refused to allow themselves to be needlessly slaughtered, if they were to turn their weapons against the very men who have put them into their hands – that day would see the last of war. But never will that day arrive" (Sur l'Eau).

The author perceives the full horror of war, realizes that the government is its author, that government forces men to go, slay or be slain, when there is no need for it; he realizes that the men who make up the armies might turn their weapons against the government and demand a reckoning. Still the author does not believe that this will ever happen, or that there is any possible deliverance from the existing condition of affairs.

He grants that the result of war is shocking, but he believes it to be inevitable; assuming that the never-ceasing requisition for soldiers on the part of government is as inevitable as death, then wars must follow as a matter of course.

These are the words of a writer of talent, endowed with a faculty of vividly realizing his subject, which is the essence of the poetic gift. He shows us all the cruel contradictions between creed and deed; but since he fails to offer a solution, it is evident that he feels that such a contradiction must exist, and regards it as a contribution to the romantic tragedy of life. Another and an equally gifted writer, Edouard Rod, paints with colours still more vivid the cruelty and folly of the present situation, but he, like Maupassant, feels the influence of the dramatic element, and neither suggests a remedy nor anticipates any change.

"Why do we toil? Why do we plan and hope to execute? And how can one even love one's neighbour in these troubled times, when the morrow is nothing but a menace?

Everything that we have begun, our ripening schemes, our plans for work, the little good that we might accomplish, will it not all be swept away by the storm that is gathering? Everywhere the soil quakes beneath our feet, and threatening clouds hang low on the horizon. Ah! If we had nothing more to fear than the bugbear of the Revolution!

Unable to conceive a society worse than our own, I am more inclined to distrust than to fear the one that may replace it, and if I should suffer in consequence of the change, I should console myself with the reflection that the executioners of the present were victims of the past, and the hope of a change for the better would make me endure the worst. But it is not this remote danger which alarms me. I see another close at hand and far more cruel, since it is both unjustifiable and irrational, and nothing good can come out of it. Day by day the chances of war are weighed, and day-by-day they become more pitiless.

"The human mind refuses to believe in the catastrophe which even now looms up before us, and which the close of this century must surely witness, a catastrophe which will put an end to all the progress of our age, and yet we must try to realize it. Science has devoted all her energy these twenty years to the invention of destructive weapons, and soon a few cannon balls will suffice to destroy an army; not the few thousands of wretched mercenaries, whose life-blood has been bought and paid for, but whole nations are about to exterminate each other; during conscription their time is stolen from them in order to steal their lives with more certainty. By way of stimulating a thirst for blood mutual animosities are excited, and gentle, kind-hearted men allow themselves to be deluded, and it will not be long before they attack each other with all the ferocity of wild beasts; multitudes of peace-loving citizens will obey a foolish command, God only knows on what pretext – some stupid frontier quarrel, perhaps, or it may be some colonial mercantile interest. They will go like a flock of sheep to the slaughter, yet knowing where they go, conscious that they are leaving their wives and their children to suffer hunger; anxious, but unable to resist the enticement of those plausible and treacherous words that have been trumpeted into their ears.

Unresistingly they go; although they form a mass and a force, they fail to realize the extent of their power, and that if they were all agreed they might establish the reign of reason and fraternity, instead of lending themselves to the barbarous trickeries of diplomacy.

"So self-deceived are they that bloodshed takes on the aspect of duty, and they implore the blessing of God upon their sanguinary hopes. As they march, they trample underfoot the harvests which they themselves have planted, burning the cities which they have helped to build, with songs, shouts of enthusiasm, and music. And their sons will raise a statue to those who have slain them by the most approved methods. The fate of a whole generation hangs on the hour when some saturnine politician shall make the sign, and the nations will rush upon each other. We know that the noblest among us will be cut down, and that our affairs will go to destruction. We know this, we tremble in anger,

yet are powerless. We have been caught in a snare of bureau-
cracy and waste paper from which we can only escape by measures too energetic for us. We belong to the laws which we have
made for our protection, and which oppress us. We are nothing
more than the creatures of that antinomic abstraction, the State,
which makes of each individual a slave in the name of all, each
individual of which all, taken separately, would desire the exact
contrary of what he will be made to do.

"And if it were but the sacrifice of a single generation! But
many other interests are involved.

"Paid orators, demagogues, taking advantage of the passions
of the masses, and of the simple-minded who are dazzled by
high-sounding phrases, have so embittered national hatreds that
tomorrow's war will decide the fate of a race: one of the component parts of the modern world is threatened; the vanquished
nation will morally disappear; it matters not which chances to
be the victim, a power will disappear (as though there had ever
been one too many for the good). A new Europe will then be
established on a basis so unjust, so brutal, so blood stained, that
it cannot fail to be worse than that of today – more iniquitous,
more barbarous, and more aggressive."

Thus a fearful depression hangs over us. We are like men
dashing up and down a narrow passage way, with muskets
pointed at us from all the roofs. We work like sailors executing
their last manoeuvre after the ship has begun to sink. Our pleasures are those of the prisoner to whom a choice dish is offered
a quarter of an hour before his execution. Anxiety paralyses our
thought, and the utmost we can do is to wonder, as we con the
vague utterances of ministers, or construe the meaning of the
words of monarchs, or turn over those ascribed to the diplomatists, retailed at random by the newspapers, never sure of their
information, whether all this is to happen tomorrow or the day
after, whether it is this year or next that we are all to be killed.
In truth, one might seek in vain throughout the pages of history
for an epoch more unsettled or more pregnant with anxiety" (*Le
Sens de la Vie*).

He shows us that the power is really in the hands of those
who allow themselves to be destroyed, in the hands of separate

individuals who compose the mass; that the root of all evil is the State. It would seem as if the contradiction between one's faith and one's actual life had reached its utmost limit, and that the solution could not be far to seek.

But the author is of a different opinion. All that he sees in this is the tragedy of human life, and having given us a detailed description of the horror of this state of things, he perceives no reason why human life should not be spent in the midst of this horror. Such are the views of the second class of writers, who consider only the fatalistic and tragic side of war.

There is still another view, and this is the one held by men who have lost all conscience, and are consequently dead to common sense and human feeling.

To this class belong Moltke, whose opinions are quoted by Maupassant, and nearly all military men who have been taught to believe this cruel superstition, who are supported by it, and who naturally regard war not only as an inevitable evil, but as a necessary and even profitable occupation. And there are civilians too, scientists, men of refinement and education, who hold very much the same views.

The famous academician Doucet, in reply to a query of the editor of the *Revue des Revues* in regard to his opinions on war, replies as follows in the number containing letters concerning war:

"Dear Sir, – When you ask of the least belligerent of all the academicians if he is a partisan of war, his reply is already given. Unfortunately you yourself classify the peaceful contemplations which inspire your fellow countrymen at the present hour as idle visions.

"Ever since I was born I have always heard good men protesting against this shocking custom of international carnage. All recognize this evil and lament it. But where is its remedy?

"The effort to suppress duelling has often been made. It seems to be so easy. Far from it. All that has been accomplished towards achieving this noble purpose amounts to nothing, nor will it ever amount to more. Against war and duelling the congresses of the two hemispheres vote in vain. Superior to all arbitrations, conventions, and legislations will ever remain human honour, which has always demanded the duel, and national interests, which have always called for war. Nevertheless, I wish with all my heart that the Universal Peace Congress may succeed at last in its difficult and honourable task. – Accept the assurance, etc.,

"Camille Doucet."

It amounts to this, that honour obliges men to fight, that it is for the interest of nations that they should attack and destroy one another, and that all endeavours to abolish war can but excite a smile.

Jules Claretie expresses himself in similar terms:

"Dear Sir, – A sensible man can have but one opinion on the question of war and peace. Humanity was created to live – to live for the purpose of perfecting its existence by peaceful labour. The mutual relations of cordiality which are promoted and preached by the Universal Congress of Peace may be but a dream perhaps, yet certainly is the most delightful of dreams. The vision of the land of promise is ever before the eyes, and upon the soil of the future the harvest will ripen, secure from the ploughing of the projectile, or the crushing of cannon wheels. But, alas! . . . Since philosophers and philanthropists are not the rulers of mankind, it is fit that our soldiers should guard our frontiers and our homes, and their weapons, skillfully wielded, are perhaps the surest guarantees of the peace we love so well. Peace is given only to the strong and the courageous. – Accept the assurances of, etc.,

"Jules Claretie."

The substance of this is, that there is no harm in talking about what no one intends to do and what ought not in any event to be done. When fighting is in order there is no alternative but to fight.

Émile Zola, the most popular novelist in Europe, gives utterance to his views on the subject of war in the following terms:

"I look upon war as a fatal necessity which seems to us indispensable because of its close connection with human nature and all creation. Would that it might be postponed as long as possible! Nevertheless a time will come when we shall be forced to fight. At this moment I am regarding the subject from the universal standpoint, and am not hinting at our unfriendly relations with Germany, which are but a trifling incident in the world's history. I affirm that war is useful and necessary, since it is one of the conditions of human existence. The fighting instinct is to be found not only among the different tribes and peoples, but in domestic and private life as well. It is one of the chief elements of progress, and every advancing step taken by mankind up to the present time has been accompanied by bloodshed.

"Men have talked, and still do talk, of disarmament; and yet disarmament is utterly impossible, for even though it were possible, we should be compelled to renounce it. It is only an armed nation that can be powerful and great. I believe that a general disarmament would be followed by a moral degradation, assuming the form of a widespread effeminacy which would impede the progress of humanity. Warlike nations have always been vigorous. The military art has contributed to the development of other arts. History shows us this. In Athens and Rome, for instance, commerce, industry, and literature reached their highest development when these cities ruled the world by the force of arms. And nearer to our own time we found an example in the reign of Louis XIV. The wars of the great king, so far from impeding the advance of arts and sciences, seemed rather to promote and to favour their progress."

War is useful!

But chief among the advocates of these views, and the most talented of all the writers of this tendency, is the academician Vogue, who, in an article on the military section of the Exhibition of 1889, writes as follows:

"On the Esplanade des Invalides, the centre of exotic and colonial structures, a building of a more severe order stands out from the midst of the picturesque bazaar; these various fragments of our terrestrial globe adjoin the palace of war. A magnificent theme and antithesis for humanitarian rhetoric which never loses a chance to lament a juxtaposition of this kind and to utter its 'this will kill that;' that the confederacy of nations brought about by science and labour will overpower the military instinct. Let it cherish this vision of a golden age, caressing it with fond hopes. We have no objection, but should it ever be realized, it would very soon become an age of corruption.

History teaches us that the former has been accomplished by the means of the latter, that blood is necessary to hasten and to seal the confederacy of nations. In our own time the natural sciences have strengthened the mysterious law which revealed itself to Joseph de Maistre through the inspiration of his genius and meditation on primordial dogmas; he saw how the world would redeem its hereditary fall by offering a sacrifice. Science shows us that the world is made better by struggle and violent selection; this affirmation of the same law, with varied utterance, comes from two sources. It is by no means a pleasant one. The laws of the world, however, are not established for our pleasure, but for our perfection. Let us then enter this necessary and indispensable palace of war, and we shall have the opportunity to observe how our most inveterate instinct, losing nothing of its power, is transformed in its adaptation to the various demands of historical moments."

This idea, namely, that the proof of the necessity of war may be found in the writings of De Maistre and of Darwin, two great thinkers, as he calls them, pleases Vogue so much that he repeats it.

"Sir," he writes to the editor of the *Revue des Revues*, "you ask my opinion in regard to the possible success of the Universal Peace Congress. I believe with Darwin that vehement struggle is the law governing all being, and I believe with Joseph de Maistre that it is a divine law – two different modes of characterizing the same principle. If, contrary to all expectations, a certain fraction of humanity – for example, all the civilized West – should succeed in arresting the issue of this law, the more primitive races would execute it against us; in these races the voice of nature would prevail over human intellect. And they would succeed, because the certainty of peace – I do not say peace, but the absolute certainty of peace – would in less than half a century produce a corruption and a decadence in men more destructive than the worst of wars. I believe that one should act in regard to war – that criminal law of humanity – as in regard to all criminal laws: modify it, or endeavour to make its execution as rare as possible, and use every means in our power to render it superfluous. But experience of all history teaches us that it cannot be suppressed, so long as there shall be found on earth two men, bread, money, and a woman between them. I should be very glad if the Congress could prove to me the contrary, but I doubt if it can disprove history, and the law of God and of nature. – Accept my assurance, etc.,

"E. M. de Vogue."

This may be summed up as follows: History and nature, God and man, show us that so long as there are two men left on earth, and the stakes are bread, money, and woman, just so long there will be war. That is, that no amount of civilization will ever destroy that abnormal concept of life which makes it impossible for men to divide bread, money (of all absurdities), and woman without a fight. It is odd that people meet in congresses and hold forth as to the best method of catching birds by putting salt on their tails, although they must know that this can never be done!

It is astonishing that men like Rod, Maupassant, and others, clearly realizing all the horrors of war, and all the contradictions that ensue from men not doing what they ought to do, and what it would be to their advantage to do; who bemoan the tragedy of life; and yet fail to see that this tragic element would vanish as soon as men ceased to discuss a subject which should not be discussed, and ceased to do that which is both painful and repulsive for them to do!

One may wonder at them; but men who, like Vogue and others, believe in the law of evolution and look upon war as not only unavoidable but even useful, and therefore desirable – such men are fairly shocking, horrible in their moral aberration. The former at least declare that they hate evil and love good, but the latter believe there is neither good nor evil.

All this discussion of the possibility of establishing peace instead of continual warfare is but the mischievous sentimentalism of idle talkers. There is a law of evolution which seems to prove that I must live and do wrong. What then can I do? I am an educated man, I am familiar with the doctrine of evolution; hence it follows that I shall work evil. *"Entrons au palais de la guerre."* There is a law of evolution and therefore there can be no real evil, and one must live one's life and leave the rest to the law of evolution. This is the last expression of refined civilization;

it is with this idea that the educated classes at the present day deaden their conscience.

The desire of these classes to preserve their favourite theories and the life that they have built up on them, can go no further. They lie, and by their specious arguments deceive themselves as well as others, obscuring and deadening their intuitive perceptions.

Rather than adapt their lives to their consciousness, they try by every means to befog and to silence it. But the light shines in the darkness, and even now it begins to dawn.

Significance of the Military Conscription

G ENERAL MILITARY CONSCRIPTION is not a political accident, but the extreme limit of contradiction contained in the social life-conception – Rise of power in
society – The basis of power is personal violence – The organization of armed men, an army, is required by power to enable it to
accomplish violence – The rise of power in society, that is, of violence, destroys by degrees the social life-conception – Attitude
of power towards the masses, that is to say, the oppressed – Governments endeavour to make workmen believe in the necessity of
State violence for their preservation from external foes – But the
army is needed principally to defend government from its own
subjects, the oppressed working men – Address of Caprivi – All
the privileges of the ruling classes are assured by violence – Increase of armies leads to a general military conscription – General military conscription destroys all the advantages of social
life which it is the duty of the State to guard – General military
conscription is the extreme limit of obedience, as it demands in
the name of the State the abnegation of all that may be dear to
man – Is the State needed ? – The sacrifices which it requires
from citizens through the general military conscription have
no longer any basis – Hence it is more advantageous for man to
rebel against the demands of the State than to submit to them.

The efforts which the educated men of the upper classes are
making to silence the growing consciousness that the present
system of life must be changed, are constantly on the increase,
while life itself, continuing to develop and to become more complex without changing its direction, as it increases the incongrui-
ties and suffering of human existence, brings men to the extreme
limit of this contradiction. An example of this uttermost limit is
found in the general military conscription.

It is usually supposed that this conscription, together with the
increasing armaments and the consequent increase of the taxes
and national debts of all countries, are the accidental results of

THE KINGDOM OF GOD IS WITHIN YOU

a certain crisis in European affairs, which might be obviated by certain political combinations, without change of the interior life.

This is utterly erroneous. The general conscription is nothing but an internal contradiction which has crept into the social life-conception, and which has only become evident because it has arrived at its utmost limits at a period when men have attained a certain degree of material development.

The social life-conception transfers the significance of life from the individual to mankind in general, through the unbroken continuity of the family, the tribe, and the state.

According to the social life-conception it is supposed that as the significance of life is comprised in the sum total of mankind, each individual will of his own accord sacrifice his interests to those of the whole. This in fact has always been the case with certain aggregates, like the family or the tribe.

In consequence of custom, transmitted by education and confirmed by religious suggestion, and without compulsion, the individual merges his interests in those of the group and sacrifices himself for the benefit of the whole.

But the more complex became societies, the larger they grew, conquest especially contributing to unite men in social organizations – the more individuals would be found striving to attain their ends at the expense of their fellow men; and thus the necessity for subjugation by power, or, in other words, by violence, became more and more frequent.

The advocates of the social life-conception usually attempt to combine the idea of authority, otherwise violence, with that of moral influence; but such a union is utterly impossible.

The result of moral influence upon man is to change his desires, so that he willingly complies with what is required of him. A man who yields to moral influence takes pleasure in conforming his actions to its laws, whereas authority, as the word is commonly understood, is a means of coercion, by which a man is forced to act in opposition to his wishes. A man who submits to authority does not do as he pleases; he yields to compulsion, and in order to force a man to do something for which he has an aversion, the threat of physical violence, or violence itself, must be employed; he may be deprived of his liberty, flogged, mutilated, or he may be threatened with these punishments. And this is what constitutes power both in the past and in the present.

Despite the unremitting efforts of rulers to conceal these facts, and to attribute a different significance to authority, it simply means the rope and chain where with a man is bound and dragged, the lash wherewith he is flogged, the knife or axe wherewith his limbs, nose, ears, and head are hewed off. Authority is either the menace or the perpetration of these acts. This was the practice in the times of Nero and Genghis Khan, and is still in force even in the most liberal governments, like there publics of France and America. If men submit to authority, it is only because they fear that if they were to resist, they would be subjected to violence. All the requisitions of the State, such as the payment of taxes and the fulfilment of public duties, the submission to penalties in the form of exile, fines, etc., to which men seem to yield voluntarily, are always enforced by the physical threat or the reality of physical punishment.

Physical violence is the basis of authority.

It is the military organization that makes it possible to inflict physical violence, that organization wherein the entire armed force acts as one man, obeying a single will. This assemblage of armed men, submitting to one will, forms what is called an army. The army has ever been and still is the basis of an authority, vested in the commanding generals, and the most engrossing interest of every sovereign, from the Roman Caesars to the Russian and German Emperors, has always been to protect and flatter the army, for they realize that when the army is on their side, power is also in their hands.

It is the drilling and the increase of the troops required for the maintenance of authority which has brought into the social life-conception an element of dissolution.

The aim of authority, and its consequent justification, is to restrain those men who are endeavouring, by methods which are detrimental to those of mankind in general, to promote their own interests. But whether authority has been acquired by force of arms, or by hereditary succession, or by election, men who have gained authority are in no way different from their fellowmen;

THE KINGDOM OF GOD IS WITHIN YOU

they are just like all others, not inclined to waive their own interests in favour of the many, but, since they hold power in their hands, are more likely to make the interests of the many give way to their own. Whatever measures may have been devised by way of restraining those in authority who might seek their own ends at the expense of the public, or to vest authority in the hands of infallible men, no satisfactory results have as yet been attained.

Attributing divine right to kings, hereditary succession, election, congresses, parliaments, and senates – none of these have ever yet proved effectual. Everybody knows that no expedient has ever succeeded either in committing authority into the hands of infallible men, or of preventing its abuses. On the contrary, we know that men who have the authority, be they emperors, ministers of State, chiefs of police, or even policemen, always are more liable, because of their position, to become immoral – that is, to put their own private interests before those of the public – than men who do not possess such an authority; and this is inevitable.

The social life-conception could be justified only while all men voluntarily sacrificed their private interests to those of the public in general; but no sooner did men appear who refused to sacrifice their interests, than authority, in other words violence, was required to restrain these men. Thus, there entered into the social life-conception and the organization based on it a principle containing within itself the germs of dissolution – the principle of authority, or the tyranny of the few over the many. In order that the authority held by certain men might fulfil its object, which is to restrain those who are trying to further their own interests to the detriment of society in general, it would be necessary to have it in the hands of infallible men, as is supposed to be the case in China, or as it was believed to be in the Middle Ages, and is even at the present time by those who have faith in consecration by unction. It is only under such conditions that the social organization can be justified.

But as no such conditions exist, and furthermore, as men who are in authority from the very fact of its possession must ever be far from being saints, the social organization that is based upon authority cannot possibly have any justification.

If there ever was a time when a low standard of morality, and the general tendency of men towards violence, called for an authority possessing the power to restrict this violence, an authority whose existence may have been an advantage – that is, when the violence of State was less than the violence of individuals towards each other – we cannot help seeing now that this prerogative of the State, when violence no longer exists, cannot go on for ever. Morals improved in proportion to the gradual decrease of individual violence, while the prerogative of authority lost ground in measure as it became corrupted by the possession of unbridled power.

The entire history of the last 2000 years will have been told when we have described this change in the relations between the moral development of man and the demoralization of governments. In its simplest form it runs thus: men lived together in tribes, in families, and in races, and were at enmity one with another; they employed violence, they spread desolation, they murdered one another. Thus devastation was on a scale both great and small: man fought with man, tribe with tribe, and family with family, race with race, nation with nation. The larger and more powerful communities absorbed the weaker ones, and the greater and more vigorous became the aggregation of men, the more seldom did one hear of acts of violence within these communities, and the more secure the continuity of their existence appeared.

When the members of a tribe or a family unite together to form one community, they are naturally less hostile to each other, and the tribes and families are not so likely to die out; while among the citizens of a state subjected to one authority, the contentions seem even less frequent, and hence is the life of the State on a basis still more assured.

These fusions into larger and larger aggregates took place not because men realized that it would be to their advantage, as is illustrated by the fable that tells of the falling of the Varegs in Russia, but are due rather to natural growth on the one hand, and struggle and conquest on the other.

When conquest was achieved the authority of the conqueror put an end to internal strife, and the social life-conception was justified. But this justification is only temporary. Internal feuds cease only when the pressure of authority is brought to bear with greater weight upon individuals formerly inimical to one another. The violence of the internal struggle, not annihilated by authority, is the offspring of authority itself. Authority is in the hands of men who, like all the rest, are ever ready to sacrifice the common weal if their own personal interests are at stake; with the sole difference that these men, encountering no resistance from the oppressed, are wholly subject to the corrupting influence of authority itself.

Therefore it is that the evil principle of violence relegated to authority is ever increasing, and the evil becomes in time worse than that which it is supposed to control; whereas in the individual members of society the inclination to violence is always diminishing, and the violence of authority becomes less and less necessary.

As its power increases in measure of its duration, State authority, though it may eradicate internal violence, introduces into life other and new forms of violence, always increasing in intensity. And though the violence of authority in the State is less striking than that of individual members of society towards each other, its principal manifestation being not that of strife, but of oppression, it exists none the less, and in the highest degree.

It cannot be otherwise; for not only does the possession of authority corrupt men, but, either from design or unconsciously, rulers are always striving to reduce their subjects to the lowest degree of weakness – for the more feeble the subject, the less the effort required to subdue him.

Therefore violence employed against the oppressed is pushed to its utmost limit, just stopping short of killing the hen that lays the golden egg. But if the hen has ceased to lay, like the American Indians, the Fiji Islanders, or the Negroes, then it is killed, despite the sincere protests of the philanthropists against that mode of procedure.

The most conclusive proof of this assertion, at the present time, is the position of the working men, who are in truth simply vanquished men.

Despite all the pretended efforts of the upper classes to lighten their position, all the working men of the world are subjected to an immutable iron rule, which prescribes that they shall have scarcely enough to live upon, in order that their necessities may urge them to unremitting toil, the fruits of which are to be enjoyed by their masters, in other words, their conquerors.

It has always been the case that, after the long continuance and growth of power, the advantages accruing to those who have submitted to it have failed, while the disadvantages have multiplied.

Thus it is and thus it always has been, under whatsoever form of government the nation may have lived; only that where despotism prevails authority is confined to a limited number of oppressors, and violence takes on a ruder form, while in the constitutional monarchies, and in the republics of France and America, authority is distributed among a greater number of oppressors, and its manifestations are less rude; but the result, in which the disadvantages of dominion are greater than the advantages, and the method – reduction of the oppressed to the lowest possible degree of abjection, for the benefit of the oppressors, remain ever the same.

Such has been the position of all the oppressed, but until lately they have been unaware of the fact, and for the most part have innocently believed that governments were instituted for their benefit, to preserve them from destruction, and that to permit the idea that men might live without governments would be a thought sacrilegious beyond expression; it would be the doctrine of anarchy, with all its attendant horrors.

Men believed, as in something so thoroughly proved that it needed no further testimony, that as all nations had hitherto developed into the State form, this was to remain the indispensable condition for the development of mankind forever.

And so it had gone on for hundreds, nay, thousands of years, and the governments, that is to say their representatives, have endeavoured, and still go on endeavouring, to preserve this delusion among the people.

As it was during the time of the Roman emperors, so it is now. Although the idea of the uselessness, and even of the detriment of power enters more and more into the consciousness of men, it might endure forever, if governments did not think it necessary to increase the armies in order to support their authority.

It is the popular belief that governments increase armies as a means of defence against other nations, forgetting that troops are principally needed by governments to protect them against their own enslaved subjects.

This has always been necessary, and has grown more so with the spread of education, the increase of intercourse among different nationalities, and at the present time, in view of the communist, socialist, anarchist, and labour movements, it is a more urgent necessity than ever.

Governments realize this fact and increase their principal means of defence – the disciplined army.

It was but recently that in the German Reichstag, in giving the reason why more money was needed to increase the pay of the subaltern officers, the German Chancellor answered candidly that trusty subaltern officers are needed in order to fight against socialism. Caprivi put into words what everyone knows, although it has been carefully concealed from the people. The reason why the Swiss and Scottish Guards were hired to protect the Popes and the French kings, and why the Russian regiments are so carefully shuffled, is in order that those which are posted in the interior may be recruited by men from the borders, and those on the borders by men from the interior. The meaning of Caprivi's reply, translated into simple, everyday language, means that money is needed, not to repel a foreign enemy, but to bribe the subaltern officers to hold themselves in readiness to act against the oppressed working men.

Caprivi incidentally expressed what every man knows, or if he does not know it he feels it – namely, that the existing system of life is such as it is, not because it is natural for it to be so, or that the people are content to have it so, but because violence on the part of governments, the army with its bribed subaltern officers, its captains and generals, sustains it.

If a working man has no land, if he is not allowed to enjoy the natural right possessed by every man, to draw from the soil the means of subsistence for himself and his family, it is not so because the people oppose it, but because the right to grant or to withhold this privilege from working men is given to certain individuals – namely, to the landed proprietors. And this unnatural order of things is maintained by the troops. If the enormous wealth earned and saved by working men is not regarded as common property, but as something to be enjoyed by the chosen few; if certain men are invested with the power of levying taxes on labour, and with the right of using that money for whatsoever purposes they deem necessary; if the strikes of the working men are suppressed and the trusts of the capitalists are encouraged; if certain men are allowed to choose in the matter of religious and civil education and the instruction of children; if to certain others the right is given to frame laws which all men must obey, and if they are to enjoy the control of human life and property – all this is not because the people wish it, or because it has come about in the course of nature, but because the governments will have it so for their own advantage and that of the ruling classes; and all this is accomplished by means of physical violence.

If every man is not yet aware of this, he will find it out whenever attempts are made to change the present order of things.

And therefore all the governments and the ruling classes stand in need of troops above all things, in order to maintain a system of life, which, far from having developed from the needs of the people, is often detrimental to them, and is only advantageous for the government and the ruling classes.

Every government requires troops to enforce obedience that it may profit by the labour of its subjects. But non government exists alone: side by side with it stands the government of the adjacent country, which is also profiting by the enforced labour of its subjects, and ever ready to pounce upon its neighbour and take possession of the goods which it has won from the labour of its own subjects. Hence it is that every government needs an army, not only for home use, but to guard its plunder from foreign depredations. Thus each government finds itself obliged to outdo its neighbour in the increase of its army, and, as Montesquieu said one hundred and fifty years ago, the expansion of armies is a veritable contagion.

One State makes additions to its army in order to overawe its own subjects; its neighbour takes alarm and immediately follows the example.

Armies have reached the millions which they now number, not only from the fear of foreign invasion; the increase was first caused by the necessity for putting down all attempts at rebellion on the part of the subjects of the State. The causes for the expansion of armies are contemporary, the one depending on the other; armies are needed against internal attempts at revolt, as well as for external defence. The one depends upon the other. The despotism of governments increases exactly in proportion to the increase of their strength and their internal successes, and their foreign aggression with the increase of internal despotism.

European governments try to outdo one another, ever increasing their armaments, and compelled at last to adopt the expedient of a general conscription as a means of enrolling the greatest number of troops at the smallest possible expense.

Germany was the first to whom this plan suggested itself. And no sooner was it done by one nation than all the others were forced to do likewise. Thus all the citizens took up arms to assist in upholding the wrongs that were committed against them; in fact, they became their own oppressors.

General military conscription was the inevitable and logical consummation at which it was but natural to arrive; at the same time it is the last expression of the innate contradiction of the social life-conception which sprang into existence when violence was required for its support.

General military conscription made this contradiction a conspicuous fact. Indeed, the very significance of the social life-conception consists in this, that a man, realizing the cruelty of the struggle of individuals among themselves, and the peril that the individual incurs, seeks protection by transferring his private interests to a social community; whereas the result of the system of conscription is that men, after having made every sacrifice to escape from the cruel struggle and uncertainties of life, are once more called upon to undergo all the dangers they had hoped to escape, and, moreover, the community – the State for which the individuals gave up their previous advantages – is now exposed to the same risk of destruction from which the individual himself formerly suffered. Governments should have set men free from the cruelty of the personal struggle and given them confidence in the inviolable structure of State life; but instead of doing this they impose on individuals a repetition of the same dangers, with this difference, that in the place of struggle between individuals of the same group it is a case of struggle between groups.

The establishment of a general military conscription dislike the work of a man who props a crumbling house. The walls have settled, sloping inward, he braces them; the ceiling begins to hang down, he supports that; and when the boards between give way other braces are supplied. At last it reaches the point when, although the braces hold the house together, they actually make it uninhabitable.

The same may be said of the general conscription system the general military conscription nullifies all those advantages of social life which it is expected to protect

The advantages of social life are those guarantees which it offers for the protection of property and labour, as well as cooperation for the purposes of mutual advantage; the general military conscription destroys all this.

The taxes collected from the people for purposes of war absorb the greater part of the productions of their labour, which the army ought to protect.

When men are taken from the ordinary avocations of daily life, labour is practically destroyed. Where war is ever threatening to break forth it does not seem worthwhile to improve social conditions.

If a man had formerly been told that unless he submitted to the civil authority he would run the risk of being assaulted by wicked men, that he would be in danger from domestic as well as from foreign foes, against whom he would be forced to defend himself, that he might be murdered, and therefore he would find it for his advantage to suffer certain privations if by that means he succeeded in escaping all these perils, he might have believed this, especially as the sacrifices required by the State promised him the hope of a peaceful existence within the well-established community, in whose name he had made them. But now, when these sacrifices are not only multiplied, but the promised advantages are not realized, it is quite natural for men to think that their subjection to authority is utterly useless.

But the fatal significance of the general conscription, as the manifestation of that contradiction which dwells in the social life-conception, lies not in this. Wherever military conscription exists, every citizen who becomes a soldier likewise becomes a supporter of the State system, and a participant in whatsoever the State may do, at the same time that he does not acknowledge its validity; and this may be called its chief manifestation.

Governments declare that armies are principally required for external defence, but this is untrue. They are, in the first place, needed to overawe their own subjects, and everyman who yields to military conscription becomes an involuntary participator in all the oppressive acts of government towards its subjects. It is necessary to remember what goes on in every State in the name of order and the welfare of the community, all the while enforced by military authority, to be convinced that every man who fulfils military duty becomes a participant in acts of the State of which he cannot approve. Every dynastic and political feud, all the executions resulting from such feuds, the crushing of rebellions, the use of the military in dispersing mobs, in putting down strikes, all extortionate taxation, the injustice of land ownership and the limitations of freedom of labour – all this is done, if not directly by the troops, then by the police supported by the troops. He who performs his military duty becomes a participant in all these acts, about which he often feels more than dubious, and which are inmost cases directly opposed to his conscience. Men do not wish to leave the land which they have tilled for generations; they do not wish to disperse on the bidding of the government; they do not wish to pay the taxes which are extorted from them; neither do they willingly submit to laws which they have not helped to make; they do not wish to give up their nationality. And I, if I am performing military duty, must come forward and strike these men down. I cannot take part in such proceedings without asking myself if they be right. And ought I to cooperate in carrying them out?

General military conscription is the last step in the process of coercion required by governments for the support of the whole structure; for subjects it is the extreme limit of obedience. It is the keystone of the arch that supports the walls, the abstraction of which would destroy the whole fabric. The time has come when the ever-growing abuses of governments and their mutual contests have required from all their subjects not only material but moral sacrifices, till each man pauses and asks himself, Can I make these sacrifices? And for whose sake am I to make them? These sacrifices are demanded in the name of the State. In the name of the State I am asked to give up all that makes life dear to a man – peace, family, safety, and personal dignity. What, then, is this State in whose name such appalling sacrifices are demanded? And of what use is it?

We are told that the State is necessary, in the first place, because were it not for that no man would be safe from violence and the attacks of wicked men; in the second place, without the State we should be like savages, possessing neither religion, morals, education, instruction, commerce, means of communication, nor any other social institutions; and, in the third place, because without the State we should be subject to the invasion of the neighbouring nations.

"Were it not for the State," we are told, "we should be subjected to violence and to the attacks of evil men in our own land."

But who are these evil men from whose violence and attacks the government and the army saves us? If such men existed three or four centuries ago, when men prided themselves on their military skill and strength of arm, when a man proved his valour by killing his fellowmen, we find none such at the present time; men of our time neither use nor carry weapons, and, believing in the precepts of humanity and pity for their neighbours, they are as desirous for peace and a quiet life as we are ourselves. Hence this extraordinary class of marauders, against whom the State might defend us, no longer exists. But if, when they speak of the men from whose attacks the government defends us, we understand that they mean the criminal classes; in that case we know that they are not extraordinary beings, like beasts of prey among sheep, but are men very much like ourselves, who are naturally just as reluctant to commit crimes as those against whom they commit them. We know now that threats and punishments are powerless to decrease the numbers of such men, but that their numbers may be decreased by change of environment and by moral influence. Hence the theory of the necessity of State violence, in order to protect mankind against evildoers, if it had any foundation three or four centuries ago, has none whatever at the present time. One might say quite the reverse nowadays, for the activity of governments, with their antiquated and merciless methods of punishment, their galleys, prisons, gallows, and guillotines, so far below the general plane of morality, tends rather to lower the standard of morals than to elevate it, and therefore rather to increase than to lessen the number of criminals.

It is said that "without the State there would be no institutions, educational, moral, religious, or international, there would be no means of communication. Were it not for the State we should be without organizations necessary to all of us."

An argument like this could only have had a basis several centuries ago. If there ever was a time when men had so little international communication, and were so unused to intercourse or interchange of thought that they could not come to an agreement on matters of general interest – commercial, industrial, or economical – without the assistance of the State, such is not the case at present. The widely diffused means of communication and transmission of thought have achieved this result, that when the modern man desires to found societies, assemblies, corporations, congresses, scientific, economical, or political institutions, not only can he easily dispense with the assistance of governments, but in the majority of cases governments are more of a hindrance than a help in the pursuit of such objects.

Since the end of the last century almost every progressive movement on the part of mankind has been not only discouraged but invariably hampered by governments. Such was the case with the abolition of corporal punishment, torture, and slavery, with the establishment of freedom of the press and liberty of meeting. Furthermore, State authorities and governments nowadays not only do not cooperate, but they directly hinder the activity by means of which men work out new forms of life. The solution of labour and land questions, of political and religious problems, is not only unencouraged but distinctly opposed by the government authority.

"If there were no State and government authority, nations would be subjugated by their neighbours."

It is not worthwhile to answer this last argument. It refutes itself.

We are told that the government and its armies are necessary for our defence against the neighbouring States which might subject us. But all the governments say this of one another, and yet we know that every European nation professes the same principles of liberty and fraternity, and therefore needs no defence against its neighbour. But if one speaks of defence against barbarians, then one per cent, of the troops under arms at the present time would suffice. It is not only that the increase of armed force fails to protect us from danger of attack from our neighbours, it actually provokes the very attack which it deprecates.

Hence no man who reflects on the significance of the State, in whose name he is required to sacrifice his peace, his safety, and his life, can escape the conviction that there is no longer any reasonable ground for such sacrifices.

Even regarding the subject theoretically, a man must realize that the sacrifices demanded by the State are without sufficient reason; and when he considers the matter from a practical point of view, weighing all the different conditions in which he has been placed by the State, every man must see that so far as he himself is concerned, the fulfilment of the requirements of the State and his own subjection to military conscription is indubitably and in every case less advantageous for him than if he refused to comply with it. If the majority of people prefer obedience to insubordination, it is not because they have given the subject dispassionate consideration, weighing the advantages and disadvantages, but because they are, so to speak, under the influence of hypnotic suggestion. Men submit to demands like this without using their reason or making the least effort of the will. It requires independent reasoning, as well as effort, to refuse submission – effort which some men are incapable of making. But supposing we exclude the moral significance of submission and non-submission, and consider only their advantages, then non-submission will always prove more advantageous than submission. Whoever I may be, whether I belong to the well-to-do

– the oppressing class – or to the oppressed labouring class, in either case the disadvantages of non-submission are less numerous than the disadvantages of submission, and the advantages of non-submission greater than those of submission.

If I belong to the oppressive, which is the smallest class, and refuse to submit to the demands of the government, I shall be tried as one who refuses to fulfil his obligations: I shall be tried, and in case my trial terminates favourably, I shall either be declared not guilty, or I may be dealt with as they treat the Mennonites in Russia – that is, be compelled to serve my term of military service by performing some non-military work; if, on the contrary, an unfavourable verdict is rendered, I shall be condemned to exile or imprisonment for two or three years (I am speaking of cases in Russia); or possibly my term of imprisonment may be longer. And I may even be condemned to suffer the penalty of death, although that is not at all probable. Such are the disadvantages of non-submission.

The disadvantages of submission are as follows: if I am fortunate I shall not be sent to murder men, neither shall I run the risk myself of being disabled or killed; they will simply make a military slave of me. I shall be arrayed in the garments of a clown; my superior officers, from the corporal to the field marshal, will order me about. At their word of command I shall be put through a series of gymnastic contortions, and after being detained from one to five years I shall be released, but still obliged for ten years longer to hold myself in readiness at any moment I may be summoned to execute the orders these people give me. And if I am less fortunate I shall be sent to the wars, still in the same condition of slavery, and there I shall be forced to slay fellow men of other countries who never did me any harm. Or I may be sent to a place where I may be mutilated or killed; perhaps find myself, as at Sevastopol, sent to certain death; these things happen in every war. Worse than all things else, I may be sent to fight against my fellow-countrymen and compelled to kill my own brethren for some matter dynastic or governmental, and to me of foreign interest. Such are the comparative disadvantages.

The comparative advantages of submission and non-submission are as follows: For him who has submitted the advantages are these: after he has subjected himself tall the degradations and committed all the cruel deeds required of him, he may, provided he be not killed, receive some scarlet or golden bauble to decorate his clown's attire; or if he be especially favoured, hundreds of thousands of just such brutal men like himself may be put under his command, and he be called field marshal and receive large sums of money.

By refusing to submit he will possess the advantages of preserving his manly dignity, of winning the respect of good men, and, above all, he will enjoy the assurance that he is doing God's business, and therefore an unquestionable benefit to mankind.

Such are the advantages and disadvantages on either side; for the oppressor, a member of the wealthy class. For a man of the working class – a poor man – the advantages and disadvantages are about the same, if we include one important addition to the disadvantages. The special disadvantage for a man of the working class who has not refused to perform military service is that when he enters the service his participation and his tacit consent go towards confirming the oppression in which he finds himself.

But the question concerning the State, whether its continued existence is a necessity, or whether it would be wiser to abolish it, cannot be decided by discussion on its usefulness for the men who are required to support it by taking part in the military service, and still less by weighing the comparative advantages and disadvantages of submission or non-submission for the individual himself. It is decided irrevocably and without appeal by the religious consciousness, by the conscience of each individual, to whom no sooner does military conscription become a question than it is followed by that of the necessity or non-necessity of the State.

CHAPTER VIII

Certainty of the Acceptance of the Christian Doctrine of Non-Resistance to Evil by Violence by the Men of Our World

CHRISTIANITY IS NOT A legislation but a new life-conception; hence it was not obligatory, nor has it been accepted by all men in its full meaning, but only by a few; the rest have accepted it in a corrupted form – Moreover, Christianity is a prophecy of the disappearance of the pagan life, and therefore of the necessity of accepting the Christian doctrine – Non-resistance of evil by violence is one of the principles of the Christian doctrine which must inevitably be accepted by men at the present day – Two methods of solving every struggle – The first method consists in believing the general definitions of evil to be binding upon all, and to resist this evil by violence – The second, the Christian method, consists in not resisting evil by violence – Although the failure of the first method was recognized in the first centuries of Christianity, it is still employed ; but as humanity advanced it has become more evident that there is not, nor can there be, a general definition of evil – Now this has become evident to all, and if the violence which is destined to combat evil exists, it is not because it is considered necessary, but because men do not know how to dispense with it – The difficulty of dispensing with it is due to the skillfulness and complexity of political violence – This violence is supported by four methods: by threats, bribes, hypnotism, and the employment of military force – Deliverance from State violence cannot be accomplished by overthrowing the State – Through experience of the misery of pagan life men are compelled to acknowledge the doctrine of Christ, with its non-resistance to evil – a doctrine which they have hitherto ignored – To this same necessity of acknowledging the Christian doctrine we are brought by the consciousness of its truth – This consciousness is in utter contradiction to our life, and is especially evident in regard to general military conscription; but, in consequence of habitant the four methods of State violence, men do not see this inconsistency of Christianity with the duties of a soldier – Men do not see it even when the authorities themselves show them plainly all the immorality of the duties of a soldier – The call of the general conscription is the extreme trial for every man; the command to choose between the Christian doctrine of non-resistance or servile submission to the existing organization of the State – Men generally submit to the demands of the State organization, renouncing all that is sacred, as though there were no other issue – For men of the pagan life-conception, indeed, no other issue does exist; they are compelled to acknowledge it, regardless of all the dreadful calamities of war – Society composed of such men must inevitably perish, and no social changes can save it – The pagan life has reached its last limits; it works its own destruction.

It is frequently said that if Christianity be a truth, it would have been accepted by all men on its first appearance, and would straightway have changed and improved the lives of men. One might as well say that if the seed is alive it must instantly sprout and produce its flower or its fruit.

The Christian doctrine is not a law which, being introduced by violence, can forthwith change the life of mankind. Christianity is a life-conception more lofty and excellent than the ancient; and such a new conception of life cannot be enforced; it must be adopted voluntarily, and by two processes, the spiritual or interior process, and the experimental or external process.

Some men there are – but the smaller proportion – who instantly, and as though by prophetic intuition, divine the truth, surrender themselves to its influence, and live up to its precepts; others – and they are the majority – are brought to the knowledge of the truth and the necessity for its adoption by a long series of errors, by experience and suffering.

It is to this necessity of adopting the doctrine by the external process of experience that Christendom has at last arrived.

Now and then one wonders why the mistaken presentment of Christianity, which even at the present time prevents men from accepting it in its true significance, could have been necessary.

And yet the very errors, having brought men to their present position, have been the medium through which it has become possible for the majority to accept Christianity in its true meaning.

If instead of that corrupted form of Christianity which was given to the people, it had been offered to them in its purity, the greater portion of mankind would have refused it, like the Asiatic peoples to whom it is yet unknown. But having once accepted it in its corrupted form, the nations embracing it were subjected to its slow but sure influence, and by a long succession of errors, and the suffering that ensued there from, have now been brought to the necessity of adopting it in its true meaning.

The erroneous presentation of Christianity, and its acceptance by the majority of mankind, with all its errors, was then a necessity, just as the seed, if it is to sprout, must for a time be buried in the soil.

The Christian doctrine is the doctrine of truth as well as of prophecy.

Eighteen hundred years ago the Christian doctrine revealed to men the true conduct of life, and at the same time foretold the result of disobeying its injunctions and of continuing to pursue their former course, guided only by the precepts which were taught before the dawn of Christianity; and it also showed them what life may become if they accept the Christian doctrine and obey its dictates.

Having taught in the Sermon on the Mount those precepts by which men should order their daily lives, Christ said: *"Therefore whosoever heareth these sayings of mine, and doeth them, I will liken him unto a wise man, which built his house upon a rock: and the rain descended, and the floods came, and the winds blew, and beat upon that house; and it fell not: for it was founded upon a rock. And every one that heareth these sayings of mine, and doeth them not, shall be likened unto a foolish man, which built his house upon the sand: and the rain descended, and the floods came, and the wind blew, and beat upon that house; and it fell: and great was the fall of it." Matthew vii: 24–27.*

And thus, after eighteen centuries, the prophecy has been fulfilled. As the result of the abandonment of Christ's teachings, having disregarded the principle of non-resistance to evil, men have unwittingly fallen into the condition of imminent peril foretold by Christ to those who refused to follow his precepts.

Men often think that the question of resistance or non-resistance to evil by violence is an artificial question, which may be evaded. And yet this is the question that life presents to mankind in general, and to each thinking man in particular, and it is one that must be solved. In social life, ever since Christianity was first preached, this question has been like the doubt that confronts the traveller when he comes to a place where the road which he has followed divides, and he knows not which branch to choose. He must pursue his way, and he can no longer go on without pausing to deliberate, because there are now two roads from which to choose, whereas before there was but one; he must make up his mind which he will take.

In like manner, since the doctrine of Christ has been made known to men, they can no longer say, I will go on living as I did before, without deciding the question of resistance or non-resistance to evil by violence. One must decide at the beginning of every fresh struggle whether one ought or ought not to resist by violence that which one believes to be evil.

The question of resistance or non-resistance of evil by violence arose with the first contest among men, for every contest is simply the resistance by violence of something which each combatant believes to be an evil. But before the time of Christ men did not understand that resistance by violence of whatever the individual believed to be evil – only the same action which seems evil to one man may seem good to another – is simply one mode of settling the difficulty, and that the other method consists in not resisting evil by violence.

Before the appearance of the doctrine of Christ men believed that there could be but one way of deciding the contest, that of resisting evil by violence, and acted accordingly, while each combatant strove to persuade himself and others that what he regarded as evil was in fact the actual and absolute evil. For this purpose, dating from the oldest times, men began to invent certain definitions of evil which should be obligatory for all, and for the purpose of establishing definitions which should be thus binding were issued either certain laws supposed to have been

THE KINGDOM OF GOD IS WITHIN YOU

received in a supernatural manner, or commands of individuals or of bodies of men, to whom an infallible wisdom was ascribed. Men used violence against their fellow men and assured themselves and others that they were but using such violence against an evil acknowledged by all.

This was the custom from the most ancient times, particularly among men who had usurped authority, and men have been long in seeing its baselessness.

But the longer mankind existed the more complex grew its mutual relations, and the more evident it became that to resist by violence everything that is considered evil is unwise; that the struggle is not diminished thereby, and that no human wisdom can ever define an infallible standard of evil.

When Christianity first appeared in the Roman Empire it had already become evident to most men that whatever Nero or Caligula called evil and sought to overcome by violence was not necessarily an evil for the rest of mankind. Even then men had already began to realize that the human laws for which a divine origin was claimed were really written by men; that men cannot be infallible no matter with what external authority they may be invested, and that fallible men will not become infallible because they meet together and call themselves a Senate, or any other similar name. Even then this had been perceived and understood by many. And it was then that Christ preached his doctrine, which not only embodied the principle of non-resistance, but which revealed a new conception of life, of which the application to social life would lead to the suppression of strife among men, not by obliging one class to yield to whatsoever authority shall ordain, but by forbidding all men, and especially those in power, to employ violence against others.

The doctrine was at that time embraced by a very limited number of disciples, while the majority of men, particularly those who were in authority, although they nominally accepted Christianity, continued to follow the practice of resisting by violence whatever they regarded as evil. So it was during the times of the Roman and Byzantine emperors, and so it went on in later times.

The inconsistency of an authoritative definition of evil and its resistance by violence, already apparent in the first centuries of

Christianity, had grown still more evident at the time of the dissolution of the Roman Empire and its subdivision into numerous independent states hostile to one another and torn by internal dissensions.

But men were not yet ready to accept the law of Christ, and the former method of defining an evil to be resisted by the establishment of laws, enforced by coercion and binding upon all men, continued to be employed. The arbiter, whose office it was to decide upon the nature of the evil to be resisted by violence, was alternately the Emperor, the Pope, the elected body, or the nation at large. But both within and without the State men were always to be found who refused to hold themselves bound either by those laws which were supposed to be the expression of the divine will, or by the human laws which claimed to manifest the will of the people; – men whose views on the subject of evil were quite at variance with those of the existing authorities, men who resisted the authorities, employing the same methods of violence that had been directed against themselves.

Men invested with religious authority would condemn as evil a matter which to men and institutions invested with a temporal authority commended itself as desirable, and vice versa, and more and more furious grew the struggle. And the oftener men had recourse to violence in settling the difficulty, the more evident it became that it was ill chosen, because there is not, nor can there ever be, a standard authority of evil to which all mankind would agree.

Thus matters went on for eighteen centuries, and at last arrived at their present condition, which is, that no man can dispute the fact that an infallible definition of evil will never be made. We have reached the point when men have ceased not only to believe in the possibility of finding a universal definition which all men will admit, but they have even ceased to believe in the necessity of such a definition. We have reached the point when men in authority no longer seek to prove that that which they consider evil is evil, but candidly acknowledge that they consider that to be evil which does not please them, and those who are subject to authority obey, not because they believe that the definitions of evil made by authority are just, but only because they have no power to resist. The annexation of Nice to France, Lorraine to Germany, the Czechs to Austria, the partition of Poland, the subjection of Ireland and India to the English rule, the waging of war against China, the slaughter of Africans, the expulsion of the Chinese, the persecution of the Jews in Russia, or the derivation of profits by landowners from land which they do not cultivate, and by capitalists from the results of labour performed by others – none of all this is done because it is virtuous or because it will benefit mankind and is essentially opposed to evil, but because those who hold authority will have it so. The result at the present time is this: certain men use violence, no longer in the name of resistance to evil, but from caprice or because it is for their advantage; while certain other men submit to violence, not because they believe, like those of former ages, that violence is used to defend them from evil, but simply because they cannot escape it.

If a Roman, or a man of the Middle Ages, or a Russian, such a man as I can remember fifty years ago, believed implicitly that the existing violence of authority was needed to save him from evil, that taxes, duties, serfdom, prisons, the lash, the knout, galleys, executions, military conscription, and wars were unavoidable, it would be difficult to find a man at the present time who believes that all the violence committed saves a single man from evil; on the contrary, not one could be found who had not a distinct assurance that most of the violations to which he is subjected, and in which he himself participates, are in themselves a great and unprofitable calamity.

There is hardly a man to be found at the present time who fails to realize all the uselessness and absurdity of collecting taxes from the labouring classes for the purpose of enriching idle officials; or the folly of punishing weak and immoral men by exile or imprisonment, where, supported as they are, and living in idleness, they become still weaker and more depraved; or, again, the unspeakable folly and cruelty of those preparations for war, which can neither be explained nor justified, and which ruin and imperil the safety of nations. Nevertheless these violations continue, and the very men, who realize and even suffer from their uselessness, absurdity, and cruelty, contribute to their encouragement.

If fifty years ago it was possible that the wealthy man of leisure and the illiterate labourer should both believe that their positions, the one a continual holiday, the other a life of incessant labour, were ordained by God – in these days, not only throughout Europe, and even in Russia, owing to the activity of the people, the growth of education, and the art of printing, it is hardly possible to find a man either rich or poor who in one way or another would not question the justice of such an order of things. Not only do the rich realize that the possession of wealth is in itself a fault, for which they strive to atone by donations to science and art, as formerly they redeemed their sins by endowing churches; but even the majority of the labouring class now understand that the existing order is false, and should be altered, if not abolished. Men who profess religion, of whom we have millions in Russia, the so-called sectarians, acknowledge, because they interpret the Gospel doctrine correctly, that this order of things is false and should be destroyed. The working men consider it false because of the socialistic, communistic, or anarchical theories that have already found way into their ranks. In these days the principle of violence is maintained, not because it is considered necessary, but simply because it has been so long in existence, and is so thoroughly organized by those who profit by it – that is to say, by the governments and ruling classes, that those who are in their power find it impossible to escape.

Nowadays every government, the despotic as well as the most liberal, has become what Herzen has so cleverly termed a Genghis Khan with a telegraphic equipment, that is, with an organization of violence, having for basis nothing less than the most brutal tyranny, and converting all the means invented by science for the inter-communication and peaceful activities of free and equal men, to its own tyrannous and oppressive ends.

The existing governments and the ruling classes no longer care to present even the semblance of justice, but rely, thanks to scientific progress, on an organization so ingenious that it is able to enclose all men within a circle of violence through which it is impossible to break. This circle is made up of four expedients, each connected with and supporting the other like the rings of a chain.

The first and the oldest expedient is intimidation. It consists in representing the actual organization of the State, whether it be that of a liberal republic or of an arbitrary despotism, as something sacred and immutable, which therefore punishes by the most cruel penalties any attempt at revolution. This expedient has been put into practice recently wherever a government exists: in Russia against the so-called Nihilists, in America against the Anarchists, in France against the Imperialists, Monarchists, Communists, and Anarchists. Railroads, telegraphs, telephones, photography, the improved method of disposing of criminals by imprisoning them in solitary confinement for the remainder of their lives in cells, where, hidden from human view, they die forgotten, as well as numerous other modern inventions upon which governments have the prior claim, give them such power, that if once the authority fell into certain hands, and the regular and secret police, administrative officials, and all kinds of procurers, jailors, and executioners laboured zealously to support it, there would be no possibility whatsoever of overthrowing the government, however cruel or senseless it might be.

The second expedient is bribery. This consists in taking the property of the labouring classes by means of taxation and distributing it among the officials, who, in consideration of this, are bound to maintain and increase the bondage of the people. The bribed officials, from the prime ministers to the lowest scribes form one unbroken chain of individuals, united by a common interest, supported by the labour of the people, fulfilling the will of the government with a submission proportionate to their gains, never hesitating to use any means in any department of business to promote the action of that governmental violence on which their well-being rests.

The third expedient I can call by no other name than hypnotism. It consists in retarding the spiritual development of men, and, by means of various suggestions, influencing them to cling to the theory of life, which mankind has already left behind, and upon which rests the foundation of governmental authority. We have at the present time a hypnotizing system, organized in a most complex manner, beginning in childhood and continued until the hour of death. This hypnotism begins during the early years of a man's life in a system of compulsory education. Children receive in school the same ideas in regard to the universe which their ancestors entertained, and which are in direct contradiction to contemporary knowledge. In countries where a State religion exists, children are taught the senseless and sacrilegious utterances of church catechisms, with the duty of obedience to authorities; in public they are taught the absurd superstition of patriotism, and the same obligation of obedience to the government. In mature years this hypnotizing process is continued by the encouragement of religious and patriotic superstition. Religious superstition is encouraged by the erection of churches built from money collected from the people, by holidays, processions, painting, architecture, music, by incense that stupefies the brain, and, above all, by the maintenance of the so-called clergy, whose duty consists in befogging the minds of men and keeping them in a continual state of imbecility, what with the solemnity of their services, their sermons, their intervention with the private lives of men in time of marriage, birth, and death. The patriotic superstition is encouraged by the governments and the ruling classes by instituting national festivals, spectacles, and holidays, by erecting monuments with money collected from the people, which will influence men to believe in the exclusive importance and greatness of their own state or country and its rulers, and encourage a feeling of hostility and even of hatred towards other nations. Furthermore, autocratic governments directly forbid the printing and circulation of books and the delivery of speeches that might enlighten men; and those teachers who have the power to rouse the people from its torpor are either banished or imprisoned. And every government, without exception, conceals from the masses all that would tend to set them free, and encourages all that would demoralize them – all those writings, for instance, that tend to confirm them in the crudeness of their religious and patriotic superstition; all kinds of sensual pleasures, shows, circuses, theatres; and all means for producing physical stupor, especially those, like tobacco or brandy, which are among the principal sources of national income. Even prostitution is encouraged; it is not only recognized, but organized by the majority of governments. Such is the third expedient. The fourth expedient consists in this: certain individuals are selected from among the mass of enslaved and stupefied beings; and these, after having been subjected to a still more vigorous process of brutalization, are made the passive instruments of the cruelties and brutalities indispensable to the government. This state of brutality and imbecility is produced by taking men in their youth, before they have yet had time to gain any clear conception of morality; and then, having removed them from all the natural conditions of human life, from home, family, birthplace, and the possibility of intelligent labour, by shutting them up together in barracks, where, dressed in a peculiar uniform, to the accompaniment of shouts, drums, music, and the display of glittering gewgaws, they are daily forced to perform certain prescribed evolutions. By these methods they are reduced to that hypnotic condition when they cease to be men and become imbecile and docile machines in the hands of the hypnotizer. These physically strong young men thus hypnotized (and at the present time, with the general conscription system, all young men answer to this description), supplied with murderous weapons, ever obedient to the authority of the government, and ready at its command to commit any violence whatsoever, constitute the fourth and the principal means for subjugating men. So the circle of violence is completed.

Intimidation, bribery, and hypnotism force men to become soldiers; soldiers give power and make it possible to execute and to rob mankind (with the aid of bribed officials), as well as to hypnotize and to recruit men who are in their turn to become soldiers.

The circle is complete, and there is no possibility of escape from it.

If some men believe that deliverance from violence, or even a certain abatement of its energy, may be the result of its overthrow by the oppressed, who will then replace it by a system which will require no such violence and subjugation; and if, so believing, they attempt to bring this about, they only deceive themselves and others. So far from improving the position, these attempts will only render things worse.

The activity of such men only strengthens the despotism of

governments by giving the latter a convenient pretext for increasing their defences. For even when, following a train of circumstances highly demoralizing to the government – take the case of France in 1870, for example – a government is overthrown by violence and the authority passes into other hands, this new authority is by no means likely to be less oppressive than the former. On the contrary, obliged to defend itself from its exasperated and overthrown enemies, it will be even more cruel and despotic than its predecessor, as has ever been the casein periods of revolution.

If socialists and communists believe that the possession of individual capital is a pernicious influence in society, and anarchists regard government itself as an evil, there are, on the other hand, monarchists, conservatives, and capitalists who look upon the social and communal state as an evil order of society, no less than anarchy itself; and all these parties have nothing better to offer by way of reconciling mankind than violence. Thus, whichever party gains the upper hand, it will be forced, in order to introduce and maintain its own system, not only to avail itself of all former methods of violence, but to invent new ones as well. It simply means a change of slavery with new victims and a new organization; but the violence will remain, nay increase, because human hatred, intensified by the struggle, will devise new means for reducing the conquered to subjection. This has always been the result of every revolution and violent overthrow of government. Each struggle serves but to increase the power of those in authority at the time to enslave their fellow men.

One domain of human activity, and only one, has hitherto escaped the encroachments of the governments – the domain of the family, the economical domain of private life and domestic labour. But now even this domain, in consequence of the struggle of socialists and communists, is gradually passing into the hands of the governments, so that labour and recreation, the dwellings, clothes, and food of the people will by degrees, if the desires of the reformers are accomplished, be determined and regulated by the government.

The long experiment of Christian life by nation after nation, during eighteen centuries, has inevitably brought men to the necessity of deciding whether the doctrine of Christ is to be accepted or refused, and of deciding, too, the question of social life dependent thereupon – the resistance or non-resistance of evil by violence. But there is this difference, that formerly men could either acceptor reject the decision given by Christianity, whereas now it has become imperative, because it affords the sole means of deliverance from that condition of slavery in which, as in a net, men find themselves entangled.

Nor is it alone this sad plight that brings them to this necessity.

Parallel with the negative proof of the falsehood of the pagan order of things there has been positive proof of the truth of the Christian doctrine.

Indeed, in the course of the eighteen centuries the best men in all Christendom, through an inner spiritual medium, having recognized the truths of the doctrine, have borne witness of it, regardless of threats, privations, miseries, and torture. These nobler men by their martyrdom have sealed the truth of the doctrine.

Christianity penetrated into human consciousness, not alone by the method of negative proof, that, namely, it had become impossible to go on with the pagan life; but by its simplifying process, by its explanation of, and its deliverance from superstition, and by its consequent spread among all classes of society.

Eighteen centuries of the profession of Christianity have not passed in vain for those who accepted it, even if it were but in outward form. These eighteen centuries have made men realize all the miseries of the pagan state, even though they have continued to lead a pagan existence, out of harmony with an age of humanity; and at the bottom of their hearts they believe now (and herein lies the only reason for living at all) that salvation from such an existence can be found in the fulfilment of the Christian doctrine in its true sense. As to when and where this salvation is to be accomplished opinions differ, according to the intellectual development of men and the prejudices among which they live; but every educated man recognizes that our salvation is to be found in the fulfilment of the Christian doctrine. Certain believers, those who consider the Christian doctrine divine, affirm that this salvation will be accomplished when all men believe in Christ and the time of the second advent approaches; others, who also have faith in the divinity of Christ's doctrine, believe that this salvation will come through the churches, which, having got all men within the fold, will implant in their hearts those Christian virtues which will transform their lives. Others, again, who do not accept the divinity of Christ, believe that the salvation of men will be accomplished by means of a slow, continuous progress, during which the groundwork of pagan life will be gradually replaced by the groundwork of liberty, equality, and fraternity – that is, by the basis of Christianity. Still others there are who preach a new social organization, and who believe that this salvation will be brought about when, by means of a violent revolution, men are forced to a community of goods, to the abolition of governments, to collective rather than individual labour – that is, by the realization of one of the aspects of Christianity. Thus after one fashion or another all men of our epoch not only renounce the existing order of life as no longer suited to the times, but acknowledge, often without realizing it, and regarding themselves as enemies of Christianity, that our salvation lies only in the adaptation to life of a whole or a part of the Christian doctrine in its true sense.

For the majority of men Christianity, as its Teacher has expressed it, could not be comprehended at once, but was to grow, like unto a huge tree, from the tiniest seed. *"The kingdom of heaven is like to a grain of mustard seed, . . .*which indeed is the least of all seeds: but when it is grown, it is the greatest among herbs, and becometh a tree." And thus it has grown and continues to grow, if not in manifestation, then in human consciousness.

It is no longer reserved for the minority of men, who have always understood Christianity by its veritable truth; but it is acknowledged by the great majority, who, if we are to judge by their social life, are far removed from it.

Look at the private life of individuals, listen to their estimation of human actions as they pronounce judgment on each other; listen not only to public sermons and orations, but to the precepts which parents and teachers offer to their charges, and you will see that, however far removed from the practice of Christian truths may be the political or social existence of men who are in

177

bonds to violence, yet Christian virtues are admired and exalted by all; while, on the contrary, the anti-Christian vices are unhesitatingly condemned as harmful to all mankind. Those who sacrifice their lives in the service of humanity are looked upon as the better men; while those who take advantage of the misfortune of their neighbours to further their own selfish interests are universally condemned.

There may still be men who, insensible to Christian ideals, have set up for themselves other ideals, such as power, courage, or wealth; but these ideals are passing away; they are not accepted by all, nor by the men of the better class. Indeed, the Christian ideals are the only ones which are recognized as obligatory for all.

The position of our Christian world, looked at from without, with its cruelty and slavery, is indeed appalling. But if we consider it from the standpoint of human consciousness, it presents a very different aspect. All the evil of our life seems to exist only because it always has existed from all ages, and the men whose actions are evil have had neither the time nor the experience to overcome their evil habits, although all are willing to abandon them. Evil seems to exist by reason of some cause apparently independent of the consciousness of men.

Strange and contradictory as it may seem, modern men hate the very order of things which they themselves support.

I believe it is Max Müller who describes the astonishment of an Indian converted to Christianity, who, having apprehended the essence of the Christian doctrine, came to Europe and beheld the life of Christians. He could not recover from his astonishment in the presence of the reality, so different from the state of things he had expected to find among Christian nations.

If we are not surprised at the contradiction between our convictions and our actions, it is only because the influences which obscure this contradiction act upon us. We have but to look at our life from the standpoint of the Indian who understood Christianity in its true significance, without any concessions or adaptations, and to behold the barbarous cruelties with which our life is filled, in order to be horrified at the contradictions in the midst of which we live, without noticing them.

One has but to remember the preparations for war, the cartridge boxes, the silver-plated bullets, the torpedoes, and – the Red Cross; the establishment of prisons for solitary confinement, experiments with electrocution, and – the care for the welfare of the prisoners; the philanthropic activity of the rich, and – their daily life, which brings about the existence of the poor, whom they seek to benefit. And these contradictions arise not, as it might seem, because men pretend to be Christians while they are actually heathens, but because they lack something, or because there is some power which prevents them from being what they really desire to be, and what they even conscientiously believe themselves to be. It is not that modern men merely pretend to hate oppression, the inequality of class distinctions, and all kinds of cruelty, whether practised against their fellow men or against animals. They are sincere in their hatred of these abuses; but they do not know how to abolish them, or they lack the courage to alter their own mode of life, which depends upon all this, and which seems to them so important.

Ask, indeed, any individual if he considers it praiseworthy or even honourable for a man to fill a position for which he receives a salary so high as to be out of all proportion to the amount of his labour, as, for instance, that of collecting from the people, often from beggars; taxes which are to be devoted to the purchase of cannon, torpedoes, and other instruments for murdering the men with whom we wish to live in peace, and who wish to live in peace with us; or, to receive a salary for spending his life either in perfecting these instruments of murder, or in the military exercises by which men are trained for slaughter? Ask whether it be praiseworthy or compatible with the dignity of man, or becoming to a Christian, to undertake, also for money, to arrest some unfortunate man, some illiterate drunkard, for some petty theft not to be compared with the magnitude of our own appropriation, or for manslaughter not conducted by our advanced methods; and for such offences to throw people into prison, or put them to death? Ask whether it be laudable and becoming in a man and a Christian, also for money, to teach the people foolish and injurious superstitions instead of the doctrine of Christ? Whether, again, it be laudable and worthy of a man to wrench from his neighbour, in order to gratify his own caprice, the very necessaries of life, as the great landowners do; or to exact from his fellowman an excessive and exhausting toil for the purpose of increasing his own wealth, as the mill-owners and manufacturers do; or to take advantage of human necessities to build up colossal fortunes, as the merchants do?

Every individual would reply not, especially if the question regarded his neighbour. And at the same time the very man who acknowledges all the ignominy of such deeds, when the case is presented to him, will often, of his own accord, and for no advantage of a salary, but moved by childish vanity, the desire to possess a trinket of enamel, a decoration, a stripe, voluntarily enter the military service, or become an examining magistrate, justice of the peace, a minister of state, an uriadnik, a bishop, accepting an office whose duties will oblige him to do things, the shame and ignominy of which he cannot help realizing.

Many of these men will, I am sure, defend themselves on the ground of the lawfulness and necessity of their position; they will argue that the authorities are of God, that the functions of State are indispensable for the good of mankind, that Christianity is not opposed to wealth, that the rich youth was bidden to give up his goods only if he wished to be perfect, that the present distribution of wealth and commerce is beneficial to all men, and that it is right and lawful. But however much they may try to deceive themselves and others, they all know that what they do is opposed to the highest interests of life, and at the bottom of their hearts, when they listen only to their consciences, they are ashamed and pained to think of what they are doing, especially when the baseness of their deeds has been pointed out to them. A man in modern life, whether he does or does not profess to believe in the divinity of Christ, must know that to be instrumental either as a czar, minister, governor, or policeman, as in selling a poor family's last cow to pay taxes to the treasury, the money of which is devoted to the purchase of cannon or to pay the salaries or pensions of idle and luxurious officials, is to do more harm than good ;or to be a party to the imprisonment of the father of a family, for whose demoralization we are ourselves responsible, and to bring his family to beggary; or to take part in piratical and murderous warfare; or to teach absurd superstitions of idol-worship instead of the doctrine of Christ; or to impound a stray cow belonging to a man who has no land; or to deduct the value of an accidentally injured article from the wages of a mechanic; or to sell something to a poor man for double its value, only because he is in dire necessity; the men of our modern life cannot but know that all such deeds are wrong, shameful, and that they ought not to commit them. They do all know it. They know that they are doing wrong, and would abstain from it, had they but the strength to oppose those forces which blind them to the criminality of their actions while drawing them on to do wrong.

But there is nothing that demonstrates so vividly the degree of contradiction to which human life has attained as the system that embodies both the method and the expression of violence – the general conscription system. It is only because a general armament and military conscription have come imperceptibly and by slow degrees, and that governments employ for their support all the means of intimidation at their disposal – bribery, bewilderment, and violence – that we do not realize the glaring contradiction between this state of affairs and those Christian feelings and ideas with which all modern men are penetrated.

This contradiction has become so common that we fail to see the shocking imbecility and immorality of the actions, not only of those men who, of their own accord, choose the profession of murder as something honourable, but of those unfortunates who consent to serve in the army, and of those who in countries where military conscription has not yet been introduced, give of their own free will the fruits of their labour to be used for the payment of mercenaries and for the organization for murder. All these men are either Christians or men professing humanitarianism and liberalism, who know that they participate in the most imbecile, aimless, and cruel murders; yet still they go on committing them. But this is not all. In Germany, where the system of general military conscription originated, Caprivi has revealed something that has always been carefully hidden: that the men who run the risk of being killed are not only foreigners, but are quite as likely to be fellow countrymen, workingmen, from which class most of the soldiers are obtained. Nevertheless, this admission neither opened men's eyes nor shocked their sensibilities. They continue just as they did before, to go like sheep and submit to anything that is demanded of them. And this is not all. The German Emperor has recently explained with minute precision the character and vocation of a soldier, having distinguished, thanked, and rewarded a private for killing defenceless prisoner who attempted to escape. In thanking and rewarding a man for an act which is looked upon even by men of the lowest type of morality as base and cowardly, Wilhelm pointed out that the principal duty of a soldier, and one most highly prized by the authorities, is that of an executioner – not like the professional executioners who put to death condemned prisoners only, but an executioner of the innocent men whom his superiors order him to kill.

Yet more. In 1891, this same Wilhelm, the enfant terrible of State authority, who expresses what other men only venture to think, in a talk with certain soldiers, uttered publicly the following words, which were repeated the next day in thousands of papers:

'Recruits! You have given me the oath of allegiance before the altar and the servant of the Lord. You are still too young to comprehend the true meaning of what has been said here, but first of all take care ever to follow the orders and instructions that are given to you. You have taken the oath of allegiance to me; this means, children of my guards, that you are now my soldiers, that you have given yourselves up to me, body and soul.

"But one enemy exists for you – my enemy. With the present socialistic intrigues it may happen that I shall command you to shoot your own relatives, your brothers, even your parents (from which may God preserve us!), and then you are in duty bound to obey my orders unhesitatingly"

This man expresses what is known but carefully concealed by all wise rulers. He says outright that the men who serve in the army serve him and his advantage, and should be ready for that purpose to kill their brothers and fathers.

Roughly but distinctly he lays bare all the horror of the crime, for which men who become soldiers prepare themselves – all that abyss of self-abasement into which they fling themselves when they promise obedience. Like a bold hypnotizer, he tests the depth of the slumber; he applies red hot iron to the sleeper's body; it smokes and shrivels, but the sleeper does not awaken.

Poor, sick, miserable man, intoxicated with power, who by these words insults all that is sacred to men of modern civilization! And we, Christians, liberals, men of culture, so far from feeling indignant at this insult, pass it over in silence. Men are put to the final test in its rudest form; but they hardly observe that a test is in question, that a choice is put before them. It seems to them as if there were no choice, but only the one necessity of slavish submission. It would seem as if these insane words, offensive to all that a civilized human being holds sacred, ought to rouse indignation – but nothing of the kind happens. Year after year every young man in Europe is subjected to the same test, and with very few exceptions they all forswear what is and should be sacred to every man; all manifest a readiness to kill their brothers and even their fathers, at the order of the first misguided man who wears a red and gold livery, asking only when and whom they are to be ordered to kill – for they are ready to do it.

Even by savages certain objects are held sacred, for whose sake they are ready to suffer rather than submit. But what is sacred for the man of the modern world? He is told: be my slave, in a bondage where you may have to murder your own father; and he, oftentimes a man of learning, who has studied all the sciences in the university, submissively offers his neck to the halter. He is dressed in a clown's garments, ordered to leap, to make contortions, to salute, to kill – and he submissively obeys; and when at last allowed to return to his former life he continues to hold forth on the dignity of man, freedom, equality, and brotherhood.

"But what is to be done?" we often hear men ask in perplexity. If every man were to refuse, it would be a different matter; but as it is, I should suffer alone without benefiting any one." And they are right, for a man who holds the social life-conception cannot refuse. Life has no significance for him except as it concerns his personal welfare; it is for his advantage to submit, therefore he does so.

To whatever torture or injury he may be subjected he will

submit, because he can do nothing alone; he lacks the foundation which alone would enable him to resist violence, and those who are in authority over him will never give him the chance of uniting with others.

It has often been said that the invention of the terrible military instruments of murder will put an end to war, and that war will exhaust itself. This is not true. As it is possible to increase the means for killing men, so it is possible to increase the means for subjecting those who hold the social life-conception. Let them be exterminated by thousands and millions, let them be torn to pieces, men will still continue like stupid cattle to go to the slaughter, some because they are driven thither under the lash, others, that they may win the decorations and ribbons which fill their hearts with pride.

And it is with material like this that the public leaders – conservatives, liberals, socialists, anarchists – discuss the ways and means of organizing an intelligent and moral society, with men who have been so thoroughly confused and bewildered that they will promise to murder their own parents. What kind of intelligence and morality can there be in a society organized from material like this? Just as it is impossible to build a house from bent and rotten timber, however manipulated, so also is it impossible with such materials to organize an intelligent and moral society. They can only be governed like a drove of cattle, by the shouts and lash of the herdsman. And so, indeed, they are governed.

Again, while on the one hand we find men, Christians in name, professing the principles of liberty, equality, and fraternity, on the other hand we see these same men ready, in the name of liberty, to yield the most abject and slavish obedience; in the name of equality, to approve of the most rigid and senseless subdivision of men into classes; and in the name of fraternity, ready to slay their own brothers.

The contradiction of the moral consciousness, and hence the misery of life, has reached its utmost limit, beyond which it can go no further. Life, based on principles of violence, has culminated in the negation of the basis on which it was founded. The organization, on principles of violence, of a society whose object was to insure the happiness of the individual and the family, and the social welfare of humanity, has brought men to such a pass that these benefits are practically annulled.

The first part of the prophecy in regard to those men and their descendants who adopted this doctrine has been fulfilled, and now their descendants are forced to realize the justice of its second part.

The Acceptance of the Christian Life-Conception Delivers Men from the Miseries of Our Pagan Life

T HE EXTERNAL LIFE OF Christian nations remains pagan, but they are already penetrated by the Christian life-conception – The issue from this contradiction is in the acceptance of the Christian life-conception – In it alone is every man free, and it alone frees him from all human authority – This deliverance is brought about, not by a change of external conditions, but only by a change in the conception of one's life – The Christian life-conception demands the renunciation of violence, and in delivering the man who accepts it, it frees the world from all external authority – The issue from the present apparently hopeless position consists in every man accepting the Christian life-conception and living accordingly – But men consider this method too slow, and see their salvation in change of the material conditions of life made with the aid of the authority of the State – This method will have no issue, because men themselves cause the evil from which they suffer – This is especially evident in regard to the submissive acceptance of military duty, for it is more advantageous for a man to refuse than accept – Human freedom will be brought about only through the liberation of each individual man, and already there are signs of this liberation, which threatens to destroy State organization – The repudiation of the un-Christian demands of governments undermines their authority and makes men free – Therefore instances of such refusals are feared by governments more than conspiracies or violence – Instances, in Russia, of refusals to take the oath of allegiance, to pay taxes, to accept passports or positions in the police, to take part in courts of law, or to be drafted as soldiers – Similar instances in other countries – Governments know not how to dispose of men who refuse to obey their requirements because of the Christian doctrine – These men destroy without a struggle the foundations of governments from the inside – To punish them would mean for governments to deny Christianity themselves, and to contribute to the diffusion of that consciousness from which such refusals spring – Hence the position of governments is a desperate one, and men who preach the uselessness of personal deliverance only arrest the destruction of the existing system of government founded on violence.

The Christian nations of the present day are in a position no less cruel than that of pagan times. In many respects, especially in the matter of oppression, their position has grown worse.

A contrast like that of modern and ancient times maybe seen in the vegetation of the last days of autumn as compared with that of the early days of spring. In the autumn the outward decay and death correspond to the interior process, which is the suspension of life; in the spring the apparent lifelessness is in direct contradiction to the real vitality within and the approaching transition to new forms of life.

And thus it is as regards the apparent resemblance between pagan life and that of the present day. It exists only in appearance. The inner lives of men in the times of paganism were quite unlike those of the men of our days.

In the former the external aspect of cruelty and slavery corresponded with the inner consciousness of men, a conformity which only increased as time went on; in the latter the external condition of cruelty and slavery is in utter contradiction to the Christian consciousness of men, a contradiction which grows more and more striking every year.

The misery and suffering resulting there from seem so useless. It is like prolonged suffering in child labour. Everything is ready for the coming life, and yet no life appears.

Apparently the situation is without deliverance. It would indeed be so were it not that to men, and therefore to the world, there has been vouchsafed the capacity for a loftier conception of life, which has the power to set free, and at once, from all fetters, however firmly riveted.

And this is the Christian life-conception presented to men 1800 years ago.

A man has but to assimilate this life-conception and he will be set free as a matter of course from the fetters that now restrain him, and feel free as a bird who spreads his wings and flies over the wall that has kept him a prisoner.

They talk of setting the Christian Church free from the State, of granting freedom to or withholding it from Christians. Such thoughts and expressions are strangely misleading. Liberty can neither be granted to nor withheld from a Christian or Christians.

But if there is a question of granting or withholding liberty, then evidently it is not the true Christians who are meant, but only men who call themselves by that name. A Christian cannot help being free, because in the pursuit and attainment of his object no one can either hinder or retard him.

A man has but to understand his life as Christianity teaches him to understand it; that is, he must realize that it does not belong to himself, nor to his family, nor to the State, but to Him who sent him into the world; he must therefore know that it is his duty to live not in accordance with the law of his own personality, nor of that of his family or State, but to fulfil the infinite law of Him who gave him life, in order to feel himself so entirely free from all human authority that he will cease to regard it as a possible obstacle.

A man needs but to realize that the object of his life is the fulfilment of God's law; then the pre-eminence of that law, claiming as it does his entire allegiance, will of necessity invalidate the authority and restrictions of all human laws.

The Christian who contemplates that law of love implanted in every human soul, and quickened by Christ, the only guide for all mankind, is set free from human authority.

A Christian may suffer from external violence, may be deprived of his personal freedom, may be a slave to his passions – the man who commits sin is the slave of the sin – but he cannot be controlled or coerced by threats into committing an act contrary to his consciousness. He cannot be forced to this, because the privations and sufferings that are so powerful an influence over men who hold the social life-conception have no influence whatever over him. The privations and sufferings that destroy the material welfare which is the object of the social life-conception produce no effect upon the welfare of the Christian's life, which rests on the consciousness that he is doing God's will – nay, they may even serve to promote that welfare when they are visited upon him for fulfilling that will.

A Christian, therefore, who submits to the inner, the divine law, is not only unable to execute the biddings of the outward law when they are at variance with his consciousness of God's law of love, as in the case of the demands made upon him by the government; but he cannot acknowledge the obligation of obeying any individual whomsoever, cannot acknowledge himself to be what is called a subject. For a Christian to promise to subject himself to any government whatsoever – a subjection which may be considered the foundation of state life – is a direct negation of Christianity; since an individual who promises beforehand to obey implicitly every law that men may enact, by that promise utters an emphatic denial of Christianity, whose very essence is obedience in all contingencies to the law which he feels to be within him – the law of love.

With the pagan life-conception it was possible to promise to obey the will of temporal authorities without violating the laws of God, which were supposed to consist in carrying out such customs as circumcision, the observance of the Sabbath, the utterance of prayer at certain periods, abstinence from certain kinds of food, etc. The one did not contradict the other. But Christianity differs from paganism inasmuch as its requirements are not of an external or negative character; on the contrary, they are such as reverse man's former relations towards his fellow men, and may call for acts on his part which could not be anticipated, and consequently are not defined. Hence it is that a Christian can neither promise to obey nor to disobey the will of another, ignorant as he must be of the nature of its requirements; not only must he refuse to obey human laws, but he cannot promise to do or abstain from doing anything definite at any given time, because he can never tell at what hour or in what manner the Christian law of love, on which his life-conception is based, will demand his cooperation. A Christian promising in advance to obey unconditionally the laws of men, admits by that promise that the inner law of God does not constitute for him the sole law of his life.

When a Christian promises to obey the commands or laws of men, he is like a craftsman who, having hired himself out to one master, promises at the same time to execute the orders of other persons. No man can serve two masters.

A Christian is freed from human authority by acknowledging the supremacy of one authority alone, that of God, whose law, revealed to him through Christ, he recognizes within himself, and obeys – that and no other.

And this deliverance is accomplished neither by means of a struggle, nor by the destruction of previous customs of life, but only through a change in his life-conception. The deliverance proceeds, in the first place, from the Christian's acknowledgment of the law of love, as revealed to him by his Teacher, which suffices to determine the relations of men, and according to which every act of violence seems superfluous and unlawful. Secondly, because those privations and miseries, or the anticipations of such, which influence a man who holds the social life-conception and reduces him to obedience, seem to him no more than the inevitable consequences of existence, which he would never dream of opposing by violence, but bears patiently, as he would bear disease, hunger, or any other misery; which, indeed, have no possible influence over his actions. The Christian's only guide must be the divine indwelling element, subject neither to restriction nor to control.

A Christian lives in accordance with the words spoken by the Master: "He shall not strive, nor cry; neither shall any man hear his voice in the streets. A bruised reed shall he not break, and smoking flax shall he not quench, *till he send forth judgment unto victory." Matthew vii: 19–20.*

A Christian enters into no dispute with his neighbour, he neither attacks nor uses violence; on the contrary, he suffers violence himself without resistance, and by his very attitude towards evil not only sets himself free, but helps to free the world at large from all outward authority.

"And ye shall know the truth, and the truth shall make you free." John viii: 32.

If there were any doubt of the truth of Christianity there could be no more indubitable proof of its authenticity than the complete freedom, recognizing no fetters, which a man feels as soon as he assimilates the Christian life-conception.

Human beings in their present condition may be likened to bees in the act of swarming, as we see them clinging in a mass to a single bough. Their position is a temporary one, and must inevitably be changed. They must rise and find themselves a new abode. Every bee knows this, and is eager to shift its own position, as well as that of the others, but not one of them will do so until the whole swarm rises. The swarm cannot rise, because one bee clings to the other and prevents it from separating itself from the swarm, and so they all continue to hang. It might seem as if there were no deliverance from this position, precisely as it seems to men of the world who have become entangled in the social net. Indeed, there would be no outlet for the bees if each one were not a living creature possessed of a pair of wings. Neither would there be any issue for men if each one were not a living individual being gifted with a capacity for assimilating the Christian life-conception.

If among these bees who are able to fly not one could be found willing to start, the swarm would never change its position. And it is the same among men. If the man who has assimilated the Christian life-conception waits for others before he proceeds to live in accordance with it, mankind will never change its attitude. And as all that is needed to change a solid mass of bees into a flying swarm is for one bee to spread its wings and fly away, when the second, the third, the tenth, and the hundredth will follow suit; so all that is needed to break through the magic circle of social life, deliverance from which seems so hopeless, is, that one man should view life from a Christian standpoint and begin to frame his own life accordingly, whereupon others will following his footsteps.

But men think that the deliverance of mankind by this method is too slow a process, and that a simultaneous deliverance might be effected by some other method Just as if bees, when the swarm was ready to rise, were to decide that it would be too long a process if they waited for each bee to spread its wings and rise separately, and that some means must be devised whereby the swarm may rise all at once, whenever it pleases. But that is impossible. Not until the first, second, third, and hundredth bee has unfolded its wings and flown away, can the swarm take flight and find for itself a new home. Not until each individual man adopts the Christian life-conception, and begins to live in conformity with its precepts, will the contradictions of human life be solved and new forms of life become established.

One of the most striking events of our time is the propaganda of slavery which is spread among the masses, not only by the government, to whom it is of use, but by those exponents of socialistic theories who consider themselves the champions of freedom.

These men preach that the amelioration in the conditions of life, the reconciliation between actuality and consciousness, will not be brought about by the personal efforts of individual men, but that it will evolve itself out of a certain forced reorganization of society by some unknown influence. Their theory is that men should not proceed of their own accord to the place where they wish to go, but that they should have a platform built under their feet, upon which they may be carried to the spot they desire to reach. Hence they must not move as far as their strength will permit, but all their efforts must be directed towards building this imaginary platform without stirring from their position.

There is a theory in economics preached in these days, of which the essential principle is this: the worse the condition of affairs, the better the prospect; the greater the accumulation of capital and oppression of the working man resulting there from, the nearer the day of deliverance; and therefore any effort on the part of the individual to free himself from the oppression of capital is useless. In regard to the government it is declared that the greater its authority, which, according to this theory, should include the domain of private life, hitherto uninvaded, the better it will be, and hence one should solicit the interference of governments with private life. In regard to international politics, it is declared that the increase of armies and modes of extermination will lead to the necessity of a general disarmament through the agency of congresses, arbitration, etc. And the most surprising part of all is that human lethargy is so profound that men credit these theories, although the whole structure of life and every stage of human progress, demonstrate their fallacy.

Men suffer from oppression, and by way of deliverance certain expedients are suggested for the improvement of their condition, these means of relief to be administered by authority, to which they continue to submit. This will naturally tend to augment authority and to increase the consequent oppression of government.

Of all the errors of humanity there is none that so retards its progress as this. Men will do anything in the world to achieve their purpose save the one simple deed, which it is every man's duty to perform. Men will invent the most ingenious devices for changing the position which is burdensome to them, but never dream of the simple remedy of abstaining from the acts which cause it.

I was told of an incident which happened to an intrepid *stanovoy* or police officer who, on arriving in a village where the peasants had revolted, and whither troops had been sent, undertook, like the Emperor Nicholas I, to quell the disturbance by his personal influence. He ordered several loads of rods to be brought, and having gathered all the peasants into the barn, he entered himself, shut himself in with them, and so terrified them by his shouts and threats that in compliance with his commands they began to flog each other. And so they went on flogging one another until some fool revolted, and shouting to his comrades, bade them leave off. It was not until then that the flogging ceased and the *stanovoy* escaped from the barn.

It is this very advice of the fool, that men who believe in the necessity of civil government seem unable to follow. They are unable to stop punishing themselves, and setting an absurd example for others to imitate. Such is the consummation of merely human wisdom.

Is it possible, indeed, to imagine a more striking imitation of those men flogging one another than the meekness with which the men of these days fulfil those social duties that lead them into bondage, especially the military conscription? It is clear that men enslave themselves; they suffer from this slavery, and yet they believe it inevitable; they also believe that it will not affect the ultimate emancipation of mankind, which they declare the final outcome, in spite of the fact that slavery is ever in creasing.

The man of modern times, whoever he may be (I do not mean a true Christian), educated or ignorant, a believer or an unbeliever, rich or poor, married or single, does his work, takes his pleasures, and dreads all restrictions and privations, all enmity and suffering. Thus he is living, peaceably. Suddenly men come to him and say: "First, promise on your oath that you will obey us like a slave in all that we command; believe that whatever we tell you is unquestionably true, and submit to all that we shall call laws. Or secondly, give us a share in the product of your labour, that we may use it to keep you in bondage and prevent you from revolting against our commands. Or thirdly, choose, or be chosen among, the so-called officials of the government, knowing that the government will go on quite regardless of the foolish speeches which you, or others like you, may utter; that it will be carried on in accordance with our wishes and the wishes of those who control the army. Or fourthly, come to the law courts, and take part in all the senseless cruelties which we commit against men who are erring and depraved men, and who have become so through our fault – in the form of imprisonment, exile, solitary confinement, and execution. Or lastly, although you may be on the most friendly terms with men who belong to other nations, you must be ready at a moment's notice, whenever the command is issued, to look upon such of themes we shall indicate as your enemies, and either personally or by substitute contribute to the ruin, robbery, and murder of these men, of old men, women and children – even, if we require it, of your fellow countrymen and your parents."

One would think that in these days there could be but one reply from any man in his senses.

"Why must I do all this? Why must I promise to obey all the orders of Salisbury today, those of Gladstone tomorrow; Boulanger today, and tomorrow the orders of an assembly composed of men like Boulanger; Peter III today, Catherine tomorrow, and the next day Pugatchov; today the insane King of Bavaria, tomorrow the Emperor William. Why should I promise this to men whom I know to be wicked or foolish, or men whom I know nothing at all about? Why should I, in the form of taxes, hand over to them the fruits of my labour, knowing that this money will be used to bribe officials, to support prisons, churches, and armies, to pay for the execution of evil acts destined for my oppression? In other words, why should I apply the rod to my own back? Why should I go on, wasting my time, averting my eyes, helping to give a semblance of legality to the acts of wrong-doers, play a part in elections and pretend to participate in the government, when I know perfectly well that the country is ruled by those who control the army? Why should I go into the courts and be a party to the infliction of tortures and executions upon my erring fellow beings, knowing, if I am a Christian, that the law of love has been substituted for the law of vengeance, and if I am an educated man, that punishment, so far from reforming its victims, serves only to demoralize them? Why should I, in person or in substitute, go and kill and despoil, and expose myself to the dangers of war, simply because the key of the temple of Jerusalem happens to be in the keeping of one bishop rather than in that of another; because Bulgaria is to be ruled by one German prince instead of another; or because the privileges of the seal fishery are reserved for the English to the exclusion of the American merchants. Why should I regard as my enemies the inhabitants of a neighbouring country, with whom up to the present day I have lived, and still wish to live in peace and amity – why should I go myself, or pay for soldiers to murder and ruin them?

"And above all, why should I contribute, whether in person or by paying for military service, to the enslavement and destruction of my brothers and parents? Why should I scourge myself? All this is of no use to me; on the contrary, it does me harm. It is altogether degrading, immoral, mean, and contemptible. Why, then, should I do all this? If I am told that I shall be made to suffer in any event, I reply that in the first place there can be no possible suffering greater than that which would befall me were I to execute your commands. And in the second place, it is perfectly evident to me that if we refuse to scourge ourselves no one else will do it for us. Governments are but sovereigns, statesmen, officials who can no more force me against my will, than the *stanovoy* could force the peasants; I should be brought before the court, or thrown into prison, or executed, not by the sovereign, or the high officials, but by men in the same position as myself; and as it would be equally injurious and disagreeable for them to be scourged as for me, I should probably open their eyes, and they would not only refrain from injuring me, but would doubt-less follow my example. And in the third place, though I were made to suffer for this, it would still be better for me to be exiled or imprisoned, doing battle in the cause of commonsense and truth, which must eventually triumph, if not today, then tomor-row, or before many days, than to suffer in the cause of folly and evil. It would rather be to my advantage to risk being exiled, im-prisoned, or even executed, than remain through my own fault a lifelong slave of evil men, to be ruined by an invading enemy, or mutilated like an idiot, or killed while defending a cannon, a useless territory, or a senseless piece of cloth called a flag. I have no inclination to scourge myself; it would be of no use. You may do it yourselves if you choose – I refuse."

It would seem as though not only the religious and moral el-ement in human nature, but ordinary commonsense and wise counsel, would influence every man of the present day thus to make reply and to suit the action to the word. But no. Men who hold the social life-conception consider such a course not only useless but even prejudicial to the object in view – the deliver-ance of mankind from slavery. They advise us to go on, like the peasants, punishing one another, comforting ourselves with the reflection that our chatter in parliaments and assemblies, our trade unions, our First of May demonstrations, our conspiracies and covert threats to the governments that scourge us, must re-sult in our final deliverance, even though we go on strengthen-ing our fetters. Nothing so hampers human liberty as this won-derful delusion. Instead of making individual efforts to achieve freedom, every man for himself devoting all his energies to that object, through the attainment of a new life-conception, men are looking for a universal scheme of deliverance, and are in the meanwhile sinking deeper and deeper into slavery. It is as if a man were to declare that in order to obtain heat one must merely place every lump of coal in a certain position, never minding whether it kindled or not. And yet, that the liberation of mankind can only be accomplished by means of the deliverance of the individual grows more and more evident.

The liberation of individuals from the dominion of the State, in the name of the Christian life-conception, which was formerly an exceptional occurrence and one that attracted but little attention, has attained in these days a menacing significance for the authority of State.

If in the days of ancient Rome it happened that a Christian, professing his faith, refused to take a part in sacrifices, or in the worship of the emperors or the gods, or in the Middle Ages refused to worship icons or to acknowledge the temporal authority of the Pope, such refusals were the exception; a man might be obliged to confess to his faith, but he might perhaps live all his life without being forced to do so. But now all men without exception are subjected to trial of faith. Every man of modern times is obliged either to participate in the cruelties of pagan life or to repudiate them. And secondly, in those days any refusal to bow before the gods, the icons, or the Pope, was of no consequence to the State. Whether those who bowed before the gods, the icons, or the Pope were many or few, the State lost none of its power. Whereas at the present time every refusal to execute the unchristian demands of the government undermines the authority of the State, because the authority of the State rests on the fulfilment of these anti-Christian requirements.

Temporal authority, in order to maintain itself, has been forced by the conditions of life to demand from its subjects certain actions which it is impossible for men who profess true Christianity to perform. Therefore at the present time every man who professes it helps to undermine the authority of the government, and will eventually pave the way for the liberation of mankind.

Of what apparent importance are such acts as the refusal of a score or two of fools, as they are called – men who decline to take the oath of allegiance, to pay taxes, or to take part in courts of law, or to serve in the army? Such men are tried and condemned, and life remains unchanged. These occurrences may seem unimportant, and yet these are precisely the factors that undermine the authority of the government more than any others, and thus prepare the way for the liberation of mankind. These are the bees who are the first to separate themselves from the swarm, and still hovering near, they wait for the whole swarm to rise and follow them. The governments are aware of this, and look upon such occurrences with more apprehension than upon all the socialists, anarchists, and communists, with their conspiracies and their dynamite bombs.

A new regime is inaugurated. Each subject, according to custom, is required to take the oath of allegiance to the new government. A proclamation is issued, and all are bidden to assemble in the cathedral to take the oath. Suddenly one man in Perm, another in Tula, a third in Moscow, a fourth in Kaluga, refuse to take the oath and(without preconcerted action) justify their refusal by the same argument – that the Christian law forbids the oath; but, even were the oath not forbidden, they could not, according to the spirit of this law, promise to perform such evil deeds as the oath requires – such as reporting those antagonistic to the interests of the government, defending that government by armed force, or attacking its enemies. They are summoned to appear before the *stanovoys, spravniks,* priests, governors; they are reasoned with, coaxed, threatened, and punished; yet they adhere to their determination and refuse to take the oath. They are asked, "Is it true that you never took the oath?" "It is."

"And what was done to you?" "Nothing."

Every subject is required to pay his taxes, and the taxes are paid. But one man in Charkov, another in Iver, and a third in Samara, refuse to comply, and, as by one accord, each man alleges the same reason. One of them says that he will pay after he has learned the object for which his money is to be used. "If it is to be used for charity he will give of his own free will, and even more than is demanded of him. But if it is to be applied to evil purposes, he will give nothing of his own free will, because according to the law of Christ, which he obeys, he can take no part in doing evil." And the others who refuse to pay taxes, except on compulsion, express the same idea, perhaps in other words.

Those who have property are forced to pay, and those who have none are simply let alone.

"Then you have not paid your tax?"

"No."

"And what was done to you?" "Nothing."

The passport system is instituted. Every man who leaves his home must apply for one, and pay a tax for it. Suddenly in different places are to be found those who declare that passports should not be used, that a man should not acknowledge his dependence upon the State which is supported by violence; and these men take no passports, consequently they pay no tax for them. And again, there are no means of coercing them to comply with the demand. They are imprisoned, but when after a time they find themselves at liberty again, they go on living without passports.

Every peasant is expected to perform police duty as *sotsky* or *dessiatsky*, etc; but some peasant in Charkov refuses to fulfil this duty, because, as he says in explanation of his refusal, the law of Christ, which he professes, forbids him to arrest, imprison, or transport his fellow men. Another peasant in Iver or in Tambov makes the same statement. The peasants are threatened, beaten, and imprisoned, but they adhere to their resolution and refuse to perform actions contrary to their religious belief. And they cease to be elected *sofsky*, and are gradually left in peace.

It is the duty of every citizen to serve on the jury. All at once men of widely different classes – carriage-makers, professors, merchants, peasants, nobles – as if moved by a single impulse, refuse to fulfil this duty, not for reasons valid in the eyes of the law, but because the tribunal itself is, in their opinion, illegal and unchristian, and ought not to exist. These men are fined, and false reasons are ascribed for their refusal, the true ones meanwhile remaining hidden from the public. The same treatment is employed in regard to those who, for similar reasons, refuse to appear as witnesses in courts of law. These too are finally left undisturbed.

Every man at the age of twenty-one must draw lots. Suddenly there is found a man in Moscow, another in Iver, another in Charkov, and still another in Kiev, who, as it were by agreement, go to the department and declare that they will neither take the oath of allegiance nor serve in the army, because they are Christians. Here are the details of an affair which was among the earlier cases – of late these refusals have begun to multiply – a case with which I am myself familiar, which is but one example among many.

In the City Hall of Moscow a young man of average education gives his reasons for refusing to comply. His words are not heeded, and he is bidden to repeat the words of the oath with the other men. He still persists in his refusal, and quotes a certain passage in the Bible that forbids men to take an oath. No attention is paid to his arguments, and again he is ordered to take the oath, which he declines to do. Whereupon it is taken for granted that he is a sectarian, and therefore misunderstands Christianity; in other words, that he differs from the priests paid by the State. He is then sent under guard to the priests that they may convince him, which they endeavour to do; but the arguments uttered in the name of Christ, by which they strive to persuade him to deny Christ, evidently have no effect on the young man. So they declare him incorrigible and send him back to the army. Still he openly refuses to take the oath and to fulfil his military duties.

It is a case not anticipated by the law. A refusal to comply with the demands of the government cannot be overlooked; neither can this case be called one of ordinary insubordination. After conferring, the military authorities decide that, in order to rid themselves of this objectionable youth, the better way will be to consider him as a rebel and forward him under military escort to the Department of the Secret Police. The police officials and the gendarmes question the young man, but his replies will not serve to classify his offence under the heading of any crime that comes within their jurisdiction; they cannot either accuse him of revolutionary motives or of conspiracy, because he declares that he has no desire to destroy anything whatsoever; on the contrary, he opposes all violence. He says that he has nothing to conceal; he desires only an opportunity for saying and doing all things in the most open manner. And as it resulted with the clergy, so also with the gendarmes, who, though rarely embarrassed as to how to put the law in operation, can find no pretext for an accusation against the young man, and send him back to the ranks. Once more there is a conference, and his superiors decide that, although he has not taken the oath of allegiance, he is to be regarded as a soldier. He is put into uniform, his name is entered on the lists, and he is sent under convoy to his post. Here his immediate superiors once more order him to perform his military duty, and still he refuses to obey, and in the presence of the other soldiers he states his reasons, saying that, as a Christian, he cannot of his own free will prepare himself to commit murder, which was forbidden even by the law of Moses.

All this takes place in a provincial city. The occurrence excites the interest and the sympathy not only of outsiders but even of the officers, and therefore there is hesitation about employing the usual punishment for contumacy. However, for the sake of appearances, he is thrown into gaol, and a request is sent to the higher military authorities for further instructions in the case. From an official standpoint this refusal to take part in a military organization, in which the Czar himself serves, and which is blessed by the Church, must be regarded as insanity, and therefore the message is received from St. Petersburg that the young man is probably insane, and that before any violent measures are used against him he must be sent to the insane hospital. Thither he is sent in the hope that he will remain there, as happened some ten years ago in the case of a young man from Iver, who also refused to serve, and who was tortured in the hospital until at last he was subdued. But in the present instance even this measure fails to relieve the military authorities from this troublesome young man. The doctors examine him, become interested in him, and discovering no symptoms of insanity they return him to his post. He is received, and pretending that his refusal and its causes are forgotten, he is once more invited to join the drill, and again he refuses in the presence of other soldiers, stating his reasons for his refusal. The affair attracts more and more notice from soldiers as well as from civilians. Again the question is referred to St. Petersburg, and thence comes the order to transfer the young man to the frontier, where the troops are in active service, and where, if he refuses to obey orders, he may be shot without exciting attention, as there are but few Russians and Christians in that faraway territory, the majority being foreigners and Mohammedans. This is done. The young man is ordered to join the Trans-Caspian troops, and with other criminals he is delivered into the hands of commanders noted for their severity and determination.

Meanwhile, during all these transportations from place to place, the young man has suffered from harsh treatment, from cold, hunger, and filth, and his life has been made miserable. Yet all these trials do not weaken his resolution. In the Trans-Caspian province, when he is once more ordered to serve as a sentry under arms, he refuses to obey. He consents to stand where he is sent, beside the hayricks, but declines to take a weapon in his hand, declaring that on no account will he use violence against any one whomsoever. All this occurs in the presence of the soldiers. Such contumacy cannot go unpunished; consequently he is court-martialled for an infringement of military discipline, convicted and sentenced to two years' confinement in a military prison. And once again with the criminals he is sent by *etape* to the Caucasus and then thrown into prison, his fate being left to the discretionary power of the gaoler. There he is tortured for a year and a half, but still his resolution to avoid the use of weapons remains unchanged, and he continues to explain to every one whom he meets the reasons for his refusal. Towards the end of the second year, before his term has really expired, he is set at liberty; and although not in accordance with the law, they are so anxious to rid themselves of him, that his imprisonment is accepted as an equivalent of further active service.

And in various parts of Russia others are found who, as if by a concerted plan, imitate his example, and in every case the action of the government is undecided, vacillating, and underhanded. Some of these men are confined in the insane hospitals, some are appointed military clerks and sent to serve in Siberia, some are made foresters, others are thrown into prison, others are fined. At the present time several of these men are imprisoned, not for their substantial offence, denying the legality of the acts of the government, but for disobeying the particular orders of their superiors. For instance, an officer of the reserve recently failed to give information of the place of his residence, and declined to serve further in the army; he was fined thirty roubles for disobeying the orders of the authorities – and this he declined to pay except under compulsion. Several peasants and soldiers who refused to take part in a drill and to use weapons were put under arrest for disobedience and contention.

Such instances of a refusal to comply with the demands of the State when opposed to Christianity, especially refusals to perform military service, occur not only in Russia but everywhere. I know that in Servia, men from the so-called sect of Nazarenes steadily refuse to enter the army, and the Austrian government has for several years made futile attempts to convert them by means of imprisonment. In 1885 there were 130 refusals of this kind. I know that in Switzerland in 1890 there were men in confinement in the castle of Chillon for refusing to perform military duty, whose determination was not to be influenced by punishment. Such refusals have occurred in Sweden; the men there also were imprisoned, and the government carefully concealed the affairs from the people. Similar instances occurred in Prussia. I know of one subaltern officer in the guards who, in 1891, in Berlin, announced to his superiors that he, as a Christian, could not continue his military service, and in spite of all remonstrances and threats he adhered to his resolution. In the South of France a community of men called the Hinschist has recently been established (my information is derived from the *Peace Herald* of July 1891), who, as professing the Christian doctrine, refuse to perform military duty. At first they were told off to serve in hospitals, but now, with the increase of the sect, they are punished for insubordination, while they still refuse to bear arms.

Socialists, communists, and anarchists, with their bombs and their revolutions, are far less dangerous to governments than these men, who from different places proclaim their refusals, all based upon the same doctrine familiar to all. Every government knows how to defend itself from revolutionists; it holds the means in its own hands, and therefore does not fear these external foes. But what can a government do to protect itself from men who declaim against all authority as useless, superfluous, and injurious, offering, however, no opposition to authority, merely rejecting its offices, dispensing with its services, and therefore refusing to participate in it?

The Revolutionists say: "State organization is bad, either for one reason or for another; it should be destroyed and replaced by such and such a system." But a Christian says: "I know nothing of State organization, whether it be good or bad, and it is for this very reason that I do not wish to support it. And I cannot undertake submission, because such submission is contrary to my conscience."

All the institutions of the State are opposed to the conscience of a Christian: the oath of allegiance, taxation, courts of law, and armies; while the whole authority of government is dependent upon them. Revolutionary foes struggle against the government, but Christianity enters not into this contest; internally, it destroys the principles on which government is based.

With the Russian people, in whose midst, particularly since the time of Peter I, the protest of Christianity against the State has never ceased; in the midst of this people, where the conditions of life are such that whole communes emigrate to Turkey, China, and uninhabited portions of the globe, who, so far from needing the government, always consider it an unnecessary burden, and only endure it as a calamity, whether it be Russian, Chinese, or Turkish – the cases of isolated individuals who from Christian motives have liberated themselves from the control of government have grown more and more frequent in these latter days. Such manifestations are particularly dreaded by the government at the present time, because the men who protest often belong not to the so-called lower, the uneducated classes, but are men of average and even superior education, and because these men explain their refusals, not by some mystical belief peculiar to the individual, as in olden times, nor do they complicate them with superstition and fanaticism, like the sects of the Self-burners or Bieguni, but assign as the reason for their refusals the simplest, most obvious of truths, patent to and admitted by all the world.

Thus men refuse to pay taxes of their own free will, because the money is used to promote violence; in other words, to pay the wages of the violators in the army, for building prisons and fortresses, or for manufacturing cannon – in all of which, as

Christians, they consider it wrong and immoral to take a part.

They refuse to take the oath of allegiance, for were they to promise to obey the authorities – that is, men who use violence; they must contradict the sense of the Christian doctrine.

They refuse to swear in court because an oath is distinctly forbidden by the Gospel.

They decline police duties, because in that office they would be compelled to use violence against their brethren and to distress them, and a Christian cannot do this.

They refuse to take part in courts of law, because they look upon every tribunal as a vehicle for the law of vengeance, and therefore incompatible with the Christian law of forgiveness and love.

They decline to have anything to do with military preparations, or to enter the ranks of the army, because they neither can nor will be executioners, nor prepare themselves for such an office.

And the reasons alleged for these refusals are of such a nature, that however arbitrary the governments may be, they cannot punish openly those who refuse.

Were the governments to punish men for such refusals they would be forced to abjure forever both justice and virtue, those principles by which, as they assure us, all their authority is supported.

What are governments to do with these men? Of course they have the power to execute, to imprison, and to condemn to transportation and penal servitude all enemies who attempt to overthrow them by violence; they can obtain by bribery half the men they need, and have at their command millions of armed soldiers, who are ready to put to death all the enemies of authority. But what can be done with men who wish neither to destroy nor to establish anything, whose sole desire is to avoid in their own private lives any act that may be opposed to the Christian law, and who consequently refuse to perform duties which are regarded by the government as the most natural and obligatory of all? If they were revolutionists preaching violence and practising it, it would be an easy matter to oppose them. Some might be bribed, some deceived, others intimidated, and those who could

neither be bought, deceived, nor intimidated would be manifestly criminals, enemies of society, who as such could be executed
or beaten to death; and the people would approve the acts of the
government. If they were fanatics belonging to some particular
sect, one might, in view of the superstitions inherent in their
doctrine, refute at the same time what truth their arguments
contained. But what is to be done with men who neither preach
rebellion nor any special dogmas, who wish to live in peace with
all mankind, who refuse to take the oath of allegiance or to pay
taxes, or to take part in tribunals, to perform military service
and the various duties of a similar nature, on which the whole
organization of the State is founded? What is to be done with
them? They cannot be bribed. The very risk they are willing to
take shows their integrity. Neither can they be deceived when
these things are represented as the commands of God, because
their refusal is based on the indubitable law of God, by which
the very men who are trying to coerce them to disobey this law
profess to hold themselves bound. It is vain to hope to intimidate
them by threats, because the very suffering and privations which
they endure for righteousness' sake serve but to strengthen their
devotion to their faith, whose law distinctly commands them
first of all to obey God, to fear not them that kill the body, but to
fear those who can kill both body and soul. Neither can they be
executed or imprisoned for life. Their past lives, their thoughts
and actions, their friends, speak for them; every one knows them
to be gentle, kindly, and harmless men, and it is impossible to
represent them in the light of criminals whose suppression is
needed for the salvation of society. Moreover, the execution of
men acknowledged by all to be virtuous would arouse defenders,
who would endeavour to explain the causes for their disobedience. And when all men are made to recognize the reasons why
these Christians refuse to obey the demands of the State, they
cannot fail to acknowledge the same obligation, and to admit
that all men should long since have refused obedience.

Confronted with these insubordinations, governments find
themselves in a desperate plight. They realize that the prophe-
cies of Christianity are about to be fulfilled, that it is loosening
the fetters of them that are in bonds and setting men free; they

realize that such freedom will inevitably destroy those who have held mankind in bondage. Governments realize this; they know that their hours are counted, that they are helpless to resist. All that they are able to do is to retard the hour of dissolution. And this they try to do; but their position is still a desperate one.

It is like the predicament of a conqueror who wishes to preserve the town set on fire by the inhabitants. No sooner does he put the fire out in one place than two other fires break out; when he separates the burning portion from the main body of a large building the flames burst out at both extremities. These outbreaks are not, as yet, of frequent occurrence, but the spark has been kindled, and the fire will burn steadily until all is consumed.

The position of governments in the presence of men who profess Christianity is so precarious that very little is needed to shake to pieces their power, built up through so many centuries, and apparently so solid in structure. And it is now that the sociologist comes forward, preaching that it is useless, and even hurtful and immoral, for the individual to emancipate himself alone.

Let us suppose that men have been working for a long time to divert the course of a river; they have at last succeeded in digging a canal, and all that remains now is to make an opening and let the water flow through it into the canal; suppose now certain other men arrive upon the scene and suggest that, instead of letting the water flow into the canal, it would be much better to erect over the river some form of machinery, by means of which the water would be poured from one side to the other.

But things have gone too far. Governments are aware of their weakness and helplessness, and men of the Christian faith are awakening from their torpor, beginning already to realize their power.

"I come to send fire on the earth," said Christ.

And this is the fire that begins to burn.

CHAPTER X

Uselessness of Violence for
the Destruction of Evil

THE MORAL ADVANCE OF Mankind is accomplished not only through the Knowledge of Truth, but also through the Establishment of Public Opinion. Christianity destroys the State – Which is more necessary, Christianity or the State? – There are men who defend the necessity of the State, and others who, on the same grounds, deny this necessity – Neither can be proved by abstract reasoning – The question decides the character of a man's consciousness, which either allows or forbids him to participate in the organization of the State – Realization of the uselessness and immorality of taking part in the organization of the State, which is contradictory to Christian doctrine, decides this question for each one, regardless of the destiny of the State – Argument of the defenders of the State, as a form of social life indispensable for the defence of the good from the wicked, until all nations, and all members of each nation, shall have become Christians – The more wicked are always those in power – History is but a recital of the usurpation of power by the bad over the good – The acknowledgment by authority of the necessity of struggle with evil by violence is equivalent to self-destruction – The annihilation of violence is not only possible, but is going on before our eyes – However, it is not destroyed by State violence, but through those men who, obtaining power by violence, and recognizing its vanity and futility, benefit by experience and become incapable of using violence – This is the process through which individual men, as well as whole nations, have passed – It is in that way that Christianity penetrates into the consciousness of men, and not only is this accomplished despite the violence used by authority, but through its agency, and therefore the abolition of authority is not only without danger, but it goes on continually as life itself – Objection of the defenders of the State system that the diffusion of

Christianity is improbable – Diffusion of Christian truth interdicting violence accomplished not only slowly and gradually, by the internal method, by individual recognition of the truth, by prophetic intuition, by the realizing of the emptiness of power and abandonment of it by individual men, but accomplished also by the external method, by which large numbers of men, inferior in intellectual development, at once, in view of their confidence in the others, adopt the new truth – The diffusion of truth at a certain stage creates a public opinion, which compels the majority of men who have previously opposed it to recognize the new truth at once – Therefore a universal renunciation of violence may very soon come to pass – namely, when a Christian public opinion shall be established – The conviction of the necessity of violence prevents the establishment of Christian public opinion – Violence compels men to discredit the moral force which can alone exalt them – Neither nations nor individual men have been conquered by violence, but by public opinion, which no violence can resist – It is possible to conquer savage men and nations only by the diffusion of Christian public opinion among them, whereas the Christian nations, in order to conquer them, do everything in their power to destroy the establishment of a Christian public opinion – These unsuccessful experiments cannot be cited as a proof of the impossibility of conquering men by Christianity – Violence which corrupts public opinion only prevents the social organization from becoming what it should be, and with the abolition of violence Christian public opinion will be established – Whatever may take place when violence has been abolished, the unknown future can be no worse than the present, and therefore one need not fear it – To penetrate to the unknown and move towards it is the essence of life.

Christianity, faithfully interpreted, saps the foundations of the civil law, and this was always understood from the very outset. It was for this that Christ was crucified; and until men felt the necessity for justifying the establishment of the Christian state, they always accepted that interpretation. The cleverly constructed theories intended to reconcile the doctrines of Christianity with that of the State date back to the time when rulers of nations adopted a nominal external Christianity. But in these times it is impossible for a sincere and earnest man not to perceive the incompatibility of the Christian doctrine of love, meekness of spirit, and forgiveness of injuries, with the despotism, the violence, and the wars of the State. The profession of true Christianity not only forbids the recognition of the State, but strikes at its very foundations.

But if it be true that Christianity is incompatible with the State, one naturally asks which is the better adapted to promote the well-being of mankind, the system prescribed by the State, or the precepts of Christianity?

There are those who affirm that the State organization is the more indispensable; they declare that its overthrow would check all human progress, that no development is possible save through the channels of civil government, and that all those evils which we find prevailing among nations who live under State laws are not the result of the organization, which permits progress and the attainment of the highest degree of civilization,

They who hold these views quote, in support of their position, certain historical, philosophical, and even religious arguments, which seem to them irrefutable. But there are others who entertain views diametrically opposed to these. For instance, they say that the fact of the world having existed at one time without a government, might be taken to prove the State to be only a temporary condition; that the time was sure to come when men would require a change, which time had now arrived. To support their theory, these men in turn adduce historical, philosophical, and religious arguments, which seem to them irrefutable.

Volumes may be and have been written in defence of the former position, and of late years a great deal has been written, and ably written too, from the opposite standpoint.

It can neither be proved on the one hand, as the partisans of the State claim, that its destruction would be followed by a general upheaval, by robberies and murders, and by the nullification of all social laws, and the return of man to a condition of barbarism: nor on the other, as the enemies of the State affirm, that man has grown so virtuous and well disposed that, preferring peace to enmity, he will no longer rob and murder his neighbour; that he is quite able, without State assistance, to establish a community, and conduct his own affairs; and that the State itself, while assuming an air of protection, is really exerting a demoralizing influence. It is impossible to prove either one or the other by abstract arguments. And naturally neither point can be proved by experience, as it is a question first of all of getting the requisite experience.

Whether or not the time has arrived for abolishing the State is a question which could not be answered were it not that we possess other means that will assist us to settle it beyond dispute.

It needs no one to tell the young birds when it is time to burst the shell; they know very well when there is no longer room for them in the eggs, and begin of their own accord to break the shell and leave it behind. So it is with this question of a change in human affairs. Has the time come for men to cast aside the customs of the State and establish a new order? When a man's inner consciousness has so developed that he feels himself hampered by the requirements of the State, and can no longer submit to the restraint, realizing at the same time that he has ceased to need its protecting care, the question whether or no men have matured sufficiently to enable them to dispense with the State is disposed of without reference to former arguments. A man who has outgrown the State can no more be coerced into submission to its laws than can the fledgling be made to re-enter its shell.

"The State may have been necessary at one time, and/or aught that I know it may even now serve the purposes you mention," says the man who holds the Christian life-conception. "I can only say that I have no need of it, nor can I conform to its requirements. You must decide for yourself whether it be advantageous or no. I shall not attempt to generalize on the subject with the expectation of proving my point. I only recognize what I need and what I don't need; what I can, and what I cannot do. I know, as far as I am myself concerned, that I do not need to separate from the men of other nations, and therefore I can neither recognize an exclusive affiliation to this or that one, nor acknowledge myself the subject of any one government. I need none of the institutions established by the State, and therefore I am not willing to surrender the fruits of my labour in the form of taxes to support institutions which I believe to be not only unnecessary but positively injurious. I know that I need neither magistrates, nor tribunals founded on and supported by violence, and therefore I can have nothing to do with them; I know that I feel no inclination to attack other nations and put their citizens to death, neither do I wish to defend myself against them by force of arms, and therefore I can take no part in wars nor in preparations for wars. Doubtless there are men who believe that all these things are an indispensable part of human life – I cannot argue with them – but I know that for me they have no meaning, and that I will have nothing to do with them.

"And this is not a matter of personal selection, but because I must obey the commands of Him who has sent me into the world, and has given me an unmistakable law by which I am to be guided through life."

Whatever arguments may be advanced to prove that harm and probably disaster will accrue from abolishing the authority of the State, the man who has already outgrown the State ideal cannot possibly be bound by it. And whatever arguments may be adduced to prove its necessity, he can never return to it. He is like the young bird that can never return to its outgrown shell.

"But granting this to be true," say the partisans of the existing' order, "we cannot dispense with the supremacy of the State until all men are Christians, because even among those who claim the title there are many who are very far from being Christians – evildoers, who seek their own gratification at the expense of their fellowmen, and if the governments were overthrown, so far from improving the condition of the people, it would greatly add to their miseries. The subversion of the State would be a misfortune not only where the minority are true Christians, but even supposing the whole people to be so, while the neighbouring nations are still non-Christian, these latter would make their lives a martyrdom by rapine and murder and all manner of violence. It would serve only to provide the vicious and unprincipled with an opportunity to oppress the innocent. Therefore the State should not be abolished until all the wicked have ceased from troubling, which will not happen just at present. Hence, however much certain individual Christians may wish to escape from the authority of the State, the greater good of the greater number demands its preservation." So say the defenders of the State principle. "If it were not," they say,

"For State authority there would be no protection against the malice and injustice of the oppressor; that authority alone makes it possible to restrain the wicked."

But in uttering these sentiments the partisans of the existing order take it for granted that they have proved the truth of what they assert. When they declare that the evildoers would ride roughshod over the defenceless and the innocent, were it not for the authority of the State, they imply that the governing power is vested at the present time in a body of virtuous men, who control all the wrongdoers. But this is a proposition which must be proved. It could only be a correct statement if we happened to resemble the inhabitants of China, where it is popularly believed, although the belief is not justified by fact, that the good are always in authority, because should it become known that the rulers are no better than those over whom they rule, it is the duty of the citizens to overthrow the government. But although this is supposed to be one of the customs of China, it is not, nor would it be possible for it to be so, since, in order to overthrow a criminal government, one needs the power as well as the right. Even in China this is a mere supposition, and in our own Christian land we have never so much as dreamed of it. As far as we are concerned, there is no reason to believe that power is in the hands of the virtuous and high-minded, rather than in those of men who took it by violence and have held it for themselves and their descendants. For surely it would be impossible for a high-minded man to usurp authority by violence and to continue to hold it.

In order to gain possession of power, and to retain it, one must have a love for it, and the love of power is incompatible with goodness; it accords with the opposite qualities of pride, duplicity, and cruelty.

Both the origin and the maintenance of power depend upon the exaltation of the individual, and the degradation of the people by means of hypocrisy and fraud, by prisons, fortresses, and murders. "If State authority were to be abolished, then would the more wicked people dominate over the less wicked," say the

THE KINGDOM OF GOD IS WITHIN YOU

upholders of State organization. But if the Egyptians conquered the Hebrews, and the Persians the Egyptians, and the Macedonians the Persians, and the Romans the Greeks, and the barbarians the Romans, is it really possible that the conquerors are always better than the conquered? And so with political changes in the State; is the power always transferred to the better men? When Louis XVI was deposed, and control passed into the hands of Robespierre, and when, later, he was in turn succeeded by Napoleon, was it the better or the worse man who held the power? Again, were they of Versailles or the Communists the better men? Charles the First or Cromwell? When Peter III reigned, or after his murder, when Catherine ruled over one part of Russia, and Pugatchov over the other – who then was good and who was wicked?

All those in authority affirm that their office is required, in order that the unprincipled may be hindered from oppressing the innocent, implying thereby that they themselves being virtuous are protecting other virtuous men from the malice of the evildoer. To possess power and to do violence are synonymous terms; to do violence means doing something to which the victim of violence objects, and which the aggressor would resent were it directed against himself. Therefore the possession of power really means doing unto others what we should not like if it were done to ourselves – that is, harm.

Obedience signifies that a man holds patience to be better than violence, and to choose patience rather than violence means to be good, or, at least, not so wicked as those who do unto others what they would not wish to have done to themselves.

Therefore all the probabilities are that those in authority were in past times, as they are in present, worse men than those they ruled over. Doubtless there are wicked men among those who submit to authority, but it is impossible that the better men should rule over the worse.

This might be thought in pagan times, when the definition of goodness was inaccurate, but with the clear and exact conception of the qualities of good and evil presented by Christianity before us we cannot imagine it. If in the pagan world they who were more or less good, and they who were more or less bad,

might not be easily distinguished, the characteristics of goodness and wickedness have been so clearly defined by the Christian conception that it is impossible to mistake them. According
to the doctrine of Christ, the good are those who submit and are
long-suffering, who do not resist evil by violence, who forgive
injuries and love their enemies; the wicked are the vainglorious,
who tyrannize, who are arrogant and violent with others. Therefore, if we are guided by the doctrine of Christ, we shall have
no difficulty in deciding where to seek the good and the wicked
among rulers and subjects. It is even absurd to speak of Christians as sovereigns or rulers.

The non-Christians – that is, those to whom life is but a matter
of temporal welfare – must always rule over the Christians, for
whom life means self-denial and disregard of temporal things.

And thus it has always been, and it has been manifested more
and more plainly as the Christian doctrine has become more
clearly defined and widespread.

The further true Christianity extended, the firmer the hold it
gained on the consciousness of men, the less possible it became
for Christians to belong to the dominant class, and the easier for
non-Christians to gain the ascendency.

"To abolish the supremacy of the State before all men have
become true Christians would only afford the wicked a chance
to tyrannize over the good and maltreat them with impunity,"
say the upholders of the existing order.

It has always been the same from the beginning of the world
until this present time, and it always will be. The wicked always
rule over the good and do violence to them. Cain did violence
to Abel, the astute Jacob betrayed the trusting Esau, and was
himself deceived by Laban; Caiaphas and Pilate sat in judgment
on Christ; the Roman emperors ruled over Seneca, Epictetus,
and other high-minded Romans of those times; Ivan IV with his
Oprichniks, the tipsy syphilitic Peter with his clowns, the prostitute Catherine with her lovers, ruled over the industrious, God-
fearing Russian people of those times and trampled upon them.
William rules the Germans, Stambulov the Bulgarians, and the
Russian officials rule over the Russian people; the Germans ruled
over the Italians, and now they rule over the Hungarians and the

Slavs. The Turks ruled over the Greeks and rule now over the Slavs, the English over the Hindus, and the Mongolians over the Chinese.

So we see that whether the tyranny of the State is or is not to be abolished, the position of the innocent, who are oppressed by the tyrants, will not be materially affected thereby.

Men are not to be frightened by being told that the wicked will oppress the good, because that is the natural course and will never change.

The whole of pagan history is a mere narrative of events wherein the wicked have got the upper hand, and once in power, by craft and cruelty have kept their hold upon men, announcing themselves meanwhile as the guardians of justice and the defenders of the innocent against the oppressor. All revolutions are but the result of the appropriation of power by the wicked and their rule over the good. When the rulers say that if their power were to be destroyed the evildoers would tyrannize over the innocent, what they really mean is that the tyrants in power are reluctant to yield to those other tyrants who would fain wrest from them their authority. When they protest that this authority of theirs, which is actually violence, is necessary to defend the people against the possible tyranny of others, they are simply denouncing themselves. The reason why violence is dangerous is that whenever it is employed all the arguments which the perpetrators advance in their own defence may be used against them with even greater force. They talk of the violence done in the past, and more frequently of future and imaginary violence, while they themselves are the real offenders. "You say that men committed robbery and murder in former times, and profess anxiety lest all men be robbed or murdered unless protected by your authority. This may or may not be true, but the fact that you allow thousands of men to perish in prisons by enforced labour, in fortresses, and in exile, that your military requisitions ruin millions of families and imperil morally and physically millions of men, this is not a suppositious but an actual violence, which, according to your own reasoning, should be resisted by violence. And therefore, by your own admission, the wicked ones, against whom one should use violence, are yourselves." Thus should the oppressed reply to their oppressors. And such are the language, the thoughts, and the actions of non-Christians. Wherever the oppressed are more wicked than the oppressor, they attack and overthrow them whenever they are able; or else, and this is more frequently the case, they enter the ranks of the oppressors and take part in their tyranny.

Thus the dangers of which the defenders of State rights make a bugbear – that if authority were overthrown the wicked would prevail over the good – potentially exist at all times. The destruction of State violence, in fact, never can, for this very reason, lead to any real increase of violence on the part of the wicked over the good.

If State violence disappeared, it is not unlikely that other acts of violence would be committed; but the sum of violence can never be increased simply because the power passes from the hands of one into those of another.

"State violence can never be abolished until all the wicked disappear," say the advocates of the existing order, by which they imply that there must always be violence, because there will always be wicked people. This could only prove true, supposing the oppressors to be really beneficent, and supposing the true deliverance of mankind from evil must be accomplished by violence. Then, of course, violence could never cease. But as, on the contrary, violence never really overcomes evil, and since there is another way altogether to overcome it, the assertion that violence will never cease is untrue. Violence is diminishing, and clearly tending to disappear; though not, as is claimed by the defenders of the existing order, in consequence of the amelioration of those who live under an oppressive government (their condition really gets worse), but because the consciousness of mankind is becoming more clear.Hence even the wicked men who are in power are growing less and less wicked, and will at last become so good that they will be incapable of committing deeds of violence.

The reason why humanity marches forward is not because the inferior men, having gained possession of power, reform their subjects by arbitrary methods, as is claimed both by Conservatives and Revolutionists, but is due above all to the fact that mankind in general is steadily, and with an ever increasing appreciation, adopting the Christian life-conception. There is a phenomenon observable in human life in a manner analogous to that of boiling. Those who profess the social life-conception are always ambitious to rule, and struggle to attain power. In this struggle the most gross and cruel, the least Christian elements of society, bubble up, as it were, and rise, by reason of their violence, into the ruling or upper classes of society. But then is fulfilled what Christ prophesied: *"Woe unto you that are rich! Woe unto you that are full! Woe unto you, when all men shall speak well of you!" Luke vi: 24–26.*

The men who have attained power and glory and riches, and who have realized all their cherished aims, live to discover that all is vanity, and gladly return to their former estate. Charles V, Ivan the Terrible, Alexander I, having realized the evils of power and its futility, renounced it, because they recognized it as a calamity, having lost all pleasure in the deeds of violence which they formerly enjoyed.

But it is not alone kings like Charles V and Alexander I who arrive at this disgust of power, but every man who has attained the object of his ambition. Not only the statesman, the general, the millionaire, the merchant, but every official who has gained the position for which he has longed this half score of years, every well-to-do peasant who has saved one or two hundred roubles, finds at last the same disillusion.

Not only individuals, but entire nations, mankind as a whole, have passed through this experience.

The attractions of power and all it brings – riches, honours, luxury – seem to men really worth struggling for only until they are won, for no sooner does a man hold them within his grasp than they manifest their own emptiness and gradually lose their charm, like clouds lovely and picturesque in outline seen from afar, but no sooner is one enveloped in them than all their beauty vanishes.

Men who have obtained riches and power, those who have struggled for them, but more particularly those who have inherited them, cease to be greedy for power or cruel in its acquisition.

Having learned by experience, sometimes in one generation,

sometimes in several, how utterly worthless are the fruits of violence, men abandon those vices acquired by the passion for riches and power, and growing more humane, they lose their positions, being crowded out by others who are less Christian and more wicked; whereupon they fall back into a stratum, which, though lower in the social scale, is higher in that of morality, thus increasing the mean level of Christian consciousness. But straightway, the worse, the rougher, and less Christian elements rise to the surface, and being subject to the same experience as their predecessors, after one or two generations these men, too, recognize the hollowness of violent ambitions, and being penetrated with the spirit of Christianity, fall back into the ranks of the oppressed. These are in turn replaced by new oppressors, less despotic than the former, but rougher than those whom they oppress. So that although the authority is to all outward seeming unchanged, yet the number of those who have been driven by the exigencies of life to adopt the Christian life-conception increases with every change of rulers. They may be harsher, crueller, and less Christian than their subjects; but always men less and less violent replace their predecessors in authority.

Violence chooses its instruments from among the worst elements of society; men who gradually become leavened, and, softened and changed for the better, are returned into society.

Such is the process by means of which Christianity takes fuller possession of men day by day. Christianity enters into the consciousness of men in spite of the violence of power, and even owing to that violence.

The argument of the defenders of the State, that if power were abolished the wicked would tyrannize over the good, not only fails to prove that the domination of the wicked is a new thing to be dreaded, as it exists already; but proves, on the contrary, that the tyranny of the State, which allows the wicked to govern the good, is itself the real evil which we ought to eradicate, and which is constantly decreasing by the very nature of things.

"But if State violence is not to cease until the rulers have become so far Christianized that they will renounce it of their own accord and no others will be found to take their places – if these things are coming to pass," say the defenders of the existing order, "when is it to happen? If 1800 years have passed and still so many long to rule, it is wholly improbable that we shall soon behold this change, if it ever takes place at all."

Even though there may be at present, as there always have been, certain individuals who would not rule if they could, who do not choose to benefit themselves in that way, still the number of those who do prefer to rule rather than to be ruled is so great that it is difficult to imagine a time when the number will be exhausted.

"In order to accomplish the conversion of all men, to induce each one to exchange the pagan for the Christian life-conception, voluntarily resigning riches and power, there being none left to profit by these, it would be necessary that not only all the rude, half barbarous people, unfitted either to accept Christianity or follow its precepts, who are always to be found in every Christian community, should become Christians, but that all savage and non-Christian nations, which are still numerous, should also become Christian," therefore were one to admit that the Christianizing process may at some future time embrace all humanity, we must still take into consideration the degree of progress that has been made in 1800 years, and realize that this can only happen after many centuries. Hence we need not for the present trouble ourselves about the overthrow of authority; all we have to do is to look to it that it is in the best hands."

Thus reply the partisans of the existing system. And this reasoning would be perfectly consistent, provided that the transition of men from one life-conception to another were only to be effected by the process of individual conversion; that is to say, that each man, through his personal experience, should realize the vanity of power, and apprehend Christian truth. This process is constantly going on, and in that way, one by one, men are converted to Christianity.

But men do not become converted to Christianity merely in this way; there is an exterior influence brought to bear which accelerates the process. The progression of mankind from one system of life to another is accomplished not only gradually, as the sand glides through the hourglass, grain by grain, until all has run out, but rather as water which enters an immersed vessel, at first slowly, atone side, then, borne down by its weight, suddenly plunges, and at once fills completely.

And this is what happens in human communities during a change in their life-conception, which is equivalent to the change from one organization to another. It is only at first that men by degrees, one by one, accept the new truth and obey its dictates; but after it has been to a certain extent disseminated, it is accepted not through intuition, and not by degrees, but generally and at once, and almost involuntarily.

And therefore the argument of the advocates of the present system, that but a minority have embraced Christianity during the last 1800 years, and that another 1800 years must pass away before the rest of mankind will accept it, is erroneous. For one must take into consideration another mode in addition to the intuitive of assimilating new truth, and of making the transition from one mode of life to another. This other mode is this: men assimilate a truth not alone because they may have come to realize it through prophetic insight or through individual experience, but the truth having been spread abroad, those who dwell on a lower plane of intelligence accept it at once, because of their confidence in those who have received it and incorporated it in their lives.

Every new truth that changes the manner of life and causes humanity to move onward is at first accepted by a very limited number, who grasp it by knowledge of it. The rest of mankind, accepting on faith the former truth upon which the existing system has been founded, is always opposed to the spread of the new truth.

But as, in the first place, mankind is not stationary, but is ever progressing, growing more and more familiar with truth and approaching nearer to it in everyday life; and secondly, as all men progress according to their opportunities, age, education, nationality, beginning with those who are more, and ending with those who are less, capable of receiving new truth; the men nearest those who have perceived the truth intuitively, pass, one by one, and with gradually diminishing intervals, over to the side of the new truth. So as the number of men who acknowledge it increases, the truth itself becomes more clearly manifested. The feeling of confidence in the new truth increases in proportion to the numbers who have accepted it. For, owing to the growing intelligibility of the truth itself, it becomes easier for men to grasp it, especially for those lower intellectually, until finally the greater number readily adopt it, and help to found a new *regime.*

The men who go over to the new truth, once it has gained a certain hold, go over en masse, of one accord, much as ballast is rapidly put into a ship to maintain its equilibrium. If not ballasted the vessel would not be sufficiently immersed, and would change its position every moment. This ballast, which at first may seem superfluous and a hindrance to the progress of the ship, is indispensable to its equipoise and motion.

Thus it is with the masses when, under the influence of some new idea that has won social approval, they abandon one system to adopt another, not singly, but in a body. It is the inertia of this mass which impedes the rapid and frequent transition from one system of life, not ratified by wisdom, to another; and which for a long time arrests the progress of every truth destined to become apart of human consciousness.

It is erroneous, then, to argue that because only a small percentage of the human race has in these eighteen centuries adopted the Christian doctrine, that many, many times eighteen centuries must elapse before the whole world will accept it – a period of time so remote that we who are now living can have no interest in it. It is unfair, because those men who stand on a lower plane of development, whom the partisans of the existing order represent as hindrances to the realization of the Christian system of life, are those men who always go over in a body to a truth accepted by those above them.

And therefore that change in the life of mankind, when the powerful will give up their power without finding any to assume it in their stead, will come to pass when the Christian life-conception, rendered familiar, conquers, not merely men one by one, but masses at a time.

"But even if it were true," the advocates of the existing order may say, "that public opinion has the power to convert the inert non-Christian mass of men, as well as the corrupt and gross who are to be found in every Christian community, how shall we know that a Christian mode of life is born, and that State violence will be rendered useless?"

After renouncing the despotism by which the existing order has been maintained, in order to trust to the vague and indefinite force of public opinion, we risk permitting those savages, those existing among us, as well as those outside, to commit robbery, murder, and other outrages upon Christians.

If even with the help of authority we have a hard struggle against the anti-Christian elements ever ready to overpower us, and destroy all the progress made by civilization, how then could public opinion prove an efficient substitute for the use of force and avail for our protection? To rely upon public opinion alone would be as foolhardy as to let loose all the wild beasts of a menagerie, because they seem inoffensive when in their cages and held in awe by red hot irons.

"Those men entrusted with authority, or born to rule over others by the divine will of God, have no right to imperil all the results of civilization, simply to make an experiment, and learn whether public opinion can or cannot be substituted for the safeguard of authority."

Alphonse Karr, a French writer, forgotten today, once said in trying to prove the impossibility of abolishing the death penalty: *"Que Messieurs les assassins commencent par nous donner l'exemple."* And I have often heard this witticism quoted by persons who really believed they were using a convincing and intellectual argument against the suppression of the penalty of death. Nevertheless, there could be no better argument against the violence of government.

"Let the assassins begin by showing us an example," say the defenders of government authority. The assassins say the same, but with more justice. They say: "Let those who have set themselves up as teachers and guides show us an example by the suppression of legal assassination, and we will imitate it." And this they say not by way of a jest, but in all seriousness, for such is in reality the situation."

We cannot cease to use violence while we are surrounded by those who commit violence."

There is no more insuperable barrier at the present time to

the progress of humanity, and to the establishment of a system that shall be in harmony with its present conception of life, than this erroneous argument.

Those holding positions of authority are fully convinced that men are to be influenced and controlled by force alone, and therefore to preserve the existing system they do not hesitate to employ it. And yet this very system is supported not by violence, but by public opinion, the action of which is compromised by violence. The action of violence actually weakens and destroys that which it wishes to support.

At best, violence, if not employed as a vehicle for the ambition of those in high places, condemns in the inflexible form a law which public opinion has most probably long ago repudiated and condemned; but there is this difference, that while public opinion rejects and condemns all acts that are opposed to the moral law, the law supported by force repudiates and condemns only a certain limited number of acts, seeming thus to justify all acts of a like order which have not been included in its formula.

From the time of Moses public opinion has regarded covetousness, lust, and cruelty as crimes, and condemned them as such. It condemns and repudiates every form that covetousness may assume, not only the acquisition of another man's property by violence, fraud, or cunning, but the cruel abuse of wealth as well. It condemns all kinds of lust, let it be profligacy with a mistress, a slave, a divorced wife, or with one's wife; it condemns all cruelty, blows, bad usage, murder, all cruelty not only towards human beings but towards animals. Whereas the law, based upon violence, attacks only certain forms of covetousness, such as theft and fraud, and certain forms of lust and cruelty, such as conjugal infidelity, assault, and murder; and thus it seems to condone those manifestations of covetousness, lust, and cruelty which do not fall within its narrow limits.

But violence not only demoralizes public opinion, it excites in the minds of men a pernicious conviction that they move onward, not through the impulsion of a spiritual power, which would help them to comprehend and realize the truth by bringing them nearer to that moral force which is the source of every progressive movement of mankind – but, by means of violence

– by the very factor that not only impedes our progress towards truth, but withdraws us from it. This is a fatal error, inasmuch as it inspires in man a contempt for the fundamental principle of his life – spiritual activity – and leads him to transfer all his strength and energy to the practice of external violence.

It is as though men would try to put a locomotive in motion by turning its wheels with their hands, not knowing that the expansion of steam was the real motive-power, and that the action of the wheels was but the effect, and not the cause. If by their hands and their levers they move the wheels, it is but the semblance of motion, and if anything, injures the wheels and makes them useless.

The same mistake is made by those who expect to move the world by violence.

Men affirm that the Christian life cannot be established save by violence, because there are still uncivilized nations outside of the Christian world, in Africa and Asia (some regard even the Chinese as a menace of our civilization), and because, according to the new theory of heredity, there exist in society congenital criminals, savage and irredeemably vicious.

But the savages whom we find in our own community, as well as those beyond its pale, with whom we threaten ourselves and others, have never yielded to violence, and are not yielding to it now. One people never conquered another by violence alone. If the victors stood on a lower plane of civilization than the conquered, they always adopted the habits and customs of the latter, never attempting to force their own methods of life upon them. It is by the influence of public opinion, not by violence, that nations are reduced to submission.

When a people have accepted a new religion, have become Christians, or turned Mohammedans, it has come to pass not because it was made obligatory by those in power (violence often produced quite the opposite result), but because they were influenced by public opinion. Nations constrained by violence to accept the religion of the conqueror have never really done so.

The same may be said in regard to the savage elements found in all communities: neither severity nor clemency in the matter of punishments, nor modifications in the prison system, nor augmenting of the police force, have either diminished or increased the aggregate of crimes, which will only decrease through an evolution in our manner of life. No severities have ever succeeded in suppressing the vendetta, or the custom of du-elling in certain countries. However many of his fellows may be put to death for thieving, the Tcherkess continues to steal out of vainglory. No girl will marry a Tcherkess who has not proved his daring by stealing a horse, or at least a sheep. When men no longer fight duels and the Tcherkess cease to steal, it will not be from fear of punishment (the danger of capital punishment adds to the prestige of daring), but because public manners will have undergone a change. The same may be said of all other crimes. Violence can never suppress that which is countenanced by gen-eral custom. If public opinion would but frown upon violence, it would destroy all its power.

What would happen if violence were not employed against hostile nations and the criminal element in society, we do not know. But that the use of violence subdues neither we do know through long experience.

And how can we expect to subdue by violence nations whose education, traditions, and even religious training all tend to glo-rify resistance to the conqueror and love of liberty as the loftiest of virtues? And how is it possible to extirpate crime by violence in the midst of communities, where the same act regarded by the government as criminal is transformed into a heroic exploit by public opinion?

Nations and races may be destroyed by violence – it has been done. They cannot be subdued.

The power transcending all others which has influenced in-dividuals and nations since time began, that power which is the convergence of the invisible, intangible, spiritual forces of all hu-manity is public opinion.

Violence serves but to enervate this influence, disintegrating it, and substituting for it one, not only useless, but pernicious to the welfare of humanity.

In order to win over all those outside the Christian fold, all the Zulus, the Manchurians, the Chinese, whom many consider uncivilized, and the uncivilized among ourselves, there is only one way. This is by the diffusion of a Christian mode of thought, which is only to be accomplished by a Christian life, Christian deeds, a Christian example. But instead of employing this one way of winning those who have remained outside the fold of Christianity, men of our epoch have done just the opposite. In order to convert uncivilized nations, who do us no harm, whom we have no motive for oppressing, we ought, above all, to leave them in peace, and act upon them only by our showing them an example of the Christian virtues of patience, meekness, temperance, purity, and brotherly love. Instead of this we begin by seizing their territory, and establishing among them new marts for our commerce, with the sole view of furthering our own interests – we, in fact, rob them; we sell them wine, tobacco, and opium, and thereby demoralize them; we establish our own customs among them, we teach them violence and all its lessons; we teach them the animal law of strife, that lowest depth of human degradation, and do all that we can to conceal the Christian virtues we possess. Then, having sent them a score of missionaries, who gabble an absurd clerical jargon, we quote the results of our attempt to convert the heathen as an indubitable proof that the truths of Christianity are not adaptable to everyday life.

And as for those whom we call criminals, who live in our midst, all that has just been said applies equally to them. There is only one way to convert them, and that is by means of a public opinion founded on true Christianity, accompanied by the example of a sincere Christian life. And by way of preaching this Christian Gospel and confirming it by Christian example, we imprison, we execute, guillotine, hang; we encourage the masses in idolatrous religions calculated to stultify them; the government authorizes the sale of brain-destroying poisons – wine, tobacco, opium; prostitution is legalized; we bestow land upon those who need it not; surrounded by misery, we display in our entertainments an unbridled extravagance; we render impossible in such ways any semblance of a Christian life, and do our best to destroy Christian ideas already established; and then, after doing all we can to demoralize men, we take and confine them like wild beasts in places from which they cannot escape, and where they will become more brutal than ever; or we murder the men we have demoralized, and then use them as an example to illustrate and prove our argument that people are only to be controlled by violence.

Even so does the ignorant physician act, who, having placed his patient in the most unsanitary conditions, or having administered to him poisonous drugs, afterwards contends that his patient has succumbed to the disease, when had he been left to himself he would have recovered long ago.

Violence, which men regard as an instrument for the support of Christian life, on the contrary prevents the social system from reaching its full and perfect development. The social system is such as it is, not because of violence, but in spite of it.

Therefore the defenders of the existing social system are self-deceived when they say that, since violence barely holds the evil and un-Christian elements of society in awe, its subversion and the substitution of the moral influence of public opinion would leave us helpless in face of them. They are wrong, because violence does not protect mankind; but it deprives men of the only possible chance of an effectual defence by the establishment and propagation of the Christian principle of life.

"But how can one discard the visible and tangible protection of the policeman with his baton and trust to invisible, intangible public opinion? And moreover, is not its very existence problematical? We are all familiar with the actual state of things; whether it be good or bad we know its faults, and are accustomed to them; we know how to conduct ourselves, how to act in the present conditions; but what will happen when we renounce the present organization and confide ourselves to something invisible, intangible, and utterly unfamiliar?"

Men dread the uncertainty into which they would plunge if they were to renounce the familiar order of things. Certainly were our situation an assured and stable one, it would be well to dread the uncertainties of change. But so far from enjoying an assured position, we know that we are on the verge of a catastrophe.

If we are to give way to fear, then let it be before something that is really fearful, and not before something that we imagine may be so.

In fearing to make an effort to escape from conditions that are fatal to us, only because the future is obscure and unknown, we are like the passengers of a sinking ship who crowd into the cabin and refuse to leave it, because they have not the courage to enter the boat that would carry them to the shore; or like sheep, who in fear of the fire that has broken out in the farmyard, huddle together in a corner and will not go out through the open gate.

How can we, who stand on the threshold of a shocking and devastating social war, before which, as those who are preparing for it tell us, the horrors of 1793 will pale, talk seriously about the danger threatened by the natives of Dahomey, the Zulus, and others who live far away, and who have no intention of attacking us; or about the few thousands of malefactors, thieves, and murderers – men whom we have helped to demoralize, and whose numbers are not decreased by all our courts, prisons, and executions?

Moreover, this anxiety, lest the visible protection of the police be overthrown, is chiefly confined to the inhabitants of cities – that is, to those who live under abnormal and artificial conditions. Those who live normally in the midst of nature, dealing with its forces, require no such protection; they realize how little avails violence to protect us from the real danger that surrounds us. There is something morbid in this fear, which arises chiefly from the false conditions in which most of us have grown up and continue to live.

A doctor to the insane related how, one day in summer, when he was about to leave the asylum, the patients accompanied him as far as the gate that led into the street.

"Come with me into town!" he proposed to them.

The patients agreed, and a little band followed him. But the farther they went through the streets where they met their sane fellowmen moving freely to and fro, the more timid they grew, and pressed more closely around the doctor. At last they begged to be taken back to the asylum, to their old but accustomed mode of insane life, to their keepers and their rough ways, to straitjackets and solitary confinement.

And thus it is with those whom Christianity is waiting to set free, to whom it offers the untrammelled rational life of the future, the coming century; they huddle together and cling to their insane customs, to their factories, courts, and prisons, their executioners, and their warfare.

They ask: "What security will there be for us when the existing order has been swept away? What kind of laws are to take the place of those under which we are now living? Not until we know exactly how our life is to be ordered will we take a single step towards making a change." It is as if a discoverer were to insist upon detailed description of the region he is about to explore. If the individual man, while passing from one period of his life to another, could read the future and know just what his whole life were to be, he would have no reason for living. And so it is with the career of humanity. If, upon entering a new period, a programme detailing the incidents of its future existence were possible, humanity would stagnate.

We cannot know the conditions of the new order of things, because we have to work them out for ourselves. The meaning of life is to search out that which is hidden, and then to conform our activity to our new knowledge.

This is the life of the individual as it is the life of humanity.

CHAPTER XI

Christian Public Opinion Already Arises in Our Society, and Will Inevitably Destroy the System of Violence of Our Life

WHEN THIS WILL COME about. The condition and organization of our society is shocking; it is upheld by public opinion, but can be abolished by it – Men's views in regard to violence have already changed; the number of men ready to serve the governments decreases, and functionaries of government themselves begin to be ashamed of their position, to the point of often not fulfilling their duties – These facts signs of the birth of a public opinion, which, in becoming more and more general, will lead finally to the impossibility of finding men willing to serve governments – It becomes more and more clear that such positions are no longer needed – Men begin to realize the uselessness of all the institutions of violence; and if this is realized by a few men, it will later be understood by all – The time when the deliverance will be accomplished is unknown, but it depends on men themselves; it depends on how much each man is willing to live by the light that is within him.

The position of the Christian nations, with their prisons, their gallows, their factories, their accumulations of capital, taxes, churches, taverns, and public brothels, their increasing armaments and their millions of besotted men, ready, like dogs, to spring at a word from the master, would be shocking indeed if it were the result of violence; but such a state of things is before all the result of public opinion; and what has been established by public opinion not only maybe, but will be, overthrown by it.

Millions and millions of money, tens of millions of disciplined soldiers, marvellous weapons of destruction, an infinitely perfected organization, legions of men charged to delude and hypnotize the people – this is all under the control of men who believe that this organization is advantageous for them, who know that without it they would disappear, and who therefore devote all their energy to its maintenance. What an indomitable array of power it seems! And yet we have but to realize whither we are fatally tending, for men to become as much ashamed of acts of violence, and to profit by them, as they are ashamed now of dishonesty, theft, beggary, cowardice; and the whole complicated and apparently omnipotent system will die at once without any struggle. To accomplish this transformation it is not necessary that any new ideas should find their way into the human consciousness, but only that the mist which now veils the true significance of violence should lift, in order that the growing Christian public opinion and methods may conquer the methods of the pagan world. And this is gradually coming to pass. We do not observe it, as we do not observe the movement of things when we are turning and everything around us is turning as well.

It is true that the social organization seems for the most part as much under the influence of violence as it seemed a thousand years ago, and in respect of armaments and war seems even more; but the Christian view of life is already having its effect. The withered tree, to all appearance, stands as firmly as ever; it seems even firmer, because it has grown harder, but it is already rotten at the heart and preparing to fall. It is the same with the present mode of life, based upon violence. The outward position of man appears the same. There are the same oppressors, the same oppressed, but the feeling of both classes in regard to their respective positions has undergone a change. The oppressors, that is, those who take part in the government, and those who are benefited by oppression, the wealthy classes, do not constitute, as formerly, the 'elite of society, nor does their condition suggest that ideal of human prosperity and greatness to which formerly all the oppressed aspired. Now, it often happens that the oppressors renounce of their own accord the advantages of their position, choosing the position of the oppressed, and endeavour, by the simplicity of their mode of life, to resemble them.

Not to speak of those offices and positions generally considered contemptible, such as that of the spy, the detective, the usurer, or the keeper of a tavern, a great many of the positions held by the oppressors, and formerly considered honourable, such as those of police officers, courtiers, judges, administrative functionaries, ecclesiastical or military, masters on a large scale, and bankers, are not only considered little enviable, but are already avoided by estimable men. Already there are men who choose to renounce such once envied positions, preferring others which, although less advantageous, are not associated with violence.

It is not merely such as these who renounce their privileges; men influenced, not by religious motives, as was the case in former ages, but by growing public opinion, refuse to accept fortunes fallen to them by inheritance, because they believe that a man ought to possess only the fruits of his own labour.

High-minded youths, not as yet depraved by life, when about to choose a career, prefer the professions of doctors, engineers, teachers, artists, writers, or even of farmers, who live by their daily toil, to the positions of judges, administrators, priests, soldiers in the pay of government; they decline even the position of living on their income.

Most of the monuments at the present day are no longer erected in honour of statesmen or generals, still less of men of wealth, but to scientists, artists, and inventors, to men who not only had nothing in common with government or authority, but who frequently opposed it. It is to their memory that the arts are thus consecrated.

The class of men who will govern, and of rich men, tends every day to grow less numerous, and so far as intellect, education, and especially morality, are concerned, rich men and men in power are not the most distinguished members of society, as was the case in olden times. In Russia and Turkey, as in France and America, notwithstanding the frequent changes of officials, the greater number are often covetous and venal, and so little to be commended from the point of view of morality that they do not satisfy even the elementary exigencies of honesty demanded in government posts. Thus one hears often the ingenuous complaints of those in government that the best men among us, strangely enough as it seems to them, are always found among those opposed to them. It is as if one complained that it is not the nice, good people who become hangmen.

Rich men of the present day, as a general thing, are mere vulgar amassers of wealth, for the most part having but little care beyond that of increasing their capital, and that most often by impure means; or are the degenerate inheritors, who, far from playing an important part in society, often incur general contempt.

Many positions have lost their ancient importance. Kings and emperors now hardly direct at all; they seldom effect internal changes or modify external policy, leaving the decision of such questions to the departments of State, or to public opinion. Their function is reduced to being the representatives of State unity and power. But even this duty they begin to neglect. Most of them not only fail to maintain themselves in their former unapproachable majesty, but they grow more and more democratic, they prefer even to be bourgeois; they lay down thus their last distinction, destroying precisely what they are expected to maintain.

The same may be said of the army. The high officers, instead of encouraging the roughness and cruelty of the soldiers, which befit their occupation, promote the diffusion of education among them, preach humanity, often sympathize with the socialistic ideas of the masses, and deny the utility of war. In the late conspiracies against the Russian government many of those concerned were military men. It often happens, as it did recently, that the troops, when called upon to establish order, refuse to fire on the people. The barrack code of ideas is frankly deprecated by military men themselves, who often enough make it the subject of derision.

The same may be said of judges and lawyers. Judges, whose duty it is to judge and condemn criminals, conduct their trials in such a fashion as to prove them innocent; thus the Russian government, when it desires the condemnation of those it wishes to punish, never confides them to the ordinary tribunals; it tries them by court-martial, which is but a parody of justice. The same may be said of lawyers, who often refuse to accuse, and, twisting round the law, defend those they should accuse. Learned jurists, whose duty it is to justify the violence of authority, deny more and more frequently the right of punishment, and in its place introduce theories of irresponsibility, often prescribing not punishment but medical treatment for so-called criminals.

Gaolers and turnkeys in convict prisons often become the protectors of those it is a part of their business to torture. Policemen and detectives are constantly saving those they ought to arrest. Ecclesiastics preach tolerance; they often deny the right of violence, and the more educated among them attempt in their sermons to avoid the deception which constitutes all the meaning of their position, and which they are expected to preach.

Executioners refuse to perform their duty; the result is that often in Russia death warrants cannot be carried out for lack of executioners, for, notwithstanding all the advantages of the position, the candidates, who are chosen from convicts, diminish in number every year. Governors, commissioners, and tax collectors, pitying the people, often try to find pretexts for remitting the taxes. Rich men no longer dare to use their wealth for themselves alone, but sacrifice a part of it to social charities. Landowners establish hospitals and schools on their estates, and some even renounce their estates and bestow them on the cultivators of the soil, or establish agricultural colonies upon them. Manufacturers and mill-owners found schools, hospitals, and savings banks, institute pensions, and build houses for the workmen; some start associations of which the profits are equally divided among all. Capitalists expend a portion of their wealth on educational, artistic, and philanthropic institutions for the public benefit. Many men who are unwilling to part with their riches during their lifetime bequeath them to public institutions.

These facts might be deemed the result of chance were it not that they all originate from one source, as, when certain trees begin to bud in the spring of the year, we might believe it accidental, only we know the cause; and that if on some trees the buds begin to swell, we know that the same thing will happen to all of them.

Even so is it in regard to Christian public opinion and its manifestations. If this public opinion already influences some of the more sensitive men, and makes each one in his own sphere decline the advantages obtained by violence or its use, it will continue to influence men more and more, until it brings about a change in their mode of life and reconciles it with that Christian consciousness already possessed by the most advanced.

And if there are already rulers who do not venture on any undertaking on their own responsibility, and who try to be like ordinary men rather than monarchs, who declare themselves ready to give up their prerogatives and become the first citizens of their country, and soldiers who, realizing all the sin and evil of war, do not wish to kill either foreigners or their fellow countrymen, judges and lawyers who do not wish to accuse and condemn criminals, priests who evade preaching lies, tax-gatherers who endeavour to fulfil as gently as possible what they are called upon to do, and rich men who give up their wealth, then surely it will ultimately come to pass that other rulers, soldiers, priests, and rich men will follow their example. And when there are no more men ready to occupy positions supported by violence, the positions themselves will cease to exist.

But this is not the only way by which public opinion leads towards the abolition of the existing system and the substitution of a new one. As the positions supported by violence become by degrees less and less attractive, and there are fewer and fewer applicants to fill them, their uselessness becomes more and more apparent.

We have today the same rulers and governments, the same armies, courts of law, tax-gatherers, priests, wealthy landowners, manufacturers, and capitalists as formerly, but their relative positions are changed.

The same rulers go about to their various interviews, they have the same meetings, hunts, festivities, balls, and uniforms; the same diplomatists have the same conversations about alliances and armies; the same parliaments, in which Eastern and African questions are discussed, and questions in regard to alliances, ruptures, "Home Rule," the eight-hour day. Changes of ministry take place just as of old, accompanied by the same speeches and incidents. But to those who know how an article in a newspaper changes perhaps the position of affairs more than dozens of royal interviews and parliamentary sessions, it becomes more and more evident that it is not these meetings, interviews, and parliamentary discussions that control affairs, but something independent of all this, something which has no local habitation.

The same generals, officers, soldiers, cannon, fortresses, parades, and evolutions. But one year elapses, ten, twenty years elapse, and there is no war. And troops are less and less to be relied on to suppress insurrection, and it becomes more and more evident that generals, officers, and soldiers are only figureheads in triumphal processions, the plaything of a sovereign, a sort of unwieldy and expensive *corps-de-ballet.*

The same lawyers and judges, and the same sessions, but it becomes more and more evident that as civil courts make decisions in a great variety of causes without anxiety about purely legal justice, and that criminal courts are useless, because the punishment does not produce the desired result, therefore these institutions have no other object than the maintenance of men incapable of doing other things more useful.

The same priests, bishops, churches, and synods, but it becomes more and more evident to all that these men themselves have long since ceased to believe what they preach, and are therefore unable to persuade any one of the necessity of believing what they no longer believe themselves.

The same tax-gatherers, but more and more incapable of extorting money from the people by force, and it becomes more and more evident that without such collectors it would be possible to obtain by voluntary contribution all that is required for social needs.

The same rich men, and yet it becomes more and more evident that they can be useful only when they cease to be personal administrators of their possessions, and surrender to society their wealth in whole or part.

When this becomes as plain to all men as it now is to a few, the question will naturally arise – Why should we feed and support all those emperors, kings, presidents, members of departments and ministers, if all their interviews and conversations amount to nothing? Would it not be better, as some wit expressed it, to set up an India-rubber queen?

And of what use to us are armies, with their generals, their musicians, their horses, and drums? Of what use are they when there is no war, when no one wishes to conquer anybody else? And even if there were a war, other nations would prevent us from reaping its advantages; while upon their compatriots the troops would refuse to fire.

And what is the use of judges and attorneys, whose decisions in civil cases are not according to the law, and who, in criminal ones, are aware that punishments are of no avail?

And of what use are tax-gatherers who are reluctant to collect the taxes, when all that is needed could be contributed without their assistance?

And where is the use of a clergy which has long ceased to believe what it preaches?

And of what use is capital in the hands of private individuals when it can be beneficial only when it becomes public property? Having once asked all these questions, men cannot but arrive at the conclusion that institutions which have lost their usefulness should no longer be supported.

And furthermore, men who themselves occupy positions of privilege come to see the necessity of abandoning them.

One day, in Moscow, I was present at a religious discussion which is usually held during St. Thomas's week, near the church in the Okhotny Ryad. A group of perhaps twenty men had gathered on the pavement, and a serious discussion concerning religion was in progress. Meanwhile, in the nobles' club near at hand, a concert was taking place, and a police officer, having noticed the group of people gathered near the church, sent a mounted policeman to order them to disperse – not that the police officer cared in the least whether the group stayed where it was or dispersed. The twenty men who had gathered inconvenienced no one, but the officer had been on duty all the morning and felt obliged to do something. The young policeman, a smart-looking fellow, with his right arm akimbo and a clanking sword, rode up to us, calling out in an imperative tone: "Disperse, you fellows! What business have you to gather there?" Every one turned to look at him, while one of the speakers, a modest-looking man in a peasant's coat, replied calmly and pleasantly: "We are talking about business, and there is no reason why we should disperse;

it might be better for you, my young friend, if you were to jump off from your horse and to listen to us. Very likely it would do you good;" and turning away he continued the conversation. The policeman turned his horse without a word and rode away.

Such scenes as this must be of frequent occurrence in countries where violence is employed. The officer was bored; he had nothing to do, and the poor fellow was placed in a position where he felt in duty bound to give orders. He was deprived of a rational human existence; he could do nothing but look on and give orders, give orders and look on, although both were works of supererogation. It will not be long before all those unfortunate rulers, ministers, members of parliaments, governors, generals, officers, bishops, priests, and even rich men will find themselves – indeed they have already done so – in precisely the same position. Their sole occupation consists in issuing orders; they send out their subordinates, like the officer who sent the policeman to interfere with the people; and as the people with whom they interfere ask not to be interfered with, this seems to their official intelligence only to prove that they are very necessary.

But the time will surely come when it will be perfectly evident to everyone that they are not only useless, but an actual impediment, and those whose course they obstruct will say gently and pleasantly, like the man in the peasant's coat: "We beg that you will let us alone." Then the subordinates as well as their instructors will find themselves compelled to take the good advice that is offered them, cease to prance about among men with their arms akimbo, and having discarded their glittering livery, listen to what is said among men, and unite with them to help to promote the serious work of the world.

Sooner or later the time will surely come when all the present institutions supported by violence will cease to be; their too evident uselessness, absurdity, and even unseemliness will finally destroy them.

There must come a time when the same thing that happened to the king in Andersen's fairy tale, *The King's New Clothes*, will happen to men occupying positions created by violence.

The tale tells of a king who cared enormously for new clothes, and to whom one day came two tailors who agreed to make him a suit woven from a wonderful stuff. The king engaged them and they set to work, saying that the stuff possessed the remarkable quality of becoming invisible to any one unfit for the office he holds. The courtiers came to inspect the work of the tailors, but could see nothing, because these men were drawing their needles through empty space. However, remembering the consequences, they all pretended to see the cloth and to be very much pleased with it. Even the king himself praised it. The hour appointed for the procession when he was to walk wearing his new garment arrived. The king took off his clothes and put on the new ones – that is, he remained naked all the while, and thus he went in procession. But remembering the consequences, no one had the courage to say that he was not dressed, until a little child, catching sight of the naked king, innocently exclaimed, "But he has nothing on!" Whereupon all the others who had known this before, but had not acknowledged it, could no longer conceal the fact.

Thus will it be with those who, through inertia, continue to fill offices that have long ceased to be of any consequence, until some chance observer, who happens not to be engaged, as the Russian proverb has it, in" washing one hand with the other," will ingenuously exclaim: "It is a long time since these men were good for anything!"

The position of the Christian world, with its fortresses, cannon, dynamite, guns, torpedoes, prisons, gallows, churches, factories, customhouses, and palaces, is monstrous. But neither fortresses nor cannon nor guns by themselves can make war, nor can the prisons lock their gates, nor the gallows hang, nor the churches themselves lead men astray, nor the custom houses claim their dues, nor palaces and factories build and support themselves; all these operations are performed by men. And when men understand that they need not make them, then these things will cease to be.

And already men are beginning to understand this. If not yet understood by all, it is already understood by those whom the rest of the world eventually follows. And it is impossible to cease to understand what once has been understood, and the masses not only can, but inevitably must follow where those who have understood have already led the way.

Hence the prophecy: that a time will come when all men will hearken unto the word of God, will forget the art of war, will melt their swords into ploughshares and their lances into reaping hooks; which, being translated means when all the prisons, the fortresses, the barracks, the palaces, and the churches will remain empty, the gallows and the cannon will be useless. This is no longer a mere Utopia, but a new and definite system of life towards which mankind is progressing with ever increasing rapidity. But when will it come?

Eighteen hundred years ago Christ, in answer to this question, replied that the end of the present world – that is, of the pagan system – would come when the miseries of man had increased to their utmost limit; and when, at the same time, the good news of the Kingdom of Heaven – that is, of the possibility of a new system, one not founded upon violence – should be proclaimed throughout the earth.

"But of that day and hour knoweth no man, no, not the angels of heaven, but my Father only," (Matthew xxiv: 36) said Christ. *"Watch therefore: for ye know not what hour your Lord doth come." Matthew xxiv: 42.*

When will the hour arrive? Christ said that we cannot know. And for that very reason we should hold ourselves in readiness to meet it, as the good man should watch his house against thieves, or like the virgins who await with their lamps the coming of the bridegroom, and moreover we should work with all our might to hasten the coming of that hour, as the servants should use the talents they have received that they may increase.

And there can be no other answer. The day and the hour of the advent of the Kingdom of God men cannot know, since the coming of that hour depends only on men themselves. Matthew xxiv: 43 and xxvi: 13, 14–30.

The reply is like that of the wise man who, when the traveller asked him how far he was from the city, answered, "Go on!"

How can we know if it is still far to the goal towards which humanity is aiming, when we do not know how it will move towards it, that it depends on humanity whether it moves steadily onward or pauses, whether it accelerates or retards its pace.

All that we can know is what we who form humanity should or should not do in order to bring about this Kingdom of God. And that we all know, for each one has but to begin to do his duty, each one has but to live according to the light that is within him, to bring about the immediate advent of the promised Kingdom of God, for which the heart of every man yearns.

CHAPTER XII

Conclusion

"Repent, For the Kingdom of Heaven is at Hand!"

I

ENCOUNTER WITH A train carrying soldiers to establish order among famine-stricken peasants – The cause of the disorder – How the mandates of the higher authorities are carried out in case of peasants' resistance – The affair at Orel as an example of violence and murder committed for the purpose of asserting the rights of the rich – All the advantages of the rich are founded on like acts of violence.

II

THE TULA TRAIN and the behaviour of the persons composing it – How men can behave as these do – The reasons are neither ignorance, nor cruelty, nor cowardice, nor lack of comprehension or of moral sense – They do these things because they think them necessary to maintain the existing system, to support which they believe to be every man's duty – On what the belief of the necessity and immutability of the existing order of things is founded – For the upper classes it is based on the advantages it affords them – But what compels men of the lower classes to believe in the immutability of this system, when they derive no advantage from it, and maintain it with acts contrary to their conscience?

The reason lies in the deceit practised by the upper classes upon the lower in regard to the necessity of the existing order, and the legitimacy of acts of violence for its maintenance – General deception – Special deception – The conscription.

THE KINGDOM OF GOD IS WITHIN YOU

III

HOW MEN RECONCILE the legitimacy of murder with the precepts of morality, and how they admit the existence in their midst of a military organization for purposes of violence which incessantly threatens the safety of society? Admitted only by the powers for whom the present organization is advantageous – Violence sanctioned by the higher authorities and carried out by the lower, notwithstanding the knowledge of its immorality, because, owing to the organization of the State, the moral responsibility is divided among a large number of participants, each of whom considers some other than himself responsible – Moreover, the loss of consciousness of moral responsibility is also due to a mistaken opinion as to the inequality of men, the consequent abuse of power by the authorities, and servility of the lower classes – The condition of men who commit acts contrary to their conscience is like the condition of a hypnotized person acting under the influence of suggestion – In what does submission to the suggestion of the State differ from submission to men of a higher order of consciousness or to public opinion? – The present system, which is the outcome of ancient public opinion, and which is already in contradiction to the modern, is maintained only through torpor of conscience, induced by auto-suggestion among the upper classes, and by the hypnotization of the lower – The conscience or intelligent consciousness of these men may awaken, and there are instances when it does awaken; therefore it cannot be said that any one of them will, or will not do what he sets out to do – Everything depends on the degree of comprehension of the illegitimacy of the acts of violence, and this consciousness in men may either awaken spontaneously or be roused by those already awakened.

IV

EVERYTHING DEPENDS UPON the strength of conviction of each individual man in regard to Christian truth – But the advanced men of the present day consider it unnecessary to explain and profess Christian truth, regarding it

sufficient for the improvement of human life to change its outward conditions within the limits allowed by power – Upon this
scientific theory of hypocrisy, which has taken the place of the
hypocrisy of religion, men of the wealthy classes base the justification of their position – In consequence of this hypocrisy,
maintained by violence and falsehood, they can pretend before
each other to be Christians, and rest content – The same hypocrisy allows men who preach the Christian doctrine to take part
in a regime of violence – No external improvements of life can
make it less miserable; its miseries are caused by disunion; disunion springs from following falsehood instead of truth – Union
is possible only in truth – Hypocrisy forbids such a union, for
while remaining hypocrites, men conceal from themselves and
others the truth they know – Hypocrisy changes into evil everything destined to ameliorate life – It perverts the conception
of right and wrong, and therefore is a bar to the perfection of
men – Acknowledged malefactors and criminals do less harm
than those who live by legalized violence cloaked by hypocrisy –
All recognize the iniquity of our life, and would long since have
modified it, if it were not covered by the cloak of hypocrisy – But
it seems as if we had reached the limits of hypocrisy, and have
but to make an effort of consciousness in order to awaken – like
the man who has a nightmare – to a different reality.

V

C AN MAN MAKE this effort? – According to the existing hypocritical theory, man is not free to change his
life – He is not free in his acts, but is always free to acknowledge or disregard certain truths already known to him –
The recognition of truth is the cause of action – The cause of
the apparent insolvability of the question of man's freedom – It
lies only in the acknowledgment of the truth revealed unto him
– No other freedom exists – The acknowledgment of the truth
gives freedom, and points the way in which a man willingly or
unwillingly must walk – The recognition of truth and of true
freedom allows man to become a participant of the work of God,
to be not the slave but a creator of life – Men have but to forego

the attempt to improve the external conditions of life, and direct all their energies towards the recognition and profession of the truth that is known to them, and the present painful system of life will vanish forthwith, and that portion of the Kingdom of God which is accessible to men would-be established – One has only to cease lying and shamming to accomplish this – But what awaits us in the future? – What will happen to mankind when they begin to obey the dictates of their conscience, and how will they exist without the customary conditions of civilization? – Nothing truly good and beneficial can perish because of the realization of the truth, but will only increase in strength when freed from the admixture of falsehood and hypocrisy.

VI

OUR SYSTEM OF LIFE has reached the limit of misery, and cannot be ameliorated by any pagan reorganization – All our life, with its pagan institutions, is devoid of meaning – Are we obeying the will of God in maintaining our present privileges and obligations? – We are in this position, not because such is the law of the universe, that it is inevitable, but because we wish it, because it is advantageous for some of us – All our consciousness contradicts this, and our deliverance consists in acknowledging the Christian truth, not to do to one's neighbour that which one would not have done to oneself – As our obligations in regard to ourselves should be subordinate to our obligations to others, so in like manner our obligations to others should be subordinate to our obligations to God – Deliverance from our position consists, if not in giving up our position and its rights at once, at least in acknowledging our guilt, and neither lying nor trying to justify ourselves – The true significance of our life consists in knowing and professing the truth, whereas our approval of, and our activity in the service of the State, takes all meaning from life – God demands that we serve Him, that is, that we seek to establish the greatest degree of union among all human beings, which union is possible only in truth.

I was just putting the finishing touches to this two year's work, when on the 9th day of September I had occasion to go by rail to visit districts in the governments of Tula and Ryazan, where certain peasants were suffering from last year's famine, and others were enduring still greater suffering from the same causes this year. At one of the stations the train in which I was a passenger met the express, which carried the Governor and troops supplied with rods and loaded rifles for torturing and murdering the famine-stricken peasants.

Although corporal punishment was legally abolished in Russia thirty years ago, the custom of flogging as a means of making the decisions of authority respected has been revived, and has of late been frequently employed. I had heard of it, had read in the papers of the frightful tortures of which the Governor of Nijni-Novgorod, Baranov, has gone so far as to boast, and of the tortures that have been inflicted in Tchernigov, Tambov, Saratov, Astrakhan, and Orel, but I had never yet witnessed, as I did now, how these things were actually done.

And I myself saw well-meaning Russians, penetrated with the spirit of Christ, but armed with muskets and carrying rods, on their way to murder and torture their starving brothers.

The pretext was as follows:

On the estate of a rich landowner, upon a piece of ground held by him in common with the peasants, a forest had been allowed to grow. (When I say that the forest "grew," I mean that the peasants had not only planted it, but had continued to take care of it.) They had always had the use of it, and therefore looked upon it as their own, or at least as common property; but the landowner, confiscating it entirely to himself, began to cut down the trees. The peasants lodged a complaint. The judge of the lower court pronounced an illegal decision (I call it illegal on the authority of the Attorney General and the Governor, who surely ought to understand the case) in favour of the landowner. The higher courts, as well as the Senate, although they could see that the case had been unfairly tried, confirmed the decision, and the wood was awarded to the landowner, who continued to fell the trees. But the peasants, believing it impossible that such an injustice could be perpetrated by the higher magistrates, refused to submit to the decision, and drove away the workmen sent to cut down the trees, saying that the forest belonged to them, and that they would appeal to the Czar himself before they would allow it to be touched.

The case was reported to St. Petersburg, from whence the Governor received the order to enforce the decision of the courts, and in order to execute the command, asked for troops.

Hence these soldiers who, armed with bayonets and provided with cartridges and rods, expressly prepared for the occasion and stored in one of the vans, were on their way to enforce the decision of the higher authorities. The execution of an order from the ruling powers can be accomplished either by threats of torture and death, or by the enforcement of those threats, according to the degree of resistance on the part of the people.

If, for instance, in Russia (it is practically the same in other lands where State authority and the rights of ownership exist), the peasants offer to resist, the result is as follows: The superior officer makes a speech and orders them to obey. The excited crowd, accustomed to be duped by those in high places, understands not a word that the representative of authority is saying in his official, conventional language, and is by no means pacified. Whereupon the commanding officer declares that unless they submit and disperse, he will be forced to have recourse to arms. If the crowd still refuses to yield and does not disperse, he orders his men to load the muskets and to fire over their heads, and then if the peasants still stand their ground he orders the soldiers to aim at the crowd; they fire, and men fall wounded and killed in the street. The crowd is dispersed, the soldiers, carrying out the orders of their commanders, having laid hands upon those whom they suppose to be the chief instigators, and arrested them. The dying, stained with blood, the wounded, mutilated, and dead, among whom are often women and children, are picked up. The dead are buried, the wounded sent to the hospitals. Those who are supposed to be the ringleaders are taken to the city and court-martialled, and if proved that they have used violence they are summarily hung. This has happened in Russia repeatedly, and similar scenes must take place wherever the system of government is based upon violence. Such is the course adopted in cases of revolt.

If, on the other hand, the peasants submit, the scene that

ensues is entirely original and peculiarly Russian. The Governor, on his arrival at the place, either quarters the soldiers in the different houses of the village, where their maintenance ruins the peasants, or, satisfied by threatening the people, he graciously pardons them and departs. Or, as more frequently happens, he addresses the multitude, upbraids it for disobedience, and announces that the ringleaders must be punished; he seizes a certain number of men considered as such, and without any form of trial causes them to be beaten with rods in his presence.

In order to give an idea of the manner in which such an affair is conducted, I will describe an instance of the kind which happened in Orel, which was approved by the higher authorities. Like the landowner in Tula, the landed proprietor at Orel chose to take possession of the peasant's property, and here too, as in the former instance, the peasants resisted. In this case the landowner, without the consent of the peasants, wished to dam up, for the benefit of his mill, the flow of water that supplied the meadows. The peasants resisted this.

The landlord lodged a complaint with the rural commissary, who illegally (as was afterwards admitted by the court) decided the case in favour of the landowner, giving him leave to divert the water. The landowner sent workmen to close the channel through which the water descended. The peasants, excited at this unfair judgment, sent their women to prevent the landowner's men from damming the channel. The women proceeded to the dam, upset the carts, and drove the workmen away. The landowner entered a complaint against them for committing a lawless act. The rural commissary gave the order to arrest and lock up in the village gaol one woman out of every family – an order rather difficult to execute, since each family included several women, and as it was impossible to tell which of them to arrest, the police could not fulfil the order. The landowner complained to the Governor of the laxity of the police. The Governor, without stopping to consider the case, gave strict orders to the Ispravnik to carry out at once the orders of the rural commissary. In obedience to his superior the Ispravnik arrived in the village, and with that contempt for the individual peculiar to Russian authorities, ordered the police to seize the first women they could. Disputes and resistance arose. The Ispravnik, paying no attention to this, persisted in his order that the police should take one woman, innocent or guilty, from every household, and put her under arrest. The peasants defended their wives and mothers; they refused to give them up, and resisted the police and the Ispravnik. Thus another and a greater offence was committed – resistance to authority – which was at once reported in town. Then the Governor, just as I saw the Governor of Tula, with a battalion of soldiers, supplied with rods and muskets, backed by all due accessories of telegraph and telephone, accompanied by a learned physician, who was to superintend the flogging from a medical standpoint, started on an express train for the spot, like the modern Genghis Khan predicted by Herten. In the Volostnoye Pravlenie were the soldiers, a detachment of police with their revolvers suspended on red cords, the principal peasants of the neighbourhood, and the men accused. Around them had collected a crowd of perhaps a thousand.

Driving up to the house of the Volostnoye Pravlenie, the Governor alighted from his carriage and delivered an address, which had been prepared in advance, after which he inquired for the criminals, and ordered a bench to be brought. No one understood what he meant, until the policeman who always accompanied the Governor and made all the arrangements for the punishments, which had already been enforced several times in the government of Orel, explained that the bench was to be used for flogging. This bench and the rods that had been brought by the party were both produced. The executioners had been previously selected from certain horse thieves taken from the same village, the military having refused to do the business.

When all was ready the Governor bade the first of the twelve men who were pointed out to him by the landowner as the ringleaders to step forward. It so happened that he was the father of a family, a man forty-five years of age, respected in the community, whose rights he had manfully defended.

He was led to the bench, stripped, and ordered to lie down.

He would have begged for mercy, but realizing how little it would avail, he made the sign of the cross and stretched himself out on the bench. Two policemen held him down, and the learned doctor stood by, ready in case of need to give his scientific assistance. The executioners having spat upon their hands, swung the rods, and the flogging began. The bench, it seemed, was too narrow, and it was found difficult to keep the writhing victim, whose muscles twitched convulsively, from falling off. Then the Governor ordered to be brought another bench, to which a plank was adjusted in such a way as to support it. The soldiers, eveready with their continual salutes and responses of "Yes, your Excellency," swiftly and obediently executed the orders, while in the meantime the half-naked, pale, and suffering man, trembling, with contracted brows and down cast eyes, stood by waiting. When the bench was readjusted, he was again stretched out upon it, and the "horse-stealers" renewed their blows. His back, his legs, and even his sides were covered with bleeding wounds, and every blow was followed by the muffled groan which he could no longer repress. In the crowd that stood by, one could hear the sobs of the wife and mother, the children and the kinsfolk of the man, as well as of all who had been called to witness the punishment.

The wretched Governor, intoxicated with power, who had no doubt convinced himself of the necessity for this performance, counted the strokes on his fingers, while he smoked cigarette after cigarette, for the lighting of which several obliging persons hastened to offer him a burning match.

After fifty blows had been given, the peasant lay motionless, without uttering a sound, and the doctor, who had been educated in a government school, that he might devote his scientific knowledge to the service of his country and his sovereign, approached the tortured man, felt his pulse, listened to the beating of his heart, and reported to the representative of authority that the victim had become unconscious, and declared that, from a scientific point of view, it might prove dangerous to prolong the punishment. But the unfortunate Governor, utterly intoxicated by the sight of blood, ordered the flogging to go on, until seventy strokes had been given, the number which he for some reason deemed necessary. After the seventieth blow the Governor said:

"That will do! Now bring on the next one!"

They raised the mutilated and unconscious man with his

swollen back, and carried him away, and the next was brought forward. The sobs and groans of the crowd increased, but the tortures were continued.

So it went on until each of the twelve men had received seventy strokes. They begged for mercy, they groaned and screamed. The sobs and moans of the women grew louder and more heartrending, and the faces of the men of the crowd more gloomy. But there stood the troops, and the torture did not cease until it had seemed sufficient to the unfortunate, half-intoxicated, erring man called the Governor.

Not only did the magistrates, the officers, and the soldiers sanction this act by their presence, but they took part in it, preventing the crowd from interfering with the order of its execution.

When I asked one of the chief officials why these tortures were inflicted after the men had already submitted, he replied with the significant air of a man who understands all the fine points of political wisdom, that it was done because it had been proved by experience that if the peasants are not punished they will soon begin again to oppose the decrees of authority, and that the punishment of a few strengthens for ever the power of authority.

And now I saw the Governor of Tula, with his clerks, officers, and soldiers, on his way to perform a similar act. Once more by murder or torture the sentence of the higher authorities was to be carried out – a sentence whose object was to enable a young landowner, the possessor of a yearly income of 100,000 roubles, to receive 3000 more for a tract of wood of which he had basely defrauded a whole community of needy and starving peasants, the price of which he would squander in a few weeks in the restaurants of St. Petersburg, Moscow, and Paris. Such was the errand of the men I met.

It would seem as if there must be some purpose in this encounter, when, after two years of incessant contemplation, of continuous thought in one direction, fate should, for the first time in my life, bring me face to face with this phenomenon, a living illustration of the theory I have so long cherished, namely, that the entire organization of our life rests not on any principle of justice, as men who occupy and enjoy advantageous positions under the existing system like to imagine, but on the rudest and most barefaced violence, on the murder and torture of human beings.

Those who possess large estates and large capital, or who receive high salaries collected from the needy working classes, from the people who often lack the necessaries of life; merchants, clerks, doctors, lawyers, artists, scientists, writers, coachmen, cooks, and valets, who earn their living in the service of rich men, fondly believe that the privileges which they enjoy are not the outcome of violence, but the natural result of a voluntary interchange of services; that these privileges are by no means the result of the outrages and floggings endured by their fellowmen, such as took place last summer in Russia, in Orel and elsewhere, as the like took place in many parts of Europe and America. They prefer to believe that the privileges they enjoy are the spontaneous result of a mutual agreement among men; that violence is only the natural result of certain universal and superior laws, judicial, political, or economic. They try not to see that the privileges they possess are only held by them inconsequence of some circumstance, not unlike that which compelled the peasants who had tended the growing fore stand greatly needed it, to surrender it to the rich landowner, who had taken no pains to preserve it, and who did not require it for his own use; men who will either be flogged or murdered if they refuse to surrender it. Now, if it is an undeniable fact that the mill in Orel was made to yield an increased income to the proprietor, and that the forest raised by the peasants was given to the landowner, only because of the flogging and the executions either threatened or actually suffered, then it must be equally evident that all the other exclusive rights of the rich, which deprive the poor of the bare necessaries of life, rest on the same basis.

If the peasants who need land in order to support their families may not cultivate the land around them, and if land, sufficient to feed a thousand families, is in the hands of one man, a Russian, an Englishman, an Austrian, a rich landowner of whatever nationality; and if the merchant who buys grain from the needy grower keeps it in his warehouses in the midst of a destitute and famishing population, or sells it for three times its value to those of whom he bought it at the lowest price, it evidently springs from the same cause.

And if, beyond a certain line called the frontier, one man is not allowed to purchase certain goods without paying duties to other men who have nothing to do with their production, and if a man is obliged to part with his last cow in order to pay taxes which are distributed by the government among its officials, or used for the support of soldiers who may kill the tax-payers, it would seem evident that all this is not the result of certain abstract rights, but of incidents like those which may even now be going on in the government of Tula, which in one form or another occur periodically all the world over, wherever State organization exists, and wherever there are rich and poor.

Owing to the fact that outrage and murder do not accompany all social relations founded on violence, those who possess the exclusive privileges of the governing classes assure themselves and others that the advantages which they enjoy are not the result of violence and bloodshed, but derived from certain vague and abstract rights. Still it ought to be evident that if those men, who realize the injustice of it all (as is the case with the working classes at the present day), continue to surrender the greater part of their earnings to the capitalist and the landowner, and if they pay taxes, knowing that such taxes are not put to a good use, they do this not because they acknowledge the justice of certain abstract rights, whose meaning is unknown to them, but only because they know that they will be whipped and put to death if they refuse to comply.

If it is not always necessary to imprison men, to flog them, or to put them to death when the landowner collects his rents, if the needy peasant pays a treble price to the merchant who deceives him, or the mechanic accept swages absurdly small in comparison with the income of his master, or the poor man parts with his last rouble for duties and taxes, it is because he remembers that men have been flogged and put to death for trying to avoid compliance with what was demanded of them. Like a caged tiger who does not touch the meat that lies before his eyes, and who when he is ordered to leap over a stick obeys at once, not because he likes it, but because he has not forgotten past hunger or the red hot iron which he felt every time he refused to obey; so it is with men, who, when they submit to a law which is not for their advantage, to a law which is disastrous to their interests, or to one which they firmly believe to be unjust, do so because they remember what they will have to suffer if they refuse to comply.

Those who benefit by privileges born of violence long since perpetrated, often forget, and are very glad to forget, how such privileges were obtained. And yet one has but to recall the annals of history – not the history of the exploits of kings, but genuine history – the history of the oppression of the majority by the minority, in order to acknowledge that the scourge, the prison, and the gallows have been the original and only sources whence all the advantages of the rich over the poor have sprung. One has but to remember the persistent and undying passion for gain among men, the mainspring of human action in these days, to become convinced that the advantages of the rich over the poor can be maintained in no other way.

At rare intervals, oppression, flogging, imprisonment, executions, the direct object of which is not to promote the welfare of the rich, may possibly occur, but we can positively declare that in our community, where for every man who lives at ease there are ten overworked, hungry, and often cruelly suffering families of working men, all the privileges of the rich, all their luxury, all their superfluities are acquired and maintained only by tortures, imprisonments, and executions.

The train that I met on the 9th day of September, carrying soldiers, muskets, ammunition, and rods to the famine-stricken peasants, in order that the wealthy landowner might possess in peace the tract of wood he had wrested from the peasants, a necessity of life to them, to him a mere superfluity, affords a vivid proof of the degree to which men have unconsciously acquired the habit of committing acts wholly at variance with their convictions and their conscience.

The express consisted of one first class carriage for the Governor, officials and officers, and several vans crowded with soldiers. The jaunty young fellows in their fresh new uniforms were crowded together either standing or sitting with their legs dangling outside the wide-open sliding doors of the vans. Some were smoking, laughing, and jesting, some cracking seeds and spitting out the shells. A few who jumped down upon the platform to get a drink of water from the tub, meeting some of the officers, slackened their pace and made that senseless gesture of lifting one hand to the forehead; then, with serious faces, as though they had been doing something not only sensible but actually important, they passed by, watching the officers as they went. Soon they broke into a run, evidently in high spirits, stamping on the planks of the platform as they ran, and chatting, as is but natural for good-natured, healthy young fellows who are making a journey together. These men, who were on their way to murder starving fathers and grandfathers, seemed as unconcerned as though they were off on the pleasantest, or at least the most everyday business in the world.

The gaily-dressed officers and officials who were scattered about on the platform and in the first class waiting room produced the same impression. At a table laden with bottles sat the Governor, the commander of the expedition, attired in his semi-military uniform, eating his luncheon and quietly discussing the weather with some friends he had met, as though the business that called him hither was so simple a matter that it could neither ruffle his equanimity nor diminish his interest in the change of the weather.

At some distance, but tasting no food, sat the chief of the police with a mournful countenance, seemingly oppressed with the tiresome formalities. Officers in gaudy gold-embroidered uniforms moved to and fro, talking loudly; one group was seated at a table just finishing a bottle of wine; an officer at the bar who had eaten a cake brushed away the crumbs that had fallen on his uniform, and with a self-sufficient air flung a coin upon the counter; some walked nonchalantly up and down in front of our train looking at the faces of the women.

All these men on their way to commit murder, or to torture the starved and defenceless peasants by whose toil they were supported, looked as if engaged upon some important business which they were really proud to execute.

What did it mean?

These men, who were within half-an-hour's ride of the spot where, in order to procure for a rich man an extra 3000 roubles, of which he had no need whatever, which he was unjustly confiscating from a community of famished peasants, might be obliged to perform the most shocking deeds that the imagination can conceive – to murder and torture as they did in Orel innocent men, their brothers. These men were now calmly approaching the time and place when these horrors were to begin.

Since the preparations had been made it could not very well be claimed that all these men, officers and privates, did not know what was before them, and what they were expected to do. The Governor had given orders for the rods; the officials had purchased the birch twigs, bargained for them, and noted the purchase in their accounts. In the military department orders had been given and received concerning ball cartridges. They all knew that they were on their way to torture and possibly to put to death their brothers exhausted by famine, and that perhaps in an hour they might begin the work.

To say, as they themselves would say, that they are acting from principle, from a conviction that the State system must be maintained, is untrue. Those men, in the first place, have rarely if ever bestowed a single thought upon political science; and in the second place, because they could never be convinced that the business on which they are engaged serves to support rather than destroy the State; and finally, because, as a matter of fact, the majority of these men, if not all of them, would not only be unwilling to sacrifice their peace and comfort to maintain the State, but would never miss the opportunity to promote their own interests at the expense of the State – therefore it is not for the sake of so vague a principle as that of maintaining the State that they do this.

What, then, does all this mean?

I know these men. I may not know them as individuals it is true, yet I know their dispositions, their past lives, their modes of thought. They have had mothers, some have wives and children. Actually, they are for the most part kindly, gentle, tender hearted men, who abhor any kind of cruelty, to say nothing of killing or torturing; moreover, every one of them professes Christianity,

THE KINGDOM OF GOD IS WITHIN YOU

and considers violence perpetrated against the defenceless a contemptible and shameful act. Each taken individually, in everyday life, is not only incapable for the sake of personal advantage of doing one-hundredth part of what was done by the Governor at Orel, but any one of them would consider himself insulted if it were suggested that he could be capable of doing anything like it in private life. And yet they are within a half-hour's ride of the spot where they will inevitably find themselves compelled to do such deeds.

What can it mean then?

It is not only the men on this train who are ready to commit murder and violence, but those others with whom the affair originated, the landowner, the steward, the judge, those in St. Petersburg who issue orders – the Minister of State, the Czar, also worthy men and professors of Christianity – how can they, knowing the consequences, conceive such a scheme and direct its execution?

How can they even who take no active part in it, the spectators, whose indignation would be aroused by accounts of private violence, even though it be but the ill-usage of a horse, how can they allow this shocking business to go on, without rising in wrath to resist it, crying aloud, "No, we will not allow you to flog or to kill starving men because they refuse to surrender their last property villainously attempted to be wrested from them!" And not only are men found willing to do these deeds, but most of them, even the chief instigators, like the steward, the landowner, the judge, and those who take part in originating prosecution and punishment, the Governor, the Minister of State, the Czar, remain perfectly calm and show no sign of remorse over such things. And they who are about to execute this crime are equally calm.

Even the spectators, who it would seem have no personal interest in the matter, look upon these men who are about to take part in this dastardly business with sympathy rather than with aversion or condemnation.

In the same compartment with me sat a merchant who dealt in timber, a peasant by birth, who in loud and decided tones expressed his approval of the outrage which the peasants were about to suffer. "The government must be obeyed; that's what it is for. If we pepper them well they will never rebel again. It is no more than they deserve!" he said.

What did it all mean?

It could not be said that all these men, the instigators, the participants, the accomplices in this business were rascals, who, in defiance of conscience, realizing the utter abomination of the act, were, either from mercenary motives or from fear of punishment, determined to commit it. Any man of them would, given the requisite circumstances, stand up for his convictions. Not one of those officials would steal a purse, or read another man's letter, or endure an insult without demanding satisfaction from the offender. Not one of those officers would cheat at cards, or neglect to pay a gambling debt, or betray a companion, or flee from the battlefield, or abandon a flag. Not one of those soldiers would dare to reject the sacrament, or even taste meat on Good Friday. Each of these men would choose to endure any kind of privation, suffering, or danger, rather than consent to do a deed which he considered wrong. Hence it is evident that they are able to resist whatever is contrary to their convictions.

Still less true would it be to pronounce these men brutes, to whom such deeds are congenial rather than repulsive. One needs but to talk with them to become convinced that all – landowner, judge, minister, Governor, Czar, officers, and soldiers – at the bottom of their hearts not only disapprove of such deeds, but when a sense of their true significance is borne in upon them, really suffer at being forced to take part in these scenes. They can only try not to think of them.

One needs but to speak to those who are actors in this business, beginning with the landowner and ending with the lowest policeman or soldier, to discover that at the bottom of their hearts they all acknowledge the wickedness of the deed and know that it would be better to abstain from it; and this knowledge makes them suffer.

A lady of liberal views in our train, seeing the Governor and the officers in the first class waiting room, and learning the object of their journey, began to talk in an ostensibly loud tone, in order that they might hear what she said, condemning the present laws and crying shame upon the men who took part in this business. This made everybody feel uncomfortable. The men knew not where to look; yet no one ventured to argue the point. The passengers pretended that remarks so senseless deserved no reply, but it was evident by the expression of their faces and their wandering eyes that they felt ashamed. I noticed the same in regard to the soldiers. They knew well enough that they were going about an evil business, and they preferred not to think of what was before them. When the timber merchant, insincerely, in my opinion, and simply by way of showing his superior knowledge, began to speak of the necessity of these measures, the soldiers who heard him turned away frowning, and pretended not to listen to him.

The landowner, his steward, the minister, the Czar, all who are parties to this business, those who were travelling by this train, even those who, taking no part in the affair, were but lookers-on, all really know it to be wicked. Why then do they do these things, why do they repeat them, why do they permit them to be?

Ask the landowner who started the affair; the judge who rendered a decision legal in form but absolutely unjust; and those who, like the soldiers and the peasants, will, with their own hands, execute this work of beating and murdering their brothers – all of them, instigators, administrators, and executioners, will make essentially the same reply.

The officials will say that the present system requires to be supported in this manner, and it is for this reason that they do these things, because the good of the country, the welfare of mankind in general, of social life and civilization, demands it.

The soldiers, men of the lower classes, who are forced to execute this violence with their own hands, will answer that the higher authorities, who are supposed to know their business, have commanded it, and that it is for them to obey. It never occurs to them to question the capacity of those who represent the higher authorities. If the possibility of error severs admitted, it is only in the case of some subordinate authority; the higher power whence all things emanate is supposed to be absolutely infallible.

Thus, while attributing their actions to various motives, both principals and subordinates agree that the existing order is the one best suited to the present time, and that it is the sacred duty of every man to maintain it.

This assurance of the necessity and immutability of the existing order is continually advanced by all participators in violence committed by the State, and that, as the existing order never can be changed, the refusal of a single individual to perform the duties imposed on him will make no difference as far as the fundamental principle is concerned, and will only result in the substitution of another who may be more cruel and do more harm.

This belief that the existing order is immutable, and that it is the sacred duty of every man to lend it support, encourages every man of good moral character to take part, with a conscience more or less clear, in such affairs as that which occurred in Orel, and the one in which those in the train for Tula were going to take part.

On what then is this belief founded?

It is but natural that it should seem pleasant and desirable to a landowner to believe that the existing order is indispensable and immutable, because it securest him the income from his hundreds and thousands of *dessiatins* by which his idle and luxurious existence is maintained.

It is also natural that the judge should willingly admit the necessity of a system through which he receives fifty times more than the most hardworking labouring man. And the same may be said in regard to the other higher functionaries. It is only while the present system endures that he, as governor, *procureur*, senator, or member of the council, can receive his salary of several thousands, without which he and his family would certainly perish – for outside the place which he fills, more or less well according to his abilities and diligence, he could command only a fraction of what he receives. The ministers, the head of the State, and every person in high authority are all alike in this, save that the higher their rank, the more exclusive their position, the more important it becomes that they should believe no order possible, except that which now exists; for were it overthrown, not only would they find it impossible to gain similar positions, but they would fall lower in the scale than other men. The man who voluntarily hires himself out as a policeman for ten roubles a month, a sum which he could easily earn in any other position, has but little interest in the preservation of the existing system, and therefore may or may not believe in its immutability.

But the king or emperor, who receives his millions, who knows that around him there are thousands of men envious to take his place, who knows that from no other quarter could he draw such an income or receive such homage, that, if overthrown, he might be judged for abuse of power – there is neither king nor emperor who can help believing in the immutability and sanctity of the existing order. The higher the position in which a man is placed, the more unstable it is; and the more perilous and frightful the possible downfall, the more firmly will he believe in the immutability of the existing order; and he is able to do wicked and cruel deeds with a perfectly peaceful conscience, because he persuades himself that they are done not for his own benefit but for the support of the existing order.

And so it is with every individual in authority, from obscure policemen to the man who occupies the most exalted rank – the positions they occupy being more advantageous than those which they might be capable of filling if the present system did not exist. All these men believe more or less in its immutability, because it is advantageous to them.

But what influences the peasants, the soldiers, who stand on the lowest rung of the ladder and who derive no advantage from the existing system, who are in the most enslaved and degraded condition; what induces them to believe that the existing order, which serves to keep them in this inferior position, is the best and one which should be maintained; and why are they willing, in order to promote this end, to violate their consciences by committing wicked deeds?

What urges them to the false conclusion that the existing order is immutable and ought therefore to be maintained, when the fact is that its immutability is due only to their own effort to maintain it?

Why do those men, taken from the plough, whom we see masquerading in ugly, objectionable uniforms, with blue collars and gold buttons, go about armed with muskets and sabres to kill their famishing fathers and brothers? They derive no advantage from their present position; they would be no losers were they deprived of it, since it is worse than the one from which they were taken.

Those in authority belonging to the higher classes, the land-owners and merchants, the judges, senators, governors, ministers, and kings, the officials in general, participate in such actions and maintain the present system, because such a system is for their interest. Often enough they are kindhearted and gentle men. They play no personal part in these acts; all they do is to institute inquiries, pronounce judgments, and issue commands. Those in authority do not themselves execute the deeds which they have devised and ordered. They but rarely see in what manner these dreadful deeds are executed. But the unfortunate members of the lower classes, who receive no benefit from the existing system, who, on the other hand, find themselves greatly despised because of the duties which they perform in order that a system which is opposed to their own interests maybe maintained – they who tear men from the bosom of their families to send them to the galleys, who bind and imprison them, who stand on guard over them, who shoot them, why do they do this? What is it that compels these men to believe that the existing order is immutable, and that it is their duty to maintain it? Violence exists only because there are those who with their own hands maltreat, bind, imprison, and murder. If there were no policemen, or soldiers, or armed men of any sort ready when bidden to use violence and to put men to death, not one of those who sign death warrants, or sentence for imprisonment for life or hard labour in the galleys, would ever have sufficient courage himself to hang, imprison, or torture one thousandth part of those whom now, sitting in their studies, these men calmly order to be hung or tortured, because they do not see it done, they do not do it themselves. Their servants do it for them in some far-away corner.

All these deeds of injustice and cruelty have become an integral part of the existing system of life, only because there are men ever ready to execute them. If there were no such men, the multitude of human beings who are now the victims of violence would be spared, and furthermore, the magistrates would never dare to issue, nor even dream of issuing, those commands which they now send forth with such assurance. If there were no men to obey the will of others and to execute commands to torture and murder, no one would ever dare to defend the declaration so confidently made by landowners and men of leisure – namely, that the land lying on all sides of the unfortunate peasants, who are perishing for the want of it, is the property of the man who does not till it, and that reserves of grain, fraudulently obtained, are to be held intact amidst a famine-stricken and dying population, because the merchant must have his profit. If there were no men ready at the bidding of the authorities to torture and murder, the landowner would never dream of seizing a forest which had been tended by the peasants; nor would officials consider themselves entitled to salaries paid to them from money wrung from the famished people whom they oppress, or which they derive for the prosecution, imprisonment, and exile of men who denounce falsehood and preach the truth.

All this is done because those in authority well know that they have always at hand submissive agents ready to obey their commands to outrage and to murder.

It is to this crowd of submissive slaves, ready to obey all orders, that we owe the deeds of the whole series of tyrants, from Napoleon to the obscure captain who bids his men fire upon the people. It is through the agency of policemen and soldiers (especially the latter, since the former can act only when supported by military force) that these deeds of violence are committed. What then has induced those who are by no means benefited by doing with their hands these dreadful deeds – what is it that has led these kindly men into an error so gross, that they actually believe that the present system, which is so distressing, so baleful, so fatal, is the one best suited to the times? Who has led them into this extraordinary aberration?

They can never have persuaded themselves that a course which is not only painful and opposed to their interests, but which is fatal to their class, which forms nine-tenths of the entire population, one which too is opposed to their conscience, is right. "What reason can you give for killing men, when God's commandment says, 'Thou shalt not kill'?" is a question I have often put to different soldiers. And it always embarrassed them to have a question put which recalled what they would rather not remember.

They knew that the divine law forbade murder – thou shalt not kill – and they had always known of this compulsory military duty, but had never thought of one as contradictory to the other. The hesitating replies to my question were usually to the effect that the act of killing a man in war and the execution of criminals by order of the government were not included in the general prohibition against murder. But when I rejoined that no such limitation existed in the law of God, and cited the Christian doctrine of brotherhood, the forgiveness of injuries, the injunction to love one's neighbour, all of which precepts are quite contrary to murder, the men of the lower class would usually agree with me and ask, "How then can it be that the government (which they believe cannot err) sends troops to war and orders the execution of criminals?" When I replied that this was a mistake on the part of the government, my interlocutors became still more uncomfortable, and either dropped the conversation or showed annoyance.

"Probably there is a law for it. I should think the bishops know more than you do," a Russian soldier once said to me. And he evidently felt relieved, confident that his superiors had found a law, one that had authorized his ancestors and their successors, millions of men like himself, to serve the State, and that the question I had asked is in the nature of a conundrum.

Every man in Christendom has undoubtedly been taught by tradition, by revelation, and by the voice of conscience, which can never be gainsaid, that murder is one of the most heinous crimes men can commit; it is thus affirmed in the Gospel, and they know that this sin of murder is not altered by conditions – that is to say, if it is sinful to kill one man, it is sinful to kill another. Any man knows that if murder be a sin, it is not changed by the character or position of the man against whom it is committed, which is the case also with adultery, theft, and all other sins, and yet men are accustomed from childhood to see murder, not only acknowledged, but blessed by those whom they're taught to regard as their spiritual directors appointed by Christ, and to know that their temporal leaders with calm assurance countenance the custom of murder, and summon all men in the name of the law and even the name of God to its participation. Men perceive the existence of an inconsistency, but finding themselves unable to discern its cause, they naturally attribute the idea to their own ignorance. The obviousness and crudity of the contradiction confirms them in this belief. They cannot imagine that their superiors and teachers, even the scientists, could advocate with so much assurance two principles so utterly at variance as the command to follow the law of Christ and the requirement to commit murder. No pure-minded, innocent child, no youth, could imagine that men who stand so high in his esteem, whom he looks upon with such reverence, could for any purpose deceive him so unscrupulously.

And yet it is this very deception which is constantly practised. In the first place, to all working men, who have personally no time to analyse moral and religious problems, it is taught from childhood by example and precept that tortures and murders are compatible with Christianity, and in certain cases they should not only be permitted but must be employed; in the second place, to certain among them, engaged in the army either through conscription or voluntarily, it is conveyed that the accomplishment with their own hands of torture or homicide is not only their sacred duty, but a glorious exploit meriting praise and recompense.

This universal deception is propagated by all catechisms or their substitutes, those books which at the present time teachers are compelled to use in the instruction of the young. It is taught that violence – outrage, imprisonment, execution – the murder that takes place in civil or in foreign war, has for its object the maintenance and security of the political organization – whether this be an absolute or a constitutional monarchy, consulate, republic, or commune – that it is perfectly legitimate, and that it is in contradiction neither to morality nor Christianity.

And men are so firmly convinced of this that they grow up, live and die in the belief, never for a moment doubting it.

So much for this universal deception. And now for another,

which is special, and practised upon soldiers and police, the instruments by whose agency outrages and murders, necessary for the support and maintenance of the existing order, are accomplished.

The military rules and regulations of every country are practically the same as those formulated in the Russian military code.

87 To fulfil exactly, and without comment, the orders of the superior officers, means – to execute orders with precision, without considering whether they are good or bad, or whether their execution be possible. Only the superior is responsible for the consequences of his order.

88 The only occasion on which the inferior should not obey the order of his superior is when he sees plainly that in obeying it. (Here one naturally thinks it will surely go on to say when he plainly sees that in fulfilling the order of his superior he violates the law of God. Not at all, it goes on to say:) sees plainly that he violates the oath of allegiance and duty to his sovereign.

It is stated in the Code that a man in becoming a soldier can and must execute all the orders, without exception, which he receives from his superior; orders which, for a soldier, are for the most part connected with murder. He may violate every law, human and divine, as long as he does not violate his oath of allegiance to him who, at a given time, happens to be in power.

Thus it stands in the Russian military code, and this is the substance of the military codes of other nations. It could not be otherwise. The foundations of the power of the State rest upon the delusion by means of which men are set free from their obligations to God and to their own consciences, and bound to obey the will of a casual superior.

This is the basis of the appalling conviction that prevails among the lower classes, that the existing system, so ruinous to them, is necessary and justifiable, and that it must be maintained by outrage and murder.

This is inevitable. In order to force the lower, the more numerous classes, to act as their own oppressors and tormentors, to commit deeds contrary to their consciences, it is necessary to deceive them.

And this is done.

Not long since I saw again put into practice this shameful deception, and again wondered to see it effected without opposition and so audaciously.

In the beginning of November, on my way through Tula, I saw at the gates of the Zemskaya Uprava the familiar dense crowd of men and women, from which issued the sounds of drunken voices blended with the heartrending sobs of the wives and mothers.

The military conscription was in progress.

As usual, I could not pass by without pausing; the sight attracts me as by fascination.

Again, I mingled with the crowd and stood looking on, questioning, and marvelling at the facility with which this most terrible of all offences is committed in broad daylight, and in the midst of a large city.

On the first day of November in every village in Russia, with its population of one hundred millions, the *starostas*, according to custom, take the men whose names are entered on the rolls, frequently their own sons, and carry them to town.

On the way the men drink freely, unchecked by the elder men; they realize that entering upon this insane business of leaving their wives and mothers, giving up everything that is sacred to them, only to become the senseless tools of murder, is too painful if one's senses are not stupefied with wine.

And thus they journey on, carousing, brawling, singing, and fighting. The night is spent in a tavern, and on this morning, having drunk still more, they assemble before the house of the Uprava.

Some in new sheepskin coats, with knit mufflers wound round their necks, some with their eyes swollen with drinking, some noisy and boisterous, by way of stimulating their courage, others silent and woebegone, they were gathered near the gates, surrounded by their wives and mothers with tear-stained faces, awaiting their turn (I happened to be there on the day when the recruits were received, that is to say, the day on which they were examined), while others were crowding the entry of the office.

Meanwhile they are hurrying on the work within. A door opens and the guard calls for Piotr Sidorov. Piotr Sidorov makes the sign of the cross, looks around with a startled gaze, and opening a glass door, he enters the small room where the recruits take off their clothes. The man before him, his friend, who has just been enrolled, has but this moment stepped out of the office stark naked, and with chattering teeth hastens to put on his clothes. Piotr Sidorov has heard, and can plainly see by the look on his face, that the man has been enlisted. He longs to question him, but he is ordered to undress as quickly as possible. He pulls off his sheep skin coat, drops his waistcoat and his shirt, and with prominent ribs, trembling and reeking with the odours of liquor, tobacco, and sweat, steps barefooted into the office, wondering what he shall do with his large sinewy hands.

A portrait of the Emperor in uniform, with a ribbon across his breast, in a large golden frame hangs in a conspicuous place, while a small icon of Christ clad in a loose garment, with the crown of thorns on his head, hangs in one corner. In the middle of the room is a table covered with a green cloth on which papers are lying, and on which stands a small three-cornered object surmounted by an eagle and called the mirror of justice. Around the table the officials sit tranquilly. One smokes, another turns over the papers. As soon as Sidorov enters a guard comes up and measures him. His chin is raised and his feet are adjusted. Then a man who is smoking a cigarette – the doctor – approaches him, and without glancing at his face, but gazing in another direction, touches his body with an expression of disgust, measures him, orders the guard to open his mouth, tells him to breathe, and then proceeds to dictate to another man who takes down the minutes. Finally, and still without even one glance at his face, the doctor says: "He will do! The next!" and with a wearied air he seats himself at the table. Once more the guard hustles him about, bidding him to make haste. Somehow or other he pulls on his shirt, fumbling for the sleeves, hastily gets on his trousers, wraps his feet in the rags he uses for stockings, pulls on his boots, hunts for his muffler and cap, tucks his sheepskin coat under his arm, and is escorted to that part of the hall which is fenced off by a bench, where the recruits who have been admitted are placed. A young countryman like himself, but from another, faraway government, who is a soldier already, with a musket to which a bayonet is attached, guards him, ready to run him through the body if he should attempt to escape.

Meanwhile the crowd of fathers, mothers, and wives, hustled by policemen, presses around the gates, trying to find out who has been taken and who rejected. A man who has been rejected comes out and tells them that Piotr has been admitted; then is heard the cry of Piotr's young wife, for whom this word means a four or five years' separation, and the dissolute life such as a soldier's wife in domestic service is.

But here comes a man with flowing hair and dressed differently from the others, who has just arrived; he descends from his *droschky* and goes towards the house of the Zemskaya Uprava, while the policemen clear a way for him through the crowd.

"The Father has arrived to swear them in." And this "Father," who has always been accustomed to believe himself a special and privileged servant of Christ, and who is usually quite unconscious of his false position, enters the room where the recruits who have been admitted are waiting for him; he puts on, as a vestment, a sort of brocade curtain, disengages from it his flowing hair, opens the Bible wherein an oath is forbidden, lifts the cross, that cross on which Christ was crucified for refusing to do what this person, his supposed servant, commands men to do, and all these defenceless and deluded young men repeat after him the lie so familiar to his lips, which he utters with such assurance. He reads while they repeat: "I promise and swear to the Lord Almighty, upon His Holy Bible," etc. to defend (that is, to murder all those whom I shall be ordered to murder) and to do whatever those men, strangers tome, who regard me only as a necessary tool to be used in perpetrating the outrages by which they oppress my brethren and preserve their own positions, command me to do. All the recruits having stupidly repeated the words, the so-called Father departs, quite sure that he has performed his duty in the most accurate and conscientious manner, while the young men deluded by him really believe that by the absurd, and to them almost unintelligible words, which they have just uttered, they are released during their term of service from all obligations to their fellowmen, and are bound by new and more imperative ties: to the duties of a soldier.

And this is done publicly, but not a man comes forward to say to the deceived and the deceivers: "Come to your senses and go your way; this is all a base and treacherous lie; it imperils not only your bodies, but your souls."

No one does this. On the contrary, as if in derision, after they have all been enrolled and are about to depart, the colonel enters the hall where these poor, drunken, and deluded creatures are locked in, and, with a solemn air, calls out to them in military fashion: "Good day, men! I congratulate you upon entering the Czar's service" And they, poor fellows, mumble in their semi-drunken way, a reply which has already been taught them, to the effect that it fills their hearts with joy.

The expectant crowd of fathers, mothers, and wives is still standing at the gates. Women, with tear-worn, wide-open eyes, watch the door. Suddenly it opens and the men come rolling out, assuming an air of bravado, the Petruhas, Vanuhas, and Makars, now enrolled, trying to avoid the eyes of their relatives, pretending not to see them. At once break out the sobs and cries of the wives and mothers. Some of the men clasp them in their arms, weeping, some put on a devil-may-care look, others make an attempt to console them. The wives, the mothers, realizing that they are now abandoned, without support, for three or four years, cry and wail bitterly. The fathers say little; they only sigh and make a clicking sound with their tongues that indicates their grief; they know that they are about to lose that help which they have reared and trained their sons to render; that when their sons return they will no longer be sober and industrious labourers, but soldiers weaned from their former life of simplicity, grown dissolute and vain of their uniforms.

Now the whole crowd has departed, driving down the street in sleighs to the taverns and inns, and louder grows the chorus of mingled sobs, songs, and drunken cries, the moaning and muttering of the wives and mothers, the sounds of the accordion, the noise of altercations.

All repair to the eating houses and taverns, from the traffic of which part of the revenue of the government is derived, and there they give themselves up to drink, stupefying their senses so that they care nothing for the injustice done to them.

Then they spend several weeks at home, drinking nearly all the time.

When the day arrives, they are driven like cattle to the appointed place, where they are drilled in military exercises by those who a few years ago, like themselves, were deceived and brutalized. During the instructions the means employed are lying, blows, and vodka. And before the year is over the good, kindly, and intelligent fellows will have become as brutal as their teachers.

"Suppose your father were arrested and attempted escape," I once suggested to a young soldier, "what would you do?"

"It would be my duty to thrust my bayonet through his body," he replied in the peculiar, meaningless monotone of the soldier. "And if he ran I should shoot," he added, taking pride apparently in thinking what he should do if his father attempted to run.

When a good young fellow is reduced to a condition lower than that of the brute, he is ready for those who wish to use him as an instrument of violence. He is ready. The man is lost, and a new instrument of violence has been created. And all this goes on throughout Russia in the autumn of every year, in broad daylight, in the heart of a great city, witnessed by all the inhabitants, and the stratagem is so skillfully managed, that though men at the bottom of their hearts realize its infamy, still they have not the power to throw off the yoke.

After our eyes are once opened, and we view this frightful delusion in its true light, it is astonishing that preachers of Christianity and morality, teachers of youth, or even those kindly and sensible parents who are to be found in every community, can advocate any principles of morality whatever in the midst of a society where torture and murder are openly recognized as constituting indispensable conditions in human life – openly acknowledged by all churches and governments – where certain men among us must be always ready to murder their brethren, and where any of us may have to do the same.

Not to speak of Christian doctrine, how are children, how are youths, how are any to be taught morality, while the principle that murder is required in order to maintain the general welfare is taught; when men are made to believe that murder is lawful, that some men, and any of us may be among them, must kill and torture their neighbours, and commit every kind of crime at the command of those in authority? If this principle is right, then there is not, nor can there be, any doctrine of morality; might is right, and there is no other law. This principle, which some seek to justify on the hypothesis of the struggle for existence, in fact dominates society.

What kind of moral doctrine can that be which permits murder for any object whatsoever? It is as impossible as a mathematical problem which would affirm that 2 = 3. It may be admitted that 2 = 3 looks like mathematics, but it is not mathematics at all. Every code of morals must be founded first of all upon the acknowledgment that human life is to be held sacred.

The doctrine of an eye for an eye, a tooth for a tooth, and a life for a life, has been revoked by Christianity because that doctrine was but the justification of immorality, a semblance of justice, but without meaning. Life is a substance which can neither be weighed, measured, nor compared; hence the taking of one life for another makes no sense. Moreover, the aim of every social law is amelioration of human life. How then can the destruction of certain lives improve the condition of other lives? The destruction of life is not an act that tends to improve it; it is suicide.

To destroy human life and call it justice may be likened to the act of a man who, having lost one arm, cuts off the other, by way of making matters even.

Not to speak of the deceit of presenting the most shocking crimes in the light of a duty, of the shocking abuse of using Christ's name and authority in order to confirm acts which he condemned, how can men, looking at the matter from the standpoint merely of personal safety, suffer the existence of the shocking, senseless, cruel, and dangerous force which every organized government, supported by the army, represents?

The most violent and rapacious band of robbers is less to be feared than such an organization. Even the authority of the leader of a band of robbers is more or less limited by the will of each individual member of the band, who, retaining a certain degree of independence, has the right to oppose acts with which he does not agree. But the authority of men who form part of an organized government, maintained by the army with its present system of discipline, is unlimited. When their master, be he Boulanger, Pugatchov, or Napoleon, issues his commands, there is no crime too hideous for those who form part of the government and the army to commit.

It must often occur to one who sees conscriptions, drills, and military manoeuvres taking place, who sees police going about with loaded revolvers, sentinels armed with bayonets – to one who hears from morning till night, as I do (in the district of Khamovniky, wherein live), the whirring balls and the concussion as they strike the target – to ask why these things are tolerated. And when one sees in the same city, where every attempt at violence is at once suppressed, where even the sale of powder or medicines is prohibited, where a doctor is not allowed to practice without a diploma – thousands of disciplined men, controlled by one individual, being trained for murder, one cannot help asking how men who have any regard for their own safety can calmly endure such a condition of affairs, and allow it to continue? Leaving aside the question of the immorality and pernicious influence of it, what could be more dangerous? What are they thinking of – I speak not now of Christians, Christian pastors, philanthropists, or moralists, but simply those who value their lives, their safety, their welfare? Granting that power is at present in the hands of a moderate ruler, it may fall tomorrow into those of a Biron, an Elizabeth, a Catherine, a Pugatchov, a Napoleon. And even though the ruler be moderate today, he may become a mere savage tomorrow; he may be succeeded by an insane or half insane heir, like the King of Bavaria or the Emperor Paul.

It is not only those who fill the highest offices, but all the lesser authorities scattered over the land, the chiefs of police, the commanders of companies, even the *stanovoys*, may commit shocking crimes before they can be dismissed; it is an everyday occurrence.

Involuntarily one asks: how can men allow these things to go on? How can they tolerate them with any regard to their own personal safety?

It may be replied that some men do oppose it. (Those who are deluded and live in subjection have nothing either to tolerate

274

or interdict.) Those who favour the continuance of the present system are only those who derive some special advantage from it. They favour it, and even with the disadvantages of having an insane or tyrannical man at the head of the government and the army, the position is less disadvantageous to them than if the present organization were abolished.

Whether his position be held under a Boulanger, a Republic, a Pugatchov, or a Catherine – the judge, the police commissioner, the governor, the officer, will remain in it. But if the system which assures their positions were overthrown they would lose them. Therefore it is a matter of indifference to these men whether one man or another be at the head of the organization of violence. What they do fear is its abolition, so they support it.

One wonders why men of independent means, who are not obliged to become soldiers, the so-called 'elite of society, enter military service in Russia, in England, in Germany, in Austria, and even in France, and desire the chance of killing? Why do parents, why do moral men send their children to military schools? Why do mothers buy them such toys as helmets, swords, and muskets? (No child of a peasant ever plays at being a soldier.) Why do kindly men and women, who can have no manner of interest in war, go into ecstasies over the exploits of a man like Skobelev? Why do men who are under no obligation to do it, and who receive no pay for it, like Marshals of Nobility in Russia, devote months to the service which demands such unremitting labour, wearying to the minds as well as to the body – the enlistment of recruits? Why do all emperors and kings wear a military dress, why do they have drills and parades and military rewards? Why are monuments built to generals and conquerors? Why do wealthy and independent men regard it as an honour to occupy the position of lackeys to kings, to flatter them and feign a belief in their special superiority? Why do men who have long since ceased to believe in the mediaeval superstitions of the church, still constantly and solemnly pretend to do so, and thus support a sacrilegious and demoralizing institution? Why is the ignorance of the people so zealously preserved not only by the government, but by men of the higher classes? Why do they so energetically denounce every attempt to overthrow popular superstition and to promote popular education? Why do historians, novelists, and poets, who can derive no benefit in exchange for their flattery, paint in such glowing colours the emperors, kings, and generals of bygone times? Why do the so-called scientists devote their lives to formulate theories that violence committed on the people by power is legitimate violence, is right ?

One often wonders why an artist or a woman of the world, neither of whom, it would seem ordinarily, take much interest in sociological or military questions – why should they condemn strikes among workmen, or advocate war with such partisan zeal?

But one ceases to feel surprise when one realizes that the members of the higher classes possess the keenest insight, an intuitive perception, as it were, concerning those conditions which are friendly and those which are hostile to the organization upon whose existence their privileges depend.

It is true that the woman of society does not deliberately argue thus: "Were there no capitalists, or armies to defend them, my husband would have no money, and I should have neither salon nor fashionable gowns;" nor does the artist tell himself in so many words, that if his pictures are to be sold there must be capitalists, defended by armies, to buy them; yet instinct, here doing duty for reason, is their surest guide. This instinct guides, with rare exceptions, all men who support those political, religious, and economic institutions which are advantageous to themselves.

But is it possible that men who belong to the higher classes defend this organization only because it is for their own advantage? They surely cannot fail to see that as an organization it is irrational, incompatible with the present consciousness of men, with public opinion, and that it is fraught with danger. Good, intelligent, honest men who belong to the ruling class cannot but suffer from such contradictions, nor can they close their eyes to the dangers that menace them.

And is it possible that the millions of men of the lower classes can go on calmly committing deeds which are so manifestly criminal, such as are the murders and tortures which they commit, simply from fear of punishment? Surely these things could not exist were not the falsehood and brutality of their actions hidden from all classes of men by the system of the political organization.

When such deeds are committed, there are so many instigators, participants, and abettors that no single individual feels himself morally responsible.

Assassins compel all the witnesses of an assassination to strike the body of the victim, with the intention of dividing the responsibility among the greatest number possible. And whenever those crimes by the aid of which the State system is maintained are to be committed, this same thing is observed. The rulers of State always endeavour to involve the greatest possible number of citizens in the participation of the crimes which it is to their interest to have committed.

In these latter days this is made especially evident by the drawing of citizens on the jury in courts of law, by drafting them into the army as soldiers, and into the communal or legislative administration as electors or elected.

As in a wicker basket all the ends are so carefully interwoven that they cannot be seen, so is it with the responsibility for crime. Individual responsibilities are so manipulated that no man perceives precisely what he is incurring.

In olden times tyrants were responsible for the crimes which were committed, but in the present age the most frightful crimes are perpetrated, such as would hardly have been possible in the time of Nero, and still no one is held responsible.

Some demand the crime, some propose it, some determine it, some confirm it, and some order it, and some execute it.

Women and old men are hung, are flogged to death – even quite innocent people, as was recently the case with us in Russia, in the affair of the factory at Uzova; or, as is done all over in Europe and America, in the struggle with anarchists and other revolutionists, hundreds, thousands of men are shot, are killed; or, as happens in time of war, millions of men are massacred; or, as is happening always, the souls of men are destroyed by solitary confinement, by the debauchery of barrack life – and no one is responsible.

On the lower scale of the social ladder are posted soldiers

armed with muskets, pistols, swords; they go about doing violence and killing, and through their doing so force other men to become soldiers like themselves, and yet they never dream that the responsibility rests on their shoulders; they shift it on to their superiors, who give the orders.

The Czars, the Presidents, the Ministers of State, the General Assemblies, order tortures, murders, conscriptions, and as they enjoy the absolute assurance that they rule by the grace of God or by the will of the society they govern, and that that society demands from them what they order, they cannot regard themselves as responsible.

Between these two classes we find a number of intermediaries, who take charge of the executions, tortures, conscriptions, and they too wash their hands of all responsibility, alleging on the one hand the orders of their superiors, and on the other that it is for such as themselves, who stand lower on the social ladder, to do these things.

The power that demands and the power that fulfils commands, the two extremes of governmental organization, unite like the two ends of a chain, each depending on, and supporting the other, and all the intervening links.

Were it not for the conviction that there are men who assume the whole responsibility of such deeds, no soldier would lift his hand to torture or murder his fellow man. Were it not for the conviction that the nation demands it, no King, Emperor, President, or Assembly would venture to issue commands for murder and torture. Were it not that he believes that there are men above him who assume the responsibility of his actions, and others below him whose welfare requires this treatment, no man of the intermediate class would ever perform the functions committed to him.

The organization of the State is such that on whatever position of the social ladder a man may stand his irresponsibility remains intact. The higher he stands the more liable he is to feel the pressure brought to bear on him from below, urging him to issue commands, and the less likely he will be to be influenced by orders from above, and vice versa.

But it is not enough that all men bound by the organization of the State transfer their responsibility from one to the other – the peasant, for instance, who becomes a soldier to the merchant who has become an officer; the officer to the noble who occupies the position of Governor; the Governor to the Minister of State; the Minister to the Sovereign; and the Sovereign who in his turn shifts the responsibility upon all – officials, nobles, merchants, peasants. Not only do men in this way merely free themselves from all sense of responsibility for their actions, but because as they adapt themselves to fulfil the requirements of political organizations they so constantly, persistently, and strenuously assure themselves and others that all men are not equal, that they begin to believe it sincerely themselves. Thus we are assured that some men are superior and must be especially honoured and obeyed; while, on the other hand, we are assured in every way that others are inferior, and therefore bound to obey without murmur the commands of their superiors.

It is to this inequality – the exaltation of some upon the abasement of others – that we may chiefly attribute the incapacity which men display for discerning the folly of the existing system, with the cruelty and deceptions committed by some and suffered by others.

There are certain men who have been made to believe that they are possessed of a peculiar importance and greatness, who have become so intoxicated by their imaginary superiority that they cease to realize their responsibility for the actions they commit; others who, on the contrary, have been told that they are insignificant beings, and that it is their duty to submit to those above them, and, as the natural result of this continual state of degradation, fall into a strange condition of stupefied servility, and in this state they too lose all sense of responsibility for their actions. And as to the intermediate class, subservient to those above them, and yet to a certain extent regarding themselves as superiors, they are apt to be both servile and arrogant, and they also lose the sense of responsibility.

One needs but to glance at any official of high rank in the act of reviewing the troops. Accompanied by his staff, mounted on a magnificently caparisoned charger, equipped in a brilliant uniform, displaying all his decorations, he rides in front of the ranks, while the band plays martial music and the soldiers present arms, standing, as they do, as though verily petrified with servility – one has but to see this to understand how in such moments, under such conditions, both generals and soldiers might commit deeds which they never would have dreamed of committing.

But the intoxication to which men succumb, under conditions like parades, pageants, religious ceremonies, and coronations, though acute, is not enduring, while there is another which is chronic, shared by all who have any authority whatsoever, from the Czar to the policemen on the street, shared, too, by the masses who submit to authority in a state of stupefied servility, and who by way of justifying their submission, after the usual manner of slaves, ascribe the greatest importance and dignity to those whom they obey.

It is this delusion in regard to human inequality and the consequent intoxication of power and stupefaction of servility which makes it possible for those who are associated in a State organization to commit crimes and suffer no remorse.

Under the influence of this intoxication – there is an intoxication of servility as well as of power – men seem to others, no less than to themselves, not the ordinary human beings which they really are, but specially privileged beings – nobles, merchants, governors, judges, officers, kings, statesmen, soldiers, having no longer ordinary human duties, but only the duties of the class to which they belong.

Thus the landed proprietor who prosecuted the peasant son account of the forest did so because he did not regard himself as an ordinary man, with the same rights as the peasants, his neighbours, but as a great landowner and a member of the nobility, and, as such, exalted by the intoxication of authority, felt himself insulted by the opposition of the peasants. And regardless of the consequences, he sends in his petition to be reinstated in his pretended rights. The judges who rendered an unfair decision in his favour, did so because they fancied themselves different from ordinary men, who are guided only by truth; under the spell of the intoxication of authority, they believed themselves the guardians of a justice which cannot err; and at the same time, under the influence of servility, they considered themselves obliged to apply certain texts set forth in a certain book and called the laws; and all the other persons who took part in this affair, from the representatives of higher authority down to the last soldier ready to fire upon his brother – they all accepted themselves in their conventionally accredited characters. Not one asked himself if he should take part in an act which his conscience reprobated, but each accepted himself as one who had simply to fulfil a certain function, let it be the Czar, anointed of God, an exceptional being called to look after the welfare of a hundred million men; let it be the noble; the priest, the recipient of grace through ordination; the soldier, bound by oath to fulfil commands without hesitation – it is the same with all.

All their activity, past, present, and future, is stimulated by a like intoxicating influence. If they had not the firm conviction that the title of king, statesman, governor, judge, landowner, marshal of nobility, officer, or soldier is of serious import and necessity, not one of them could contemplate without horror and disgust his own share in the deeds done in these latter days.

Arbitrary distinctions, established hundreds of years ago, recognized for hundreds of years, described by special names and distinguished by special dress, sanctioned by all kinds of solemnities calculated to influence men through their emotions, have been so thoroughly impressed upon the human imagination that men have forgotten the common, everyday aspects of life; they look upon themselves and others from a point of view dependent upon outward conditions, and regard their own acts and those of their neighbours accordingly.

Here, for instance, we see a man of advanced years, a man perfectly in possession of his senses, who, because he has been decorated with some bauble, and is attired in ridiculous habit, or because he is the holder of certain keys, or has received a bit of blue ribbon fitter for the wear of a coquettish child, when he is called general, chamberlain, Chevalier of the order of St. Andrew, or some such absurdity, becomes at once proud, arrogant, happy, if, on the contrary, he fails to get the gewgaw or the nickname he expected, he becomes unhappy and ill really to the point of sickness.

Or let us take a still more remarkable case. A man, morally sane, young, free, and absolutely safe from want, has no sooner received the name of district attorney, of *Zemsky Nachalnik*, than he pounces upon some luckless widow, takes her from her small children, and throws her into gaol, all because the poor woman has been secretly selling wine, and thus depriving the treasury of 25 roubles' revenue. This man feels no remorse. Another still more surprising case is that of a man, ordinarily kind and good, who, because he wears a uniform or carries a medal, and is told that he is a keeper (*garde-champetre*) or custom house officer, considers himself justified in shooting men down, and no one ever dreams of blaming him for it, nor does he think himself in the wrong; but if he failed to fire upon his fellowmen he would then indeed be culpable. I say nothing of judges and jurymen, who condemn men to death, nor of troops, who slaughter thousands without a vestige of remorse, because they are told that they are not in the position of ordinary men, but are jurymen, judges, generals, soldiers.

This abnormal and surprising state of affairs is formulated in words like these: "As a man, I sympathize with him, but as a keeper, a judge, a general, a czar, or a soldier, I must torture or murder him."

So it is in this present case; men are on the way to slaughter and torment their famine-stricken brethren, admitting all the while that in this dispute between the peasants and the landowner the former are in the right (all the superior officials told me so). They know that the peasants are miserable, poor, and hungry, and that the landowner is wealthy and one who inspires no sympathy, and yet these men are going to kill the peasants in order that this landowner may gain 3000 roubles; and all because they regard themselves at the moment not as men, but one as a governor, another as a general of gendarmerie, another as an officer, or as soldiers, as the case may be, and bound not by the eternal laws of the human conscience, but by the accidental, transitory demands of their positions.

However strange it may appear, the only explanation of this surprising phenomenon is that men are like those under hypnotic influence, who, as suggested by the hypnotizers, imagine themselves in certain conditions. Thus, for instance, when it is suggested to a hypnotized patient that he is lame, he proceeds to limp; that he is blind, he ceases to see; that he is an animal, and he begins to bite. And this is the state of all those who put their social and political duties before, and to the detriment of, their duties as human beings.

The essential characteristic of this condition is, that men, influenced by the thought that has been suggested to them, are unable to weigh their own actions, and simply obey the suggestion that has been communicated to them.

The difference between men artificially hypnotized and those under the influence of governmental suggestion consists in this, that to the former their imagined environment is suggested suddenly by one person, and the suggestion operates only for a short time; whereas to the latter, their imagined position has been the result of gradual suggestion, going on not for years but for generations, and proceeds not from a single individual but from their entire circumstances.

"But," it will be objected, "always, in all societies, the majority of men, all the children, all the women, absorbed in the duties and cares of motherhood, all the great mass of workers, who are completely absorbed by their labour, all those of weak mind, all the enfeebled, the many who have come under the subjection of nicotine, alcohol, opium, or what not – all these are not in a position to think for themselves, and consequently they submit to those who stand on a higher intellectual level, or they simply act according to domestic or social tradition, or in accordance with public opinion – and in their acting thus there is nothing abnormal or contradictory."

Indeed there is nothing unnatural in it, and the readiness with which those who reason but little submit to the guidance of men who stand on a higher plane of consciousness is a universal phenomenon, and one without which social life could not be. The minority submit to principles which they have considered for themselves, and in consequence of the accordance of these principles with their reason; the rest of men, the majority, submit to the same principles, not because of personal apprehension of their validity, but because public opinion demands it.

Such submission to public opinion of men who can think but little for themselves has nothing abnormal about it so long as public opinion maintains its unity.

But there is a period when the higher forms of truth, having been revealed to the few, are in process of transmission to the many; and when the public opinion which was based on a lower plane of consciousness has already begun to waver, to give place to the new, ready to be established. And now men begin to view their own and other men's actions in the light of their new consciousness, while, influenced by inertia and tradition, they still continue to apply principles which were the outcome of the once highest consciousness, but which are now distinctly opposed to it. Hence it is that men find themselves in an abnormal position, and that, while realizing the necessity conforming to this new public opinion, they lack courage to abandon conformity to the old one. This is the attitude which men, not only the men on the train, but the greater part of mankind, occupy toward Christian truths.

The attitude of those who belong to the upper classes, and who have all the advantages of high position, is the same as that of the lower classes who obey implicitly every command that is given to them.

Men of the ruling classes, who have no reasonable explanation of their privileges, and who in order to retain them are forced to repress all their nobler and more humane tendencies, try to persuade themselves of the necessity of their superior position; while the lower classes, stultified and oppressed by labour, are kept by the higher classes in a state of constant subjection.

This is the only possible explanation of the amazing phenomena which I witnessed on the train on the 9th of September, when men, naturally kindly and inoffensive, were to be seen going with an easy conscience to commit the most cruel, contemptible, and idiotic of crimes.

It cannot be said that they are devoid of the conscience which should forbid them to do these things, as was the case with the men who, centuries ago, tortured their fellowmen, scourged them to death, and burned them at the stake. Nay, it does exist in them, but it is kept dormant; auto-suggestion, as the psychologist calls it, keeps it thus among the upper classes, while the soldiers, the executioners, are under the hypnotic influence of the classes above them.

Conscience may slumber for a time, but it is not dead, and in spite of suggestion and auto-suggestion, it still whispers; yet a little while and it will awaken.

One might compare these men to a person under the influence of hypnotism, to whom it has been suggested that he shall commit some act contrary to his conception of right and wrong, as, for example, to murder his mother or his child. He feels himself so far coerced by the suggestion given him that he cannot refrain; and yet as the appointed time and place draw near, he seems to hear the stifled voice of conscience reviving, and he begins to draw back, he tries to awaken himself. And no one can tell whether or not hypnotic suggestion will conquer in the end; all depends on the relative strength of conflicting influences.

So it was with the soldiers on that train, so it is with all men of our period who take part in State violence and profit by it.

There was a time when, having gone forth to do violence and murder, to terrify by an example, men did not return until they had performed their mission, and then they suffered no doubt or remorse, but having done their fellowmen to death, they placidly returned to the bosom of their families, caressed their children, and with jest and laughter gave themselves up to all the pure joys of the hearth.

The men who were then benefited by violence, landed proprietors and men of wealth, believed their own interests to have a direct connection with these cruelties. It is different now, when men know, or at least suspect, the real reason why they do these things. They may close their eyes and try to silence their consciences, but neither those who commit such outrages, nor those who order them, can longer fail to discern the significance of their acts. It maybe that they do not fully appreciate it, until they are on the point of committing the deed, or in some cases not until after the deed has been done. Those soldiers, for instance, who administered the tortures during the riot at the Yuzovo factory, at Nijni-Novgorod, Saratov, and Orel, did not fully apprehend the significance of what they were doing until it was all over, and now, both they who gave the orders, and they who executed them, suffer agonies of shame in the condemnation of public opinion and of their own conscience. I have talked with some of the soldiers about it; they either tried to change the subject or spoke of it with horror and repugnance.

There are instances of men coming to their senses, however, just as they are on the point of committing deeds of the kind. I know of a sergeant who during the riots was beaten by two peasants; he reported the fact to the commander of his company, but on the following day, when he saw the tortures inflicted upon other peasants, he persuaded his superior officer to destroy his report and to allow the peasants who had beaten him to depart unpunished. I know of a case where the soldiers appointed to shoot a prisoner refused to obey; and of other occasions where the superior officers have refused to direct tortures and executions.

The men who were in the train on the 9th of September started with the intention of torturing and murdering their fellow men, but whether they would carry out their intention one could not know. However each one's share in the responsibility of this affair might be concealed from him, however strong the hypnotic suggestion among those taking part in it that they did so, not as men, but as functionaries, and so could violate all human obligations, in spite of this, the nearer they approached their destination, the more they must have hesitated about it.

It is impossible that the Governor should not pause at the moment of giving the decisive order to begin to murder and torture. He knows that the conduct of the Governor at Orel has excited the indignation of the honourable men, and he himself, influenced by public opinion, has repeatedly expressed his own disapproval of the affair; he knows that the lawyer who ought to have accompanied him distinctly refused to do so, denouncing the whole affair as shameful; he knows that changes are likely to take place in the government at any moment, the result of which would be that those who were in favour yesterday may be in disgrace tomorrow; that if the Russian press remains silent, the foreign press may give an account of this business that might cover him with opprobrium. Already he feels the influence of the new public opinion which is to supersede and destroy the old one. Moreover, he has no assurance that his subordinates may not at the last moment refuse to obey him. He hesitates; it is impossible to divine what he will do.

The functionaries and officers who accompany him feel more or less as he does. They all know at the bottom of their hearts that they are engaged in a shameful business, that their share in it stains and degrades them in the eyes of those persons whose opinion they value. They know that a man who participates in deeds like these feels shame in the presence of the woman whom he loves. And like the Governor, they too feel doubtful whether the soldiers will obey them at the last moment. What a contrast to the self-assurance of their bearing on the platform of the station! Not only do they suffer, but also they actually hesitate, and it is partly to hide their inward agitation that they assume an air of bravado. And this agitation increases as they draw nearer to their destination.

And, indeed, the entire body of soldiers, although they give no outward sign, and seem utterly submissive, are really in the same state of mind.

They are no longer like the soldiers of former days, who gave up the natural life of labour, and surrendered themselves to debauchery, rapine, and murder, as the Roman legions did, or the veterans of the Thirty Years' War, or even those soldiers of more modern times, whose term of service lasted twenty-five years. Now they are for the most part men newly taken from their families, with all the memories of the wholesome rational life from which they have been torn still fresh in their minds.

These young men, peasants for the most part, know what they are going to do; they know that the landowners generally ill-treat the peasants, and that this probably is a case in point. Furthermore, the majority of them can read, and the books they read are not always in favour of the service; some even demonstrate its immorality. They find comrades who are independent thinkers, volunteers and young officers, and the seed of doubt respecting the merit and rectitude of such deeds as they are about to commit has already been sown in their minds. True, they have all been subjected to that ingenious discipline, the work of centuries, which tends to kill the spirit of independence in every man, and are so accustomed to automatic obedience, that at the words of command, "Fire along the line!... Fire!" and so forth, their muskets are raised mechanically, and they perform the customary movements. But now: "Fire!" means something more than firing at a target; it means the murder of their abused, downtrodden fathers and brothers, who are grouped yonder in the street with their wives and children, gesticulating and crying out one does not know what.

There they are: here a man with thin beard, clad in a patched kaftan, with bast shoes on his feet, just like the father left behind in the province of Kazan or Ryazan; there another, with grey beard and bowed shoulders, leaning on a stout staff, just like the grandfather; and here a youth, with big boots and red shirt, just like himself a year ago – the soldier who is about to shoot him. And there is a woman, with her bast shoes and petticoat, like the mother he left behind him.

And he must fire upon them!

And God alone knows what each soldier will do at the supreme moment. The slightest suggestion that they ought not to do it, that they must not do it, a single word or hint, would be enough to make them pause.

Every one of these men at the moment of action will belike one hypnotized, to whom it has been suggested to chop a log, who, as he approaches the object which is told to him is a log, sees as he raises the axe that it is not a log at all, but his own brother who lies sleeping there. He may accomplish the act which has been suggested to him, or he may awake at the moment of committing it. It is the same with these men. If they do not awaken, then will a deed be done as shocking as that committed in Orel, and the reign of official hypnotism will thereby gain new power? If they awaken, then not only will the deed remain undone, but many of those who hear of their refusal to do it will free themselves from the suggestion under whose influence they have hitherto acted, or at least it will think of the possibility of doing so.

If only a few of these men come to their senses and refuse to do the deed, and fearlessly express their opinion of the wickedness of such deeds, even such a few men might enable the rest to throw off the suggestion under the influence of which they act, and such evil deeds would not be done.

And another thing: if but a few of those persons who are simply spectators of the affair would, from their knowledge of other affairs of the same kind, boldly express their opinion to those engaged in it, and point out to them their folly, cruelty, and criminality, even this would not be without a salutary influence.

This is precisely what happened in the case of Tula. Partly because certain persons expressed reluctance to take a part in the affair; because a lady passenger and others showed their indignation at a railway station; because one of the colonels whose regiment was summoned to reduce the peasants to obedience, declared that soldiers are not executioners – because of these and other apparently trifling influences the affair took on a different aspect, and the troops on arriving did not commit outrages, but contented themselves with cutting down the trees and sending them to the landowner.

Had it not been that certain of these men conceived a distinct idea that they were doing wrong, and had not the idea got abroad, the occurrences at Orel would have been repeated. Had the feeling been stronger, perhaps the Governor and his troops would not have gone so far as even to fell the trees and deliver them to the landowner. Had it been more powerful still, perhaps the Governor would not have dared even to set out for Tula; its influence might even have gone so far as to prevent the Minister from framing, and the Emperor from confirming, such decrees.

All depends, as we come therefore to see, upon the degree of consciousness that men possess of Christian truth.

Hence let all men today who wish to promote the welfare of mankind direct their efforts towards the development of this consciousness of Christian truth.

But, strange to say, those men who nowadays talk most of the amelioration of human life, and who are the acknowledged leaders of public opinion, declare this to be precisely the wrong thing to do, and that there are more effectual expedients for improving human existence. They insist that any improvement in the conditions of human life must be accomplished, not through individual moral effort, nor through the propagation of truth, but through progressive modifications in the general material conditions of life. Therefore, they say, individual effort should be devoted to the gradual reform of the everyday conditions of life; and seeing that any individual profession of the truth which may happen to be incompatible with the existing order is harmful, because it provokes, on the part of the government, an opposition which prevents the individual from continuing efforts which may be of utility to society.

According to this theory, all changes in the life of mankind proceed from the same causes that control the lives of the brute creation.

And all the religious teachers, like Moses and the Prophets, Confucius, Lao Tze, Buddha, and Christ, preached their doctrines and their followers adopted them, not because they divined and loved the truth, but because the political, social, and above all the economical conditions of the nations in whose midst these doctrines found expression were favourable to their exposition and development.

Therefore the principal activity of a man who wishes to serve the world and to improve the condition of his kind should be directed, according to this theory, not to teaching and profession of the truth, but to the improvement of the outward, political, social, and above all economic conditions of life. The change in these conditions may be accomplished by serving the government and introducing liberal and progressive principles, by contributing to the development of commerce, by propagating socialistic principles, but above all by promoting the diffusion of science.

According to this doctrine, it is a matter of no consequence whether one profess the revealed truth or not; there is no obligation to live in accordance with its precepts, or to refrain from actions opposed to them – as, for instance, to serve the government, though one considers its power detrimental; to profit by the organization of capital, though one disapproves of it; to subscribe to certain forms of religion, though one considers them superstitions. Practise in the courts of law, though one believes them to be corrupt; or enter the army, or take the oath of allegiance, or indeed lie, or do anything that is convenient. These things are trivial, for it is a matter of vital importance, instead of challenging the prevailing customs of the day, to conform to them, though they be contrary to one's convictions, satisfied meanwhile to try and liberalize the existing institutions, by encouraging commerce, propagating socialistic doctrines, and generally promoting *soi-disant* science and civilization. According to this convenient theory, it is possible for a man to remain a landowner, a merchant, a manufacturer, a judge, a functionary paid by the government, a soldier, an officer, and at the same time to be humanitarian, socialist, and revolutionary.

Hypocrisy, formerly growing only out of such religious doctrines as that of original sin, redemption, the Church, has in these latter days, by means of the new theory, gained for itself a scientific basis, and those whose intellectual habit of mind renders the hypocrisy of the Church unendurable, are yet deceived by this new hypocrisy with the cachet of science. If in old times a man who professed the doctrines taught by the Church could with a clear conscience take part in any political crime, and benefit by so doing, provided he complied with the external forms of his faith; men of the present day who deny Christianity, and view the conduct of life from a secular and scientific standpoint, are every whit as sure of their own innocence, even of their lofty morality, when they participate in and benefit by the evil-doings of government.

It is not alone in Russia, but in France, England, Germany, and America as well, that we find the wealthy landed proprietor, who, in return for having allowed the men who live on his estate and who supply him with the products of the soil, extorts from these men, who are often poverty-stricken, all that he possibly can. Whenever these oppressed labourers make an attempt to gain something for themselves from the lands which the rich man calls his own, without first asking his consent, troops are called out, who torture and put to death those who have been bold enough to take such liberties.

By methods like this are claims to the ownership of land made good. One would hardly imagine that a man who lived in such a wicked and selfish manner could call himself a Christian, or even liberal. One would think that if a man cared to seem Christian or liberal, he would at least cease to plunder and to torment his fellow men with the aid of the government, in order to vindicate his claims to the ownership of land. And such would be the case were it not for the metaphysical hypocrisy which teaches that from a religious standpoint it is immaterial whether one owns land or not, and that, from the scientific point of view, for a single individual to give up his land would be a useless sacrifice, without any effect on the well-being of mankind, the amelioration of which can only be brought about by a progressive modification of outward conditions.

Meanwhile, your modern landowner will, without the least hesitation or doubt, organize an agricultural exhibition, or a temperance society, or through his wife and daughters distribute warm underclothing and soup to three old women; and he will hold forth before the domestic circle, or in society, or as a member of committees, or in the public press, upon the gospel of love for mankind in general, and the agricultural class in particular, that class which he never ceases to torment and oppress. And those who occupy a similar position will believe in him and sing his praises, and take counsel together upon the best methods of improving the condition of those very labouring classes they spend their lives in exploiting; and for this purpose they suggest every possible expedient, save that which would effect it – namely, to desist from robbing the poor of the land necessary for their subsistence.

(A striking example of this hypocrisy was presented by the Russian landowners during the struggle with the famine of last year, a famine of which they were themselves the cause, and by which they profited, not only by selling bread at the highest price, but even by disposing of the dried potato plants for five roubles a desisting, to be used as fuel by the freezing peasants.)

The business of the merchant, again (as is the case with business of any kind), is based upon a series of frauds; he takes advantage of the necessities of men by buying his merchandise below, and selling it above its value. One would think that a man, the mainspring of whose activity is what he himself in his own language calls shrewdness, ought to feel ashamed of this, and never dream of calling himself Christian or liberal while he continues a merchant. But, according to the new metaphysic of hypocrisy, he may pass for a virtuous man and still pursue his evil career; the religious man has but to believe, the liberal man but to co-operate, in the reform of external conditions to promote the general progress of commerce; the rest does not signify. So, this merchant (who besides often sells bad commodities, adulter-ates and uses false weights and measures, or deals exclusively in commodities that imperil human life, such as alcohol or opium) frankly considers himself, and is considered by others – always provided he only does not cheat his colleagues in business and knavery, his fellow tradesmen – a model of conscientiousness and honesty. And if he spend one per cent, of his stolen money on some public institution, hospital, museum, or school, men call him the benefactor of the people on whose exploitation all his welfare depends; and if he gives but the least part of this money to the church or to the poor, then is he deemed an exemplary Christian indeed.

Take again the factory owner, whose entire income is derived from reducing the pay of his workmen to its lowest terms, and whose whole business is carried on by forced and unnatural la-bour, endangering the health of generations of men. One would suppose that if this man professed Christian or liberal principles he would cease to sacrifice human lives to his interests. But, ac-cording to the existing theory, he encourages industry, and it would be a positive injury to society if he were to abandon his operations, even supposing he were willing to do so. And, too, this man, the cruel slave-driver of thousands of human beings, having built for those injured in his service minute houses, with gardens six feet in extent, or established a fund, or a home for the aged, or a hospital, is perfectly satisfied that he has more than atoned for the moral and physical jeopardy into which he has plunged so many lives; and he continues to live calmly, proud of his work.

We find that the functionary, civil, military, or ecclesiastical, who performs his duties to gratify his selfishness or ambition, or, as is more usually the case, for the sake of the stipend, collected in the shape of taxes from an exhausted and crippled people – if, by a rare exception, he does not directly steal from the public treasury – considers himself, and is considered by his equals, a most useful and virtuous member of society.

There are judges and other legal functionaries who know that their decisions have condemned hundreds and thousands of unfortunate men to be torn from their families and thrown into prison. There these hapless beings are locked up in solitary confinement, or sent to the galleys, where they go desperate and put an end to themselves by starving themselves to death, by swallowing glass, or by some such means. And who knows what the mothers, wives, and children of these men suffer by the separation and imprisonment, and the disgrace of it – who have vainly begged for pardon for their sons, husbands, brothers, or that their lot may be a little alleviated. But the judge or other legal functionary is so primed with the current hypocrisy that he himself, his colleagues, his wife, and his friends are all quite sure, despite what he does, that he is a good and sensible man. According to the current philosophy of hypocrisy such a man performs a duty of great importance to the public. And this man, who has injured hundreds or thousands of human beings, who owe it to him that they have lost their belief in goodness and their faith in God, goes to church with a benevolent smile, listens to the Bible, makes liberal speeches, caresses his children, bestows moral lessons upon them for their edification, and grows sentimental over imaginary suffering.

Not only these men, their wives and children, but the entire community around them, all the teachers, actors, cooks, jockeys, live by preying upon the lifeblood of the working people, which in one way or another they absorb like leeches. Every one of their days of pleasure costs thousands of days in the lives of the workers. They seethe suffering and privation of these workmen, of their wives and children, of their aged and feeble. They know what punishments are visited upon those who attempt to resist the organized system of pillage, but so far from abandoning or concealing their luxurious habits, they flaunt them in the faces of those whom they oppress and by whom they are hated. All the while they assure themselves and others that they have the welfare of the working man greatly at heart. On Sundays, clad in rich garments, they drive in their carriages to churches where the mockery of Christianity is preached, and listen there to the words of men who have learned their falsehoods by heart. Some of these men wear stoles, some wear white cravats; they all preach the doctrine of love for one's neighbour, a doctrine belied by their daily lives. And they have all grown so accustomed to playing this part that they really believe themselves to be what they pretend.

This universal hypocrisy, which has become to every class of society at the present day like the air it breathes, is so familiar that men are no longer exasperated by it. It is very fitting that hypocrisy should signify acting or playing of a part. It has become so much a matter of course that it no longer excites surprise when the representatives of Christ pronounce a blessing over murderers as they stand in rank holding their guns in the position which signifies, in military parlance, "for prayers," or when the priests and pastors of various Christian sects accompany the executioner to the scaffold, and, by lending the sanction of their presence to murder, make men believe it compatible with Christianity. (One minister was present when experiments in "electrocution" took place in the United States.) At the International Prison Exposition recently held in St. Petersburg, where instruments of torture, such as chains, and models of prison cells for solitary confinement – means of torture worse than the knout or the rod – were on exhibition, sympathetic ladies and gentlemen went to see them, and seemed greatly entertained.

No one marvels to find liberal science insisting upon the equality, fraternity, and liberty of men on the one hand, while on the other it is striving to prove the necessity of armies, executions, custom houses, of censorship of the press, of legalized prostitution, of the expulsion of foreign labour, of the prohibition of emigration, and of the necessity and justice of colonization established by the pillage and extermination of whole races of so-called savages, etc.

They talk of what will happen when all men shall profess what they call Christianity (by which they mean the different conflicting creeds); when every one will be fed and clothed, when men will communicate with one another all over the world by telegraph and telephones, and will travel in balloons; when all working men will accept the doctrine of socialism, when the trades unions will embrace many millions of men and possess millions of money; when all men will be educated, will read the papers, and be familiar with all the sciences.

But what good will this do if after all these improvements men are still false to the truth?

The miseries of men are caused by disunion, and disunion arises from the fact that men follow not truth, but falsehood, of which there is no end. Truth is the only bond by which men may be united; and the more sincerely men strive after the truth the nearer they approach to true unity.

But how are men to be united in the truth, or even approach it, if they not only fail to proclaim the truth which they possess but actually think it useless to do so, and pretend to believe in something which they know to be a lie? In reality no improvement in the condition of mankind is possible while men continue to hide the truth from themselves, nor until they acknowledge that their unity, and consequently their welfare, can be promoted only by the spirit of truth; until they admit that to profess, and to act in obedience to the truth as it has been revealed to them, is more important than all things else.

Let all the material progress ever dreamt of by religious and scientific men be made; let all men accept Christianity, and let all the improvements suggested by the Bellamys and Richets, with every possible addition and correction, be carried out, and yet if the hypocrisy of today still flourishes, if men do not make known the truth that is within them, but go on pretending to believe what they know to be untrue, showing respect where they no longer feel it, their condition will never improve; on the contrary, it will become worse. The more men are raised above want, the more telegraphs, telephones, books, newspapers, and reviews they possess, the more numerous will be the channels for the diffusion of falsehood and hypocrisy, and the more at variance and miserable will men become – and it is even so at the present time.

Let all those material changes take place, and still the position of humanity will in no way be improved by them; but let every man, so far as he is able, begin at once and live up to his highest ideal of the truth, or at the least cease to defend a lie, then indeed should we see even in this year of 1893 such an advance in the establishment of the truth upon earth, and in the deliverance of mankind, as could hardly be hoped for in a hundred years.

It was not without reason that the only harsh and denunciatory words that Christ uttered were addressed to hypocrites. It is neither theft, nor robbery, nor murder, nor fornication, nor fraud, but falsehood, that particular hypocritical falsehood which destroys in men's conscience the distinction between good and evil, which corrupts them and takes from them the possibility of avoiding evil and of seeking good, which deprives them of that which constitutes the essence of a true human life – it is this which bars the way to all improvement. Those men who do evil, knowing not the truth, inspire in the beholder compassion for their victims and repugnance for themselves, but they only injure the few whom they molest. Whereas those men who, knowing the good, yet pursue the evil, wearing all the while the mantle of hypocrisy, commit a wrong not only against themselves and their victims, but also against thousands of other men who are deceived by the falsehood under which they conceal the wrong.

Thieves, robbers, murderers, rogues, who commit acts which they themselves, as well as other men, know to be evil, serve as a warning to show men what is evil, and make them hate it. Those, however, who steal, rob, torture, and murder, justifying themselves by pretended religious, scientific, or other motives, like the landowners, merchants, factory owners, and government servants of the present time, by provoking imitation, injure not only their victims but thousands and millions of men who are corrupted by their influence and who become so blinded that they cannot distinguish the difference between good and evil.

One fortune acquired by trading in the necessaries of life or in articles that tend to demoralize men, or by speculations in the stock exchange, or by the acquisition of cheap lands which subsequently rise in value by reason of the increasing needs of the people, or by the establishment of factories that endanger human health and human lives, or by rendering civil or military service to the State, or by any occupation that tends to the demoralization of mankind – a fortune acquired in any of these ways, not only permitted, but approved by the leaders of society, when, furthermore, it is supported by a show of charity, surely demoralizes men more than millions of thefts, frauds, or robberies – sins committed against the laws of the land and subject to judicial prosecution.

A single enforcement of capital punishment, ordained by men of education and wealth, sanctioned by the approval of the Christian clergy, and declared to be an act of justice essential to the welfare of the State, tends far more to degrade and brutalize mankind than hundreds and thousands of murders committed in passion by the ignorant. A more demoralizing scene than the execution suggested by Jukovsky, calculated as it is to excite a feeling of religious exaltation, it would be difficult to conceive.

A war even of the shortest duration, with all its customary consequences, the destruction of harvests, the thefts, the unchecked debauchery and murders, with the usual explanations of its necessity and justice, with the accompanying glorification and praise bestowed upon military exploits, upon patriotism, devotion to the flag, with the assumption of tenderness and care for the wounded, will do more in one year to demoralize men than thousands of robberies, arsons, and murders committed in the course of centuries by individual men carried away by passion.

The existence of one household, one not even extravagant beyond the ordinary limits, esteeming itself virtuous and innocent, which yet consumes the production of enough to support thousands of the men who live near in poverty and distress, has a more degrading influence on mankind than innumerable orgies of gross shopkeepers, officers, or workmen who are addicted to drink and debauchery, and who smash mirrors and crockery by way of amusement.

One solemn procession, one religious service, or one sermon from the pulpit, embodying a falsehood, which the preacher himself does not believe, does infinitely more harm than thousands of frauds, adulterations of food, etc.

Men talk of the hypocrisy of the Pharisees; but the hypocrisy of our contemporaries far surpasses the comparatively harmless acrimoniousness of the Pharisees. They at least had an outward religious law, whose fulfilment may perhaps have prevented them from discerning their duty towards their neighbours; indeed, those duties had not then been distinctly defined. Today there is no such law. (I do not consider such gross and stupid men as even now believe that sacraments or absolution of the Pope can free them from sins.) On the contrary, the law of the Gospel, which in one form or another we all profess, makes our duties perfectly plain. Indeed, those precepts, which were but vaguely indicated by certain of the prophets have since been so clearly formulated, have grown to be such truisms, that the very schoolboys and hack writers repeat them. Therefore men of our times cannot feign ignorance concerning them.

Those men who enjoy the advantages of the existing system, and who are always protesting love for their neighbour, without suspicion that their own lives are an injury to their neighbours, are like the robber who, caught with an uplifted knife, his victim crying desperately for help, protests that he did not know that he was doing anything unpleasant to the man whom he was in the act of robbing and about to murder. Since the denial of this robber and murderer would be of no avail, his act being patent to all observers, it would seem equally futile for our fellow citizens, who live by the sufferings of the oppressed, to assure themselves and others that they desire the welfare of those whom they never cease to rob, and that they had not realized the nature of the methods by which their prosperity had been attained.

We can no longer persuade ourselves that we do not know of the one hundred thousand men in Russia alone who have been shut up in galleys or in prisons for the purpose of securing to us our property and our peace; and that we do not know of the existence of those courts of law at which we preside, to which we bring our accusations, which sentence those men who have attacked our property or our lives to the galleys, to imprisonment, or to exile, where human beings, no worse than they who have pronounced judgment upon them, become degraded and lost; nor that we do not know that everything that we possess has been won and is preserved at the expense of murder and violence. We cannot shut our eyes and pretend that we do not see the policeman, who, armed with a revolver, paces before our window, protecting us while we are eating our excellent dinner, or when we are at the theatre seeing a new play; nor do not know of the existence of the soldiers who will appear armed with guns and cartridges whenever our property is menaced. We know perfectly well that if we finish our dinner, see the new play to it send, enjoy a merrymaking at Christmas, take a walk, go to a ball, a race, or a hunt, we owe it to the policeman's revolver or the ball in the soldier's musket, which will pierce the hungry belly of the disinherited man who, with watering mouth, peeps round the corner at our pleasures, and who might interrupt them if the policeman or the soldiers in the barracks were not ready to appear at our first call. Hence, as the man who is caught in the act of robbery in broad daylight cannot deny that he threatened his victim with a knife for the purpose of stealing his purse, it might be supposed that we could no longer represent to ourselves and to others that the soldiers and policemen whom we see around us are here not for the purpose of protecting us, but to repulse foreign enemies, to assure public order, to adorn by their presence public rejoicings and ceremonies. We cannot pretend we do not know that men are not fond of starving to death. We know that they do not like to die of hunger, being deprived of the right to earn their living from the soil upon which they live, that they are not anxious to work ten to fourteen hours a day underground, standing in water, or in overheated rooms, twelve or fourteen hours a day, or at night, manufacturing articles which contribute to our pleasures. It would seem impossible to deny what is so evident, and yet it is what we do deny.

It cannot be denied that there are people of the wealthy class, and I am glad to say that I meet them more and more frequently, particularly in the younger generation and among women, who, on being reminded by what means and at what a price their pleasures are obtained, instantly admit the truth of it, and with bowed heads exclaim: "Ah, do not tell us of it! If it is as you say, one cannot live!" If, however, there are some who are willing to admit theirs in, though they know not how to escape from it, still, the majority of men nowadays have become so confirmed in hypocrisy that they boldly deny facts that are patent to every one who has eyes.

"It is all nonsense," they say. "No one forces the people to work for the landowners or in the factories. It is a matter of mutual accommodation. Large properties and capital are indispensable, because they enable men to organize companies and provide work for the labouring classes, and the work in mills and factories is by no means so dreadful as you represent it. When real abuses are found to exist, the government and society in general take measures to abolish them and to render the labour of the working men easier and more agreeable. The working classes are used to physical labour, and are not as yet capable of doing anything else. The poverty of the people is caused neither by the landowners nor by the tyranny of the capitalists; it springs from other causes – from ignorance, disorder, and intemperance. We, the governing classes, who counteract this state of poverty by wise administration; and we, the capitalists, who counteract it by the multiplication of useful inventions; and we, the liberals, who contribute our share by instituting trade unions. And by diffusing education – these are the methods by which we promote the welfare of the people, without making any radical change in our position. We do not wish all to be poor like the poor; we wish all to be rich like the rich.

"As to torturing and killing men for the purpose of making them work for the rich, that is all sophistry; the troops are sent out to quell disturbances when men, not appreciating their advantages, rebel and disturb the peace essential for the general welfare. It is equally necessary to restrain malefactors, for whom prisons, gallows, and the like are established. We are anxious enough to abolish them as far as possible ourselves, and are working for that purpose."

Hypocrisy, which nowadays is supported by two methods, the quasi-religious and the quasi-scientific, has attained such proportions, that if we did not live in its atmosphere continually, it would be impossible to believe that humanity could sink to such depths of self-deception. Men have reached so surprising a state, their hearts have become so hardened, that they look and do not see, listen and do not hear or understand.

For a long time they have been living a life that is contrary to their conscience. Were it not for the aid of hypocrisy they would be unable so to live, for such a life, so opposed to conscience, can only continue because it is veiled by hypocrisy.

And the greater the difference between the practice and the conscience of men, the more elastic becomes hypocrisy. Yet even hypocrisy has its limits, and I believe that we have reached them. Every man of the present day, with the Christian consciousness that has involuntarily become his, may be likened to a sleeper who dreams that he is doing what even in his dream he knows he ought not to do. In the depths of his dream-consciousness he realizes his conduct, and yet seems unable to change his course, and to cease doing that which he is aware he should not do.

Then, in the progress of his dream, his state of mind becoming less and less endurable, he begins to doubt the reality of what has seemed so real, and makes a conscious effort to break the spell that holds him.

The average man of our Christian world is in exactly the same strait. He feels that everything going on around him is absurd, senseless, and impossible; that the situation is becoming more and more painful, that it has indeed reached the crisis.

It is impossible that we of the present age, endowed with the Christian conscience that has become a part of our very flesh and blood as it were, who live with a full consciousness of the dignity of man and the equality of all men, who feel our need for peaceable relations with each other and for the unity of all nations, should go on living in such a way. It is impossible that all our pleasures, all our satisfactions, should be purchased by the sufferings and the lives of our brethren; impossible that we should be ready at a moment's notice to rush upon each other like wild beasts, one nation against another, and relentlessly destroy the lives and labour of men, only because one foolish diplomatist or ruler says or writes something foolish to another.

It is impossible; and yet all men of our time see that this is what does happen every day, and all wait for the catastrophe, while the situation grows more and more strained and painful.

And as a man in his sleep doubts the reality of his dream and longs to awaken and return to real life, so the average man of our day cannot, in the bottom of his heart, believe the terrible situation in which he finds himself, and which is growing worse and worse, to be the reality. He longs to attain to a higher reality, the consciousness of which is already within him.

And like this sleeper, who has but to make the conscious effort to ask himself whether it be a dream, in order to transform its seeming hopelessness into a joyous awakening, our average man has but to make a conscious effort and ask himself, "Is not all this an illusion?" in order to feel himself forthwith like the awakened sleeper, transported from an hypocritical and horrible dream-world into a living, peaceful, and joyous real one.

And for this he has no need of any heroic achievement; he has only to make the effort prompted by his moral consciousness.

But is man able to make this effort?

According to the existing theory, one indispensable from the point of view of hypocrisy, man is not free and may not change his life.

"A man cannot change his life, because he is not a free agent. He is not a free agent, because his acts are the result of preceding causes. And whatever he may do, certain it is that preceding causes always determine that a man must act in one way rather than in another; therefore a man is not free to change his life," – thus argue the defenders of the metaphysic of hypocrisy. And they would be perfectly right if man were an unconscious and stationary being, incapable of apprehending the truth, and unable to advance to a higher state by means of it. But man is a conscious being, able to grow more and more in the knowledge of truth. Therefore if he were not free in his acts, the causes of these acts, which consist in the recognition simply of such and such truth, are yet within his mastery.

So that if a man is not free to do certain acts, he is yet free to work towards the suppression of the moral causes which prevent their performance. Tie may be likened to the engineer of a locomotive, who, though not at liberty to change the past or present motion of his engine, is yet free to determine its future progress.

No matter what an intelligent man may do, he adopts a certain course of action only because he acknowledges to himself that at the moment that course alone is the right one; or because he has formerly recognized it as such, and now continues to act as he does through force of habit, or through mental inertia.

Whether a man eats or abstains from food, whether he works

THE KINGDOM OF GOD IS WITHIN YOU

or rests, whether he avoids danger or seeks it, he acts as he does
because he considers it to be reasonable at the time, or because
previously he saw that the truth consisted in acting in that way
and not in another.

The admission or the denial of a certain truth depends not on
outward causes, but on certain conditions that man finds within himself. Thus frequently, with all the outward and, as it may
seem, favourable conditions for recognizing the truth, one may
reject it, while another may receive it under the most unfavourable conditions, and without apparent motives. As it is said in
the Gospel: "No man can come to me, except the Father which
hath sent me draw him." That is to say, the recognition of truth,
which is the cause of all the manifestations of a man's life, does
not depend on outward conditions, but on certain inherent qualities which escape recognition.

Therefore a man who is not free in his acts still feels himself
free in regard to the cause of his acts; that is, in regard to the
recognition or non-recognition of truth.

Thus a man who, under the influence of passion, has committed a deed contrary to the truth he knows, still remains free
in recognizing or denying the truth; in other words, denying the
truth, he may consider his act necessary and justify himself in
committing it, or, accepting the truth, he may acknowledge his
deed to be evil and himself guilty.

Thus a gambler or a drunkard, who has succumbed to his
passion, is free to acknowledge gambling or drunkenness either
as evils, or as amusements without consequence. In the first instance, if he cannot get rid of his passion at once, he becomes
free from it gradually, according to the depth of his conviction of
its evil. In the second instance, his passion grows and gradually
deprives him of all chance of deliverance.

So, too, with a man who, unable to endure the scorching
flames for the rescue of his friend, himself escapes from a burning house, while he recognizes the truth that a man should save
the life of his fellowman at the peril of his own, is yet free to
look upon his act as evil, and therefore to condemn himself for
it; or, denying this truth, to judge his act to be both natural and
necessary, and so justify himself in his own opinion. In the first

instance, his recognition of the truth, even though he has not acted in accordance with it, helps him to prepare for a series of self-sacrificing actions that will inevitably follow such recognition. In the second instance, he prepares for a series of actions just as selfish.

I do not say that a man is always free to recognize or not to recognize every truth. Certain truths there are long since recognized by men, and transmitted by tradition, education, and mere force of habit, until they have become second nature; and there are other truths which men perceive as but dimly and afar. A man is not free not to recognize the first of these; he is not free to recognize the second. But there is a third category of truths, which have not as yet become unquestioned motors of his activity, but have revealed themselves to man so unmistakably that he is unable to disregard them; he must inevitably consider them, and either accept or reject them. It is by his relation to these truths that a man's freedom is manifested.

Each man in his perception of truth is like a wayfarer who walks by the aid of a lantern whose light he casts before him: he does not see what as yet has not been revealed by its beams, he does not see the path he has left behind, merged again in the darkness; but at any given point he sees that which the lantern reveals, and he is always at liberty to choose one side of the road or the other.

There exist for each man certain concealed truths, as yet unrevealed to his mental vision; certain others, which he has experienced, assimilated, and forgotten; and yet others, that rise up before him demanding immediate recognition from his reason. And it is in the recognition or the disregard of these truths that what we call freedom becomes evident.

All the apparent difficulty of the question of man's liberty comes from the fact that those who seek to solve it represent man as stationary in the presence of the truth.

Undoubtedly he is not free if we look upon him as a stationary being; if we forget that the life of all humanity is an eternal procession from darkness to light, from the lower conception of truth to a higher one, from truth mingled with error to purer truth.

A man would not be free if he were ignorant of all truth; neither would he be free, nor even have any conception of liberty, if the truth were suddenly revealed to him in its entire purity and without any admixture of error.

But man is not a stationary being. And as he advances in life, every individual discovers an ever-increasing proportion of truth, and thus becomes less liable to error.

The relations of man to truth are threefold. Some truths are so familiar to him that they have become the unconscious springs of action; others have only been dimly revealed to him; again others, though still unfamiliar, are revealed to him so plainly that they force themselves upon his attention, and inevitably, in one way or another, he is obliged to consider them. He cannot ignore them, but must either recognize or repudiate them.

And it is in the recognition or in the disregard of these truths that man's free agency is manifested.

A man's freedom does not consist in a faculty of acting independently of his environment and the various influences it brings to bear upon his life, but in his power to become, through recognizing and professing the truth that has been revealed to him, a free and willing labourer at the eternal and infinite work performed by God and his universe; or, in shutting his eyes to truth, to become a slave and be forced against his will into a way in which he is loath to go.

Not only does truth point out the direction a man's life should take, but it opens the only road he can take. Hence, all men will invariably, free or not, follow the road of truth; some willingly, doing the work they have set themselves to do; others involuntarily, by submitting in spite of themselves to the law of life. It is in the power of choice that a man's freedom lies.

Freedom, in limits so narrow as these, appears to men so insignificant that they fail to perceive it. The believers in causation prefer to overlook it; the believers in unlimited free will, keeping in view their own ideal, disdain a freedom to them so insignificant. Freedom, confined between the limits of entire ignorance of the truth, or of the knowledge of only a part of it, does not seem to them to be freedom, the more so that whether a man is, or is not willing to recognize the truth revealed unto him, he will inevitably be forced to obey it in life.

A horse harnessed to a load in company with other horses is not free to remain in one place. If he does not pull the load, the load will strike him and force him to move in the direction it is going, thus compelling him to advance. Still, in spite of this limitation of freedom, the horse is still free to pull the load of his own accord or be pushed forward by it. The same reasoning can be applied to human freedom.

Be this freedom great or small as compared with the chimerical freedom for which we sigh, it is the only true freedom, and through it alone is to be found all the happiness accessible to man. And not only does this freedom promote the happiness of men, but it is the only means through which the work of the world can be accomplished.

According to the doctrine of Christ, a man who limits his observation of life to the sphere in which there is no freedom – to the sphere of effects – that is, of acts – does not live a true life. He only lives a true life who has transferred his life into the sphere in which freedom lies – into the domain of first causes – that is to say by the recognition and practice of the truth revealed to him.

The man who consecrates his life to sensual acts is ever performing acts that depend on temporary causes beyond his control. Of himself he does nothing; it only seems to him that he is acting independently, whereas in reality all that he imagines he is doing by himself is done through him by a superior force; he is not the creator of life, but its slave. But the man who devotes his life to the acknowledgment and practice of the truth revealed to him unites himself with the source of universal life, and accomplishes not personal, individual acts, that depend on the conditions of time and space, but acts that have no causes, but are in themselves causes of all else, and have an endless and unlimited significance.

Because of their setting aside the essence of true life, which consists in the recognition and practice of the truth, and directing their efforts towards the improvement of the external conditions of life, men of the pagan life-conception may be likened to passengers on a steamer, who should, in their anxiety to reach their destination, extinguish the engine fires, and instead of making use of steam and screw, try during a storm to row with oars which cannot reach the water.

The Kingdom of God is attained by effort, and it is only those who make the effort that do attain it. It is this effort, which consists in sacrificing outward conditions for the sake of the truth, by which the Kingdom of God is attained – an effort which can and ought to be made now, in our own epoch.

Men have but to understand this: that they must cease to care for material and external matters, in which they are not free; let them apply one hundredth part of the energy now used by them in outward concerns to those in which they are free – to the recognition and profession of the truth that confronts them, to the deliverance of themselves and others from the falsehood and hypocrisy which conceal the truth; and then the false system of life which now torments us, which threatens us with still greater suffering, will be destroyed at once without struggle. Then the Kingdom of Heaven, at least in that first stage, for which men through the development of their consciousness are already prepared, will be established.

As one shake is sufficient to precipitate into crystals a liquid saturated with salt, so at the present time it may be that only the least effort is needed in order that the truth, already revealed to us, should spread among hundreds, thousands, millions of men, and a public opinion become established in conformity with the existing consciousness, and the entire social organization become transformed. It depends upon us to make this effort.

If only each of us would try to understand and recognize the Christian truth, which in the most varied forms surrounds us on all sides, pleading to be admitted into our hearts, if we would cease to lie and pretend that we do not see this truth, or that we are anxious to fulfil it, excepting in the one thing that it really demands – if we would only recognize this truth which calls us, and would fearlessly profess it, we should find forthwith that hundreds, thousands, and millions of men are in the same position as ourselves, fearing like ourselves to standalone in its recognition, and waiting only to hear its avowal from others.

If men would only cease to be hypocrites they would perceive at once that this cruel organization of society, which alone hampers them and yet appears to them like something immutable, necessary, and sacred, established by God, is already wavering, and is maintained only by the hypocrisy and the falsehood of ourselves and our fellow men.

But if it be true that it depends only on ourselves to change the existing order of life, have we the right to do it without knowing what we shall put in its place? What will become of the world if the present system were destroyed?

"What is there beyond the walls of the world we leave behind us?

"Fear seizes us – emptiness, space, freedom . . . how is one to go on, not knowing whither? How is one to lose, without the hope of gain?

"Had Columbus reasoned thus he never would have weighed anchor? It was madness to attempt to cross an unknown ocean, to set sail for a country whose very existence was doubtful. But he discovered a new world through this madness. To be sure, if people had only to move from one furnished house into another and a more commodious one, it would be an easy matter, but the trouble lies in there being no one to prepare the new apartments. The future looks more uncertain still than the ocean – it promises nothing – it will only be what men and circumstances make it.

"If you are content with the old world, try to preserve it; it is sick, and will not live long. But if you can no longer live in the eternal conflict between your convictions and life, thinking one way and acting another, take it upon yourselves to leave the shelter of the blanched and ruinous arches of the Middle Ages. I am aware that this is not an easy matter. It is hard to part with all one has been accustomed to from birth. Men are ready for great sacrifices, but not those which the new life demands of them. Are they ready to sacrifice their present civilization, their mode of life, their religion, their conventional morality? Are they ready to be deprived of all the results of such prolonged efforts, the results we have boasted of for three centuries, of all the conveniences and attractions of our existence, to give the preference to wild youth rather than to civilized senility, to pull down the palace built by our fathers simply for the pleasure of laying the foundation of a new house, which, without doubt, will not be completed till long after our time." Thus wrote, almost half a century ago, a Russian author, who, with penetrating vision, clearly discerned even at that time what is recognized by every man today who reflects a little – the impossibility of continuing life on the former basis, and the necessity of establishing some new mode of existence.

It is plain from the simplest and most ordinary point of view that it is folly to remain under a roof that threatens to fall, and that one must leave it. Indeed, it is difficult to imagine a more miserable situation than that of the present Christian world, with its nations arrayed in arms one against the other, with its ever increasing taxes the purpose of supporting its growing armaments, with the burning hatred of the working classes for the rich, with war suspended above all like the Sword of Damocles ready to fall, as it may, at any moment.

It is doubtful whether any revolution could be more disastrous than the present social order, or rather disorder, with its perpetual victims of overwork, misery, drunkenness, dissipation, with all the horrors of impending war that in one year will sacrifice more lives than all the revolutions of the present century.

What will become of mankind if each one fulfils that which God demands through the conscience that is in him? Shall I be safe if, under the orders of my master, I accomplish in his great workshop the tasks he has set me, although, ignorant of his final plans, I may think it strange? Nor is it alone the question of the future that troubles men when they hesitate to do the master's bidding. They are concerned about the question as to how they are to live without the familiar conditions which we call science, art, civilization, culture. We feel individually all the burden of our present way of living; we see that were this order of things to continue, it would inevitably ruin us; and yet we are anxious to have these conditions continue, to have our science, our art, our civilization, and culture remain unchanged. It is as though a man who dwells in an old house, suffering from cold and discomfort, who is moreover aware that its walls may tumble at any moment, should consent to the remodelling of it, only on condition that he may be allowed to remain there, a condition that is equivalent to a refusal to have his dwelling rebuilt. "What, if I should leave my house," he says, "I should be temporarily deprived of its comforts; the new house may not be built after all, or it may be constructed on a new plan, which will lack the conveniences to which I have been accustomed!" But if the materials and the work men are ready, it is probable that the new house will be built, and in a better manner than the old one; while it is not only probable but certain that the old house will soon fail into ruins, crushing those who remain within its walls. In order that the old, every day conditions of life may disappear and make room for new and better ones, we must surely leave behind the old conditions, which are at length become fatal and impossible, and issue forth to meet the future.

"But science, art, civilization, and culture will cease to be!" But if all these are only diverse manifestations of truth, the impending change is to be accomplished for the sake of a further advance towards truth and its realization. "How then can the manifestations of truth disappear, in consequence of further realization of truth?" The manifestations of truth will be different, better, loftier, the error that has been in them will perish, while the verity that is in them will remain and flourish with renewed vigour.

Return to yourselves, sons of men, and have faith in the Gospel, and in its doctrine of eternal happiness! If you heed not this warning, you shall all perish like the men slain by Pilate, like those upon whom the Tower of Siloam fell; like millions of other men, who slew and were slain, who executed and suffered execution, who tortured and were tortured; as perished the man who so foolishly filled his granaries, counting on a long life, on the very night when his soul was required of him. Return, sons of men, and believe in the words which Christ uttered 1800 years ago, words which He repeats today with greater force, warning us that the evil day He foretold is at hand, and that our life has reached its last descent of folly and wickedness.

Now, after so many centuries of futile effort to protect ourselves by the methods of the pagan system of violence, it should be evident to every man that all such effort, far from insuring our safety, tends only to add a new element of danger both to individual and social existence.

No matter by what names we may be called, nor what garments we may wear, nor in the presence of what priest we may be anointed, nor how many millions our subjects may number, nor how many guards may be posted on our journey, nor how many policemen may protect our property, nor how many so-called criminals, revolutionists, or anarchists we may execute – no matter what exploits we may perform, nor what states we may establish, nor what fortresses and towers we may erect – from the Tower of Babel to the Eiffel Tower – we have before us two ever present and unavoidable conditions, that deprive our mode of life of all significance: (1) death, that may overtake each of us at any moment, and (2) the transitory nature of all our undertakings, that disappear, leaving no trace behind them. No matter what we may do, found kingdoms, build palaces and monuments, write poems and songs – all is but fleeting and leaves no trace behind. Therefore no matter how much we may attempt to conceal this from ourselves, we cannot fail to perceive that the true significance of our life lies neither in our individual, physical existence, subjected to unavoidable suffering and death, nor in any institution or social organization.

Whoever you are, you who read these lines, reflect upon your position and your duties, not upon the position of landowner, merchant, judge, emperor, president, minister, priest, or soldier, which you may assume but for a time, not upon the imaginary duties which these positions impose upon you, but upon your actual and eternal position as a being, who, after a whole eternity of non-existence, is called by the will of Some One from unconsciousness into life, and who may at any moment return whence he came by the same will. Consider your duties! Not your imaginary duties of landowner in regard to your estate, nor of merchant to your capital, nor of emperor, minister, or governor to the State, but of your real duties, of a being called forth into life and endowed with love and reason. Do that which He who has sent you into this world, and to whom you will shortly return, demands of you. Are you doing what He requires? Are you doing right when, as landowner or manufacturer, you take the products of the labour of the poor, and establish your life on this spoliation; or when, as governor or judge, you do violence in condemning men to death; or when, as soldier, you prepare for war, for fighting, robbery, and murder – are you doing right?

You say that the world is as you find it, that it is inevitable that it should be as it is, that what you do you are compelled to do. But can it be that, having so strongly rooted an aversion to the suffering of men, to violence, to murder; having such a need of loving your fellowmen, and of being loved by them – seeing clearly, too, that the greatest good possible to men comes from acknowledging human brotherhood, from one serving another: can it be that your heart tells you all this, that you are taught it by your reason, that science repeats it to you, and yet regardless of it, on the strength of some mysterious and complicated argument, you are forced to contradict it all in your daily conduct? Is it possible that, being a landowner or a capitalist, you should establish your life on the oppression of the people; that, being an emperor or a president, you should command armies, and be a leader of murderers; that, being a functionary of State, you should take from the poor their hard-earned money for your own benefit, or for the benefit of the rich; that, being a judge or juror, you should condemn erring men to torture and death, because the truth hasn't been revealed to them; or, above all, is it possible that you, a youth, should enter the army, doing that upon which all the evil of the world is founded, that, renouncing your own will, all your human sympathy, you should engage at the will of others to murder those whom they bid you murder ? It is impossible!

If you are told that all this is essential for the support of the existing system of life; that this system, with its pauperism, famine, prisons, executions, armies, wars, is necessary for society, and that if it were to be abolished worse evils would follow, you are told so only by those who benefit by this system; while those who suffer from it – and their numbers are ten times greater – all think and say the opposite. And at the bottom of your heart you know that this is false – that the existing system has had its day, and must inevitably be remodelled on new foundations; and that there is no need whatsoever to support it by the sacrifice of human life.

Even supposing that the existing system is necessary, how is it that you should have to support it by trampling upon all finer feelings? But who has made you a guardian of this crumbling structure? Neither has the State, nor society, nor has any one requested you individually to support it by occupying your position of landowner, merchant, emperor, priest, or soldier, and you are well aware that you have accepted and are holding it, not for purposes of self-denial, for the good of your fellowmen, but for your own selfish interest; for your greed of gain, vainglory, ambition, through your indolence or your cowardice. If you do not desire this position you should not persist in doing what is cruel, false, and contemptible, in order to retain it. If you would once refrain from these things, which you do continually for the purpose of retaining it, you would lose it at once. If you are a ruler or an official, make only an attempt to cease polite lying, cease to take part in violence and executions; if you are a priest, desist from deceiving; if a soldier, cease killing; if a landowner or manufacturer, cease defending your property by roguery and violence; and forthwith you will lose the position which, as you say, is forced upon you and seems to you burdensome.

It cannot be that a man should be placed against his will in a position contrary to conscience.

If you are put in such a position, it is not because it is necessary for some one to be there, but only because you are willing to accept it. And therefore, knowing that such a position is directly opposed to the mandates of your heart, your reason, your faith, and even to the teachings of that science you believe in, you cannot but pause to consider, if you wish to keep it, and especially if you try to justify it, if you are doing what you ought to do.

You might run the risk if you had but the time to see your mistake and correct it, and if you ran the risk for something worth having. But when you know for certain that you are liable to die at any moment, without the slightest possibility either for yourself or for those whom you have drawn in with you, of rectifying your mistake; and, moreover, since you know that no matter what those about you may accomplish in the material organization of the world, it will all very shortly disappear as certainly as you yourself, leaving no trace behind, it is surely obvious that you have no inducement to run the risk of making a mistake so terrible.

This would seem perfectly plain and simple if we did not veil with hypocrisy the truth that is indubitably revealed to us.

Share what you have with others; do not amass riches; be not vain; do not rob, torture, or murder men; do not to others what you would not that others should do to you – these things have been said not eighteen hundred but five thousand years ago, and there can be no doubt of the truth of them. Save for hypocrisy, it would be impossible, even if one did not obey these rules, not to acknowledge that they ought to be obeyed, and that those who do not obey them do wrong.

But you say that there is still the general well being, for the sake of which one should deviate from these rules. It is allowable for the general well being to kill, torture, and rob. "It is better that one man should perish than a whole nation," you say, like Caiaphas, when you are signing death warrants; or you load your gun to shoot your fellowman, who is to perish for the general good; or you imprison him or take away his goods.

You say that you do these cruel things because you are a part of society, of the State, and must serve your government and carry out its laws, as landowner, judge, emperor, or soldier. But if you are a part of the State and have duties in consequence, you are also a partaker of the infinite life of God's universe, and have higher duties in consequence of that.

As your duties to your family or to society are always subject to the higher duties that depend upon your citizenship in the State, so your duties of citizenship are subject to the duties arising from your relations to the life of the universe, from your son ship to God. And as it would be unwise to cut down telegraph poles in order to furnish fuel for the benefit of a family or a few people, because this would be breaking the laws that protect the welfare of the State; so it is equally unwise, in order to promote the welfare of the State, to execute or murder a man, because this is breaking the immutable laws which preserve the welfare of the world.

The obligations of citizenship must be subject to the higher and eternal obligations on your part in the everlasting life of God, and must not contradict them. As it was said eighteen hundred years ago by the disciples of Christ, *"Whether it is right in the sight of God to hearken unto you more than unto God, judge ye."* Acts iv: 19. *"We ought to obey God rather than men."* Acts v: 29.

You are told to believe that in order to maintain an ever changing system, established but yesterday by a few men in a corner of the globe, you should commit violent deeds that are against the fixed and eternal order established by God or reason. Can it be possible?

Do not fail then to reflect upon your position of landowner, merchant, judge, emperor, president, minister, priest, or soldier – associated with violence, oppression, deceit, torture, and murder; refuse to recognize the lawfulness of these crimes. I do not mean that if you are a landowner you should forthwith give your land to the poor; or if capitalist, your money or your factory to your workmen; or if a czar, a minister, a magistrate, a judge, or a general, you should forthwith abdicate all your advantages; or if a soldier, whose occupation in its very nature is based on violence, you should at once refuse to continue longer a soldier, despite all the dangers of such a refusal. Should you do this, it will indeed be a heroic act; but it may happen – and most probably – that you will not be able to do it. You have connections, a family, subordinates, chiefs; you may be surrounded by temptations so strong that you cannot overcome them: but to acknowledge the truth to be the truth, and not to lie – that you are always able to do. You can refrain from affirming that you continue to be a landowner or factory owner, a merchant, an artist, an author, because you are thus useful to men; from declaring that you are a governor, an attorney general, a czar, not because it is agreeable or you are accustomed to be such, but for the good of men; from saying that you remain a soldier, not through fear of punishment, but because you consider the army indispensable for the protection of men's lives. To keep from speaking thus falsely before yourself and others – this you are always able to do, and not only able, but in duty bound to do, because in this alone – in freeing yourself from falsehood and in working out the truth – lies the highest duty of your life. And do but this and it will be sufficient for the situation to change at once of itself.

One only thing in which you are free and all-powerful has been given you; all others are beyond you. It is this – to know the truth and to profess it. And it is only because of other miserable and erring men like yourself that you have become a soldier, an emperor, a landowner, a capitalist, a priest, or a general, that you commit evil deeds so obviously contrary to the dictates of your heart and reason; that you torture, rob, and murder men, establishing your life on their sufferings; and that, above all, instead of performing your paramount duty of acknowledging and professing the truth which is known to you, you pretend not to know it, concealing it from yourself and others, doing the very opposite of what you have been called to do.

And under what conditions are you doing this? Being liable to die at any moment, you sign a death warrant, declare war or take part in it, pass judgment, torture and rob workmen, live in luxury surrounded by misery, and teach weak and trusting men that all this is right and for you is a matter of duty, while all the time you are in danger of your life being destroyed by a bullet or a bacillus, and you may be deprived for ever of the power to rectify or counteract the evil you have done to others and to yourself; having wasted a life given you but once in all eternity, having left undone in it the one thing for which it was given you.

No matter how trite it may appear to state it, nor how we may hypocritically deceive ourselves, nothing can destroy the certainty of the simple and obvious truth that external conditions can never render safe this life of ours, so fraught with unavoidable suffering, and ended infallibly by death, that human life can have no other meaning than the constant fulfilment of that for which the Almighty Power has sent us here, and for which He has given us one sure guide in this life, namely, our conscious reason.

This Power does not require from us what is unreasonable and impossible – the organization of our temporal, material life, the life of society, or of the State. He demands of us only what is reasonable and possible – to serve the Kingdom of God, which establishes the unity of mankind, a unity possible only in the truth – to recognize and profess the truth revealed to us, which it is always in our power to do.

"Seek ye first the kingdom of God, and his righteousness; and all these things shall be added unto you." Matthew vi: 33.

The only significance of life consists in helping to establish the Kingdom of God; and this can be done only by means of the acknowledgment and profession of the truth by each one of us.

"The kingdom of God cometh not with observation: neither shall they say, Lo here! Or, lo there! For, behold, the kingdom of God is within you." Luke xvii: 20–21.

LEO TOLSTOY, YASSNAYA POLYANA, 14 MAY 1893

Also available from
White Crow Books

Marcus Aurelius—*The Meditations*
ISBN 978-1-907355-20-2

Elsa Barker—*Letters from
a Living Dead Man*
ISBN 978-1-907355-83-7

Elsa Barker—*War Letters
from the Living Dead Man*
ISBN 978-1-907355-85-1

Elsa Barker—*Last Letters
from the Living Dead Man*
ISBN 978-1-907355-87-5

Richard Maurice Bucke—
Cosmic Consciousness
ISBN 978-1-907355-10-3

G. K. Chesterton—*The
Everlasting Man*
ISBN 978-1-907355-03-5

G. K. Chesterton—*Heretics*
ISBN 978-1-907355-02-8

G. K. Chesterton—*Orthodoxy*
ISBN 978-1-907355-01-1

Arthur Conan Doyle—*The
Edge of the Unknown*
ISBN 978-1-907355-14-1

Arthur Conan Doyle—
The New Revelation
ISBN 978-1-907355-12-7

Arthur Conan Doyle—
The Vital Message
ISBN 978-1-907355-13-4

Arthur Conan Doyle with
Simon Parke—*Conversations
with Arthur Conan Doyle*
ISBN 978-1-907355-80-6

Leon Denis with Arthur Conan
Doyle—*The Mystery of Joan of Arc*
ISBN 978-1-907355-17-2

The Earl of Dunraven—*Experiences
in Spiritualism with D. D. Home*
ISBN 978-1-907355-93-6

Meister Eckhart with Simon Parke—
Conversations with Meister Eckhart
ISBN 978-1-907355-18-9

Kahlil Gibran—*The Forerunner*
ISBN 978-1-907355-06-6

Kahlil Gibran—*The Madman*
ISBN 978-1-907355-05-9

Kahlil Gibran—*The Prophet*
ISBN 978-1-907355-04-2

Kahlil Gibran—*Sand and Foam*
ISBN 978-1-907355-07-3

Kahlil Gibran—*Jesus the Son of Man*
ISBN 978-1-907355-08-0

Kahlil Gibran—*Spiritual World*
ISBN 978-1-907355-09-7

Hermann Hesse—*Siddhartha*
ISBN 978-1-907355-31-8

All titles available as eBooks, and select titles available in Audiobook format from www.whitecrowbooks.com

CPSIA information can be obtained
at www.ICGtesting.com
Printed in the USA
BVHW03*0840160318
510177BV00011B/8/P